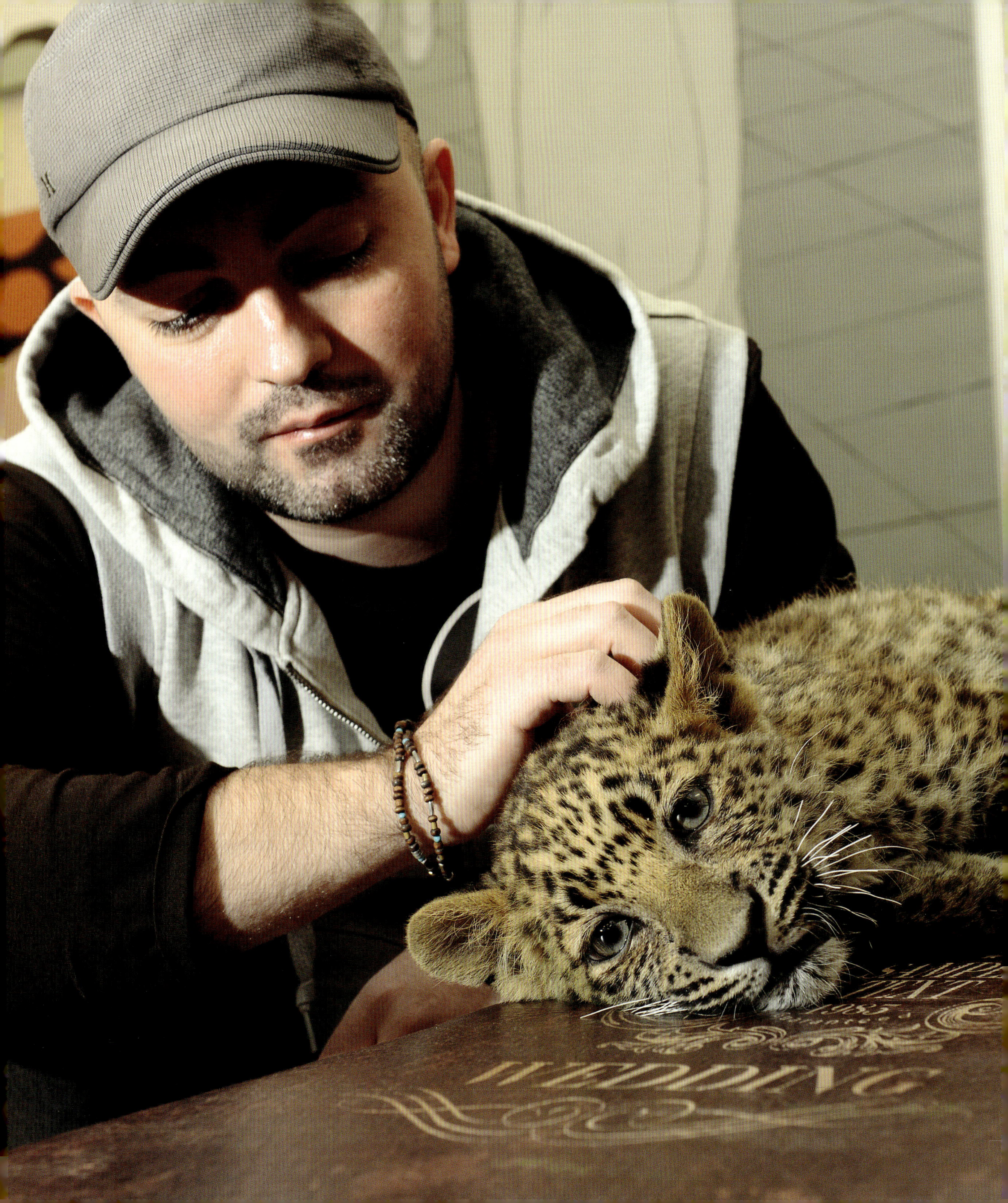

WEDDING

Demetrio Paparoni

Rafael Megall

Paintings 2009–2015

SKIRA

Cover
The Mask of History, 2015
Acrylic on canvas, 100 x 75 cm

page 2
Rafael Megall, 2015
Photo Davide Borsa

Design
Marcello Francone

Editorial Coordination
Vincenza Russo

Editing
Emily Ligniti

Layout
Antonio Carminati

Translations
Julia Heim

Iconographic Research
Paola Lamanna

*Photographs of Rafael Megall's
works by*
Zaven Khachikyan

First published in Italy in 2015 by
Skira Editore S.p.A.
Palazzo Casati Stampa
via Torino 61
20123 Milano
Italy
www.skira.net

Printed and bound in Italy. First edition
ISBN: 978-88-572-2813-6

Distributed in the world by Thames
and Hudson Ltd., 181A High Holborn,
London WC1V 7QX, United Kingdom.

*This publication was made
possible with the contribution of*

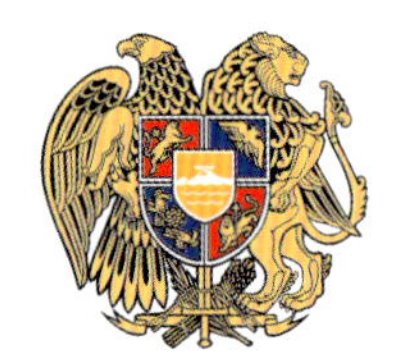

RA MINISTRY OF DIASPORA

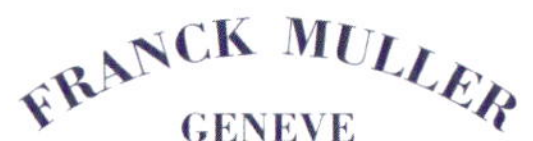

Contents

7 The Man and the Mask in Rafael Megall's
Bestiary
Demetrio Paparoni

23 Culture Stems from Attitudes Already
Present in Nature
*Elio Cappuccio in conversation
with Rafael Megall*

41 **Works**

111 **Appendix**

Biography

Exhibitions

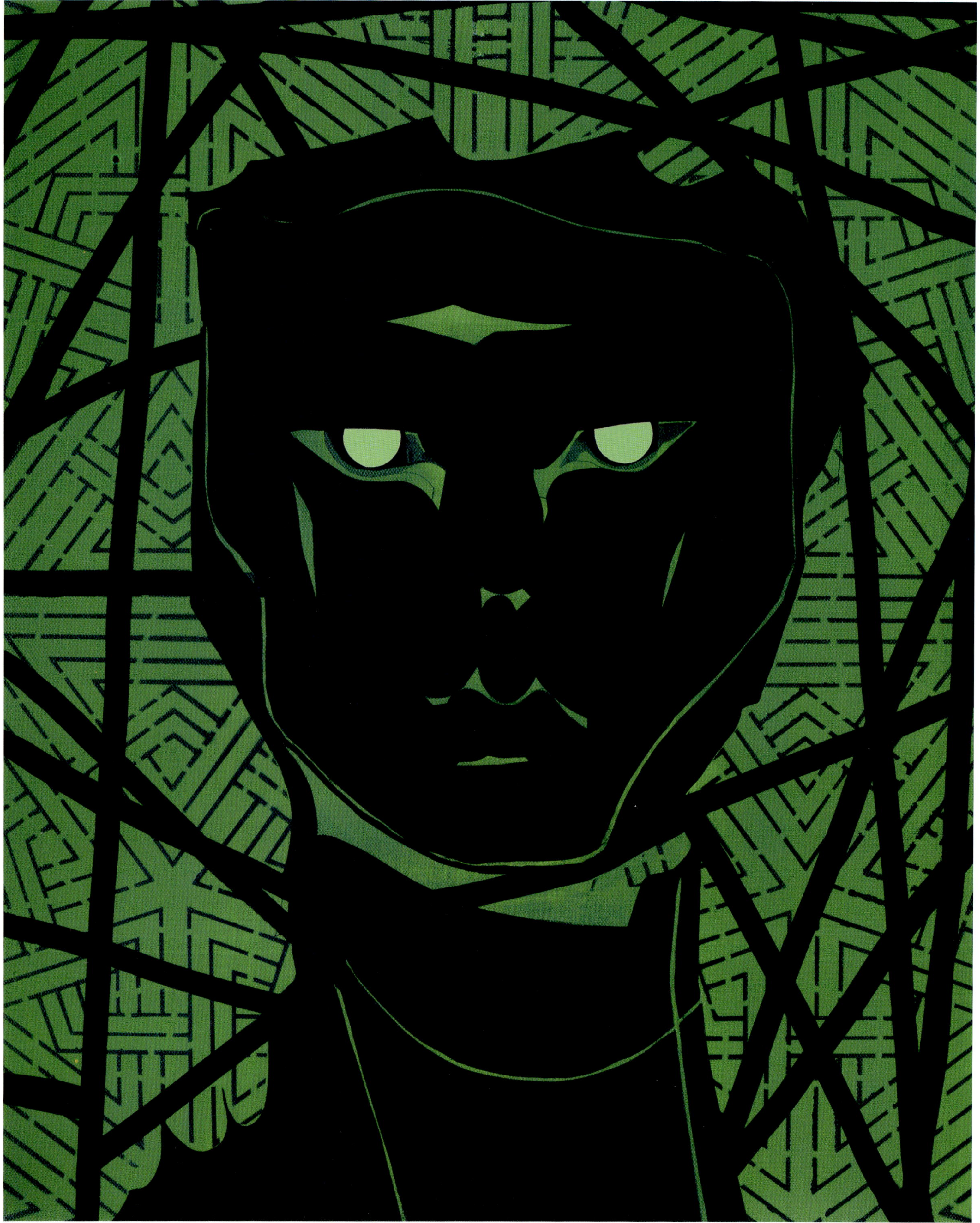

The Man and the Mask in Rafael Megall's Bestiary

Demetrio Paparoni

The complex relationship between reason and instinct is depicted through the mask in Rafael Megall's work. The mask represents the symbolic device through which man, in varying ways and forms, attempts to distance himself from impulse, in an effort to be perceived as being in a state of control and balance.

Emphasizing the condition in which the individual finds himself every time he must decide if and how to reveal himself, Megall adopts the fundamental question of existentialism, according to which, each moment of life is characterized by relationships with others. The relationship between individuals, which is expressed through both dialogue and conflict, becomes, in him, the acknowledgement of the limits of the human condition and the belief in the capacity to move beyond them. These paintings bring to light the conflict between nature and human will: on the one hand lies nature that shows its domination over man, conditioning him with the force of impulse (the animal component), whereas on the other hand there is man, seeking to dominate instincts with morality, social rules, and reason (the mask). While, as an artist, Megall grasps the tragic aspect of existence, as a man and a humanist he is involved in making visible the trust in man's ability to overcome the limits of nature with culture. This tension emerges in the representation of animal figures placed next to human ones, as if the animal represented the dark, unenlightened part of human rationality.

In *The Hunter and the Panther*, 2013, the hunter is not portrayed as a man striking the animal, but as a knight next to it, as the sword he holds is placed unthreateningly over his shoulder. Megall depicted the relationship with the animal in terms of complementarity, and not in terms of absolute domination of one over the other. In other words, in keeping his sword on his shoulder and not showing an aggressive attitude, the man expresses the power of reason over instinct. Here, the reference to medieval bestiaries is explicit and helps in understanding the conceptual and narrative dynamic that underpins the entire work of the Armenian artist. From medieval bestiaries we learn that the word "panther" derives from the Greek *pan*, meaning "all." In this case, the proximity of the hunter to the panther describes the harmonic relationship between man and creation, and references medieval iconography, according to which the animal is not considered for what it is in itself, but as an element that refers to the divine. The juxtaposition of the two figures shows that the man and the animal are complementary.

The theme of duplicity can be found, as we have already seen, in the representation of the mask. The mask does not, however, reference the relationship between the individual and nature. Instead, it refers to interpersonal relationships and social roles.

Sovereign, 2014
Acrylic on canvas, 80 x 65 cm

In *Six Faces, Six Masks*, 2012, Megall makes each face and mask correspond to social roles that man must play to make his status evident. In *The Nature of the Dog*, 2013, four dogs are presented from the front as white and from the back as black. This chromatic device introduces another important theme for the artist that is tied to the representation of the animal: the polarity of the forces of nature. Megall represents this polarity through the female figure and the bull, which, in various cultures indicates the fertile force of the male. In the painting *Minotaur*, 2014, for example, an imposing bull looks at a female figure who is taking care of a child. The figure is linked to a red stain, which instinctively hints at menstrual blood, pain, and childbirth. Despite the fact that the work has a uniform background devoid of hues or shading, the protective gaze of the bull towards the woman is evident. The two figures, both constructed by the relationship between white and black, stage the complementarity present in the symbols of the yin (black) and the yang (white), which in Chinese culture indicate the complementarity of night and day and thus the *coincidentia oppositorum* of the principles at the base of natural flux: negative/positive, feminine/masculine, water/fire. In this *coincidentia oppositorum* we also find the theme of the polarity between introversion and extroversion, which was dear to Jung. Moreover, we find the contrast, present in Chinese culture, between the tiger and the dragon, where the tiger is the female figure and the dragon, the equivalent of the bull, is the male figure.

The intricacies of the complementary relationship between opposites bear elements of the masculine within the feminine and the feminine within the masculine. While the title of the work *Minotaur* refers to Greek mythology, Megall does not wish to create ties with the Hellenic world, just as the reference to the yin and yang symbolism is not related to a particular interest in the Chinese world. Megall's interest is in the culture of the Christian world, as evidenced by his use of vine shoots, which symbolize the Christian universe. Megall eliminates any decorative intent to make it become an abstract grid. What the artist wants to bring to light is the universality of the symbol, which transcends the specificity of any single culture. In many paintings, Megall recreates similar figures, as if they had been generated by the repetitive markings of the same stamp. On the formal plane (formal, not theoretical!) the use of the plain background, divided into distinct sections, references a vast range of artistic expressions, from Matisse and Staël to post-pictorial abstraction, from concrete art to pop art, and to the aesthetic of Gilbert and George. On the theoretical plane, the repetition of the stamped image, which clones itself, refers to the cyclic alternation of generations and the roles that at times men can take on throughout their existence. However you look at them, Megall's paintings always reference the relationship between nature and culture. This vision of the world led Megall

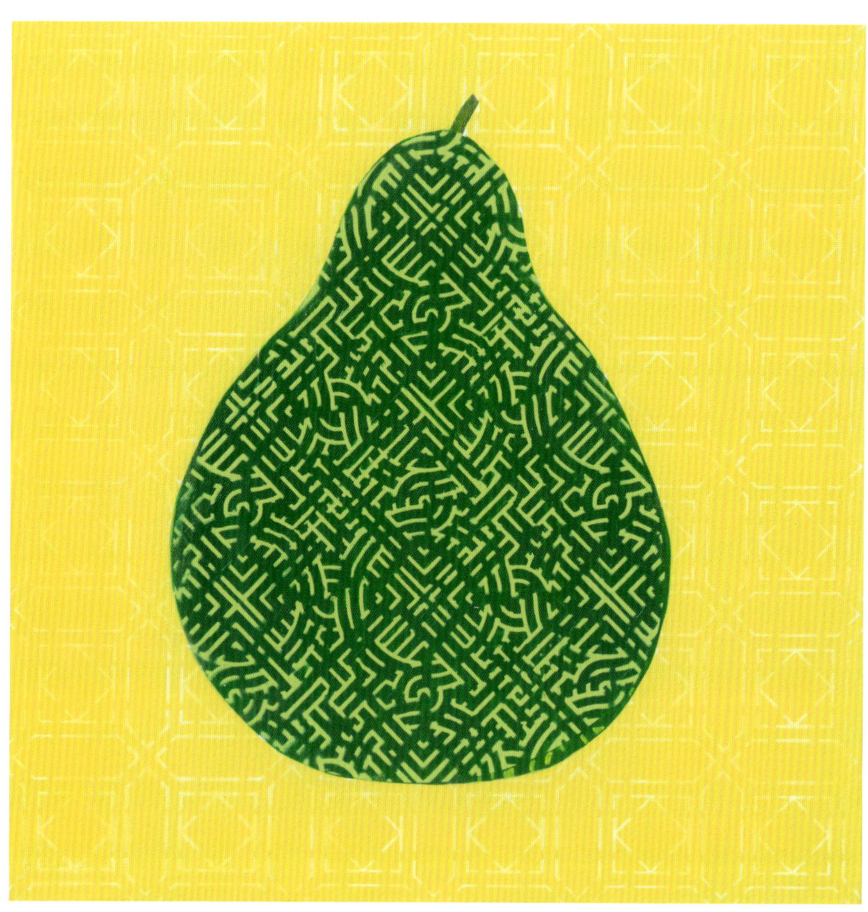

Green Pumpkin, 2014
Acrylic on canvas, 45 x 45 cm

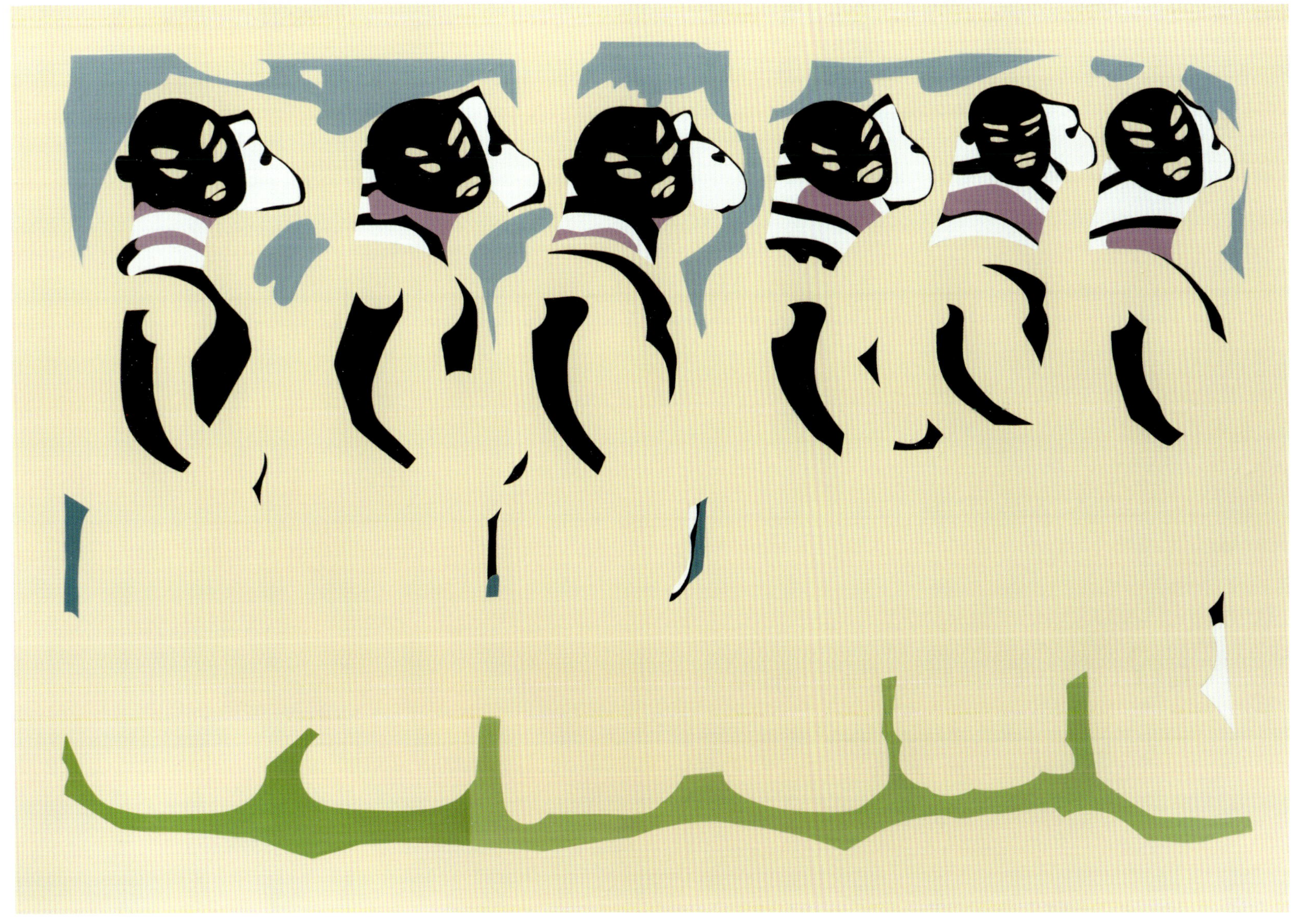

Six Faces, Six Masks, 2012
Acrylic on canvas, 140 x 200 cm

Pages 10–11
Sea Monster, 2015
Diptych
Acrylic on canvas, 80 x 65 cm each

to multiply the same subject in many of his works. Examples of this image proliferation are: *Six Faces, Six Masks*, *The Nature of the Dog, Pumpkins*, 2014, and *Rowers,* 2014.

In Rafael Megall's iteration of the subject, there is the echo of the transformation of natural elements into decorative forms that in ancient miniatures and Armenian bas-reliefs take shape through stylization, repetition, connection, and weaving. This echo becomes particularly explicit in his religious paintings, in which even the color assumes the original symbolic valiance. For Megall's sacred subjects he privileges the use of gold, all shades of blue, red, and black, which no longer have the same flatness that we find in the paintings that refer to the contemporary world. Even the color seems to come from a distant time during which those images found their form for the first time.

Megall does not conceal or disguise the original sources, because his works are not citation or rewriting. He paints something that he has always known, that he has always seen, and thus he calls into question the concept of outdatedness. The animals that appear in his paintings–at times as a symbol of the four evangelists, other times as fantastical or monstrous creatures–are as massive as those that fight in the stone bas-reliefs, or as subtle as those that come from the re-elaborations of the initial

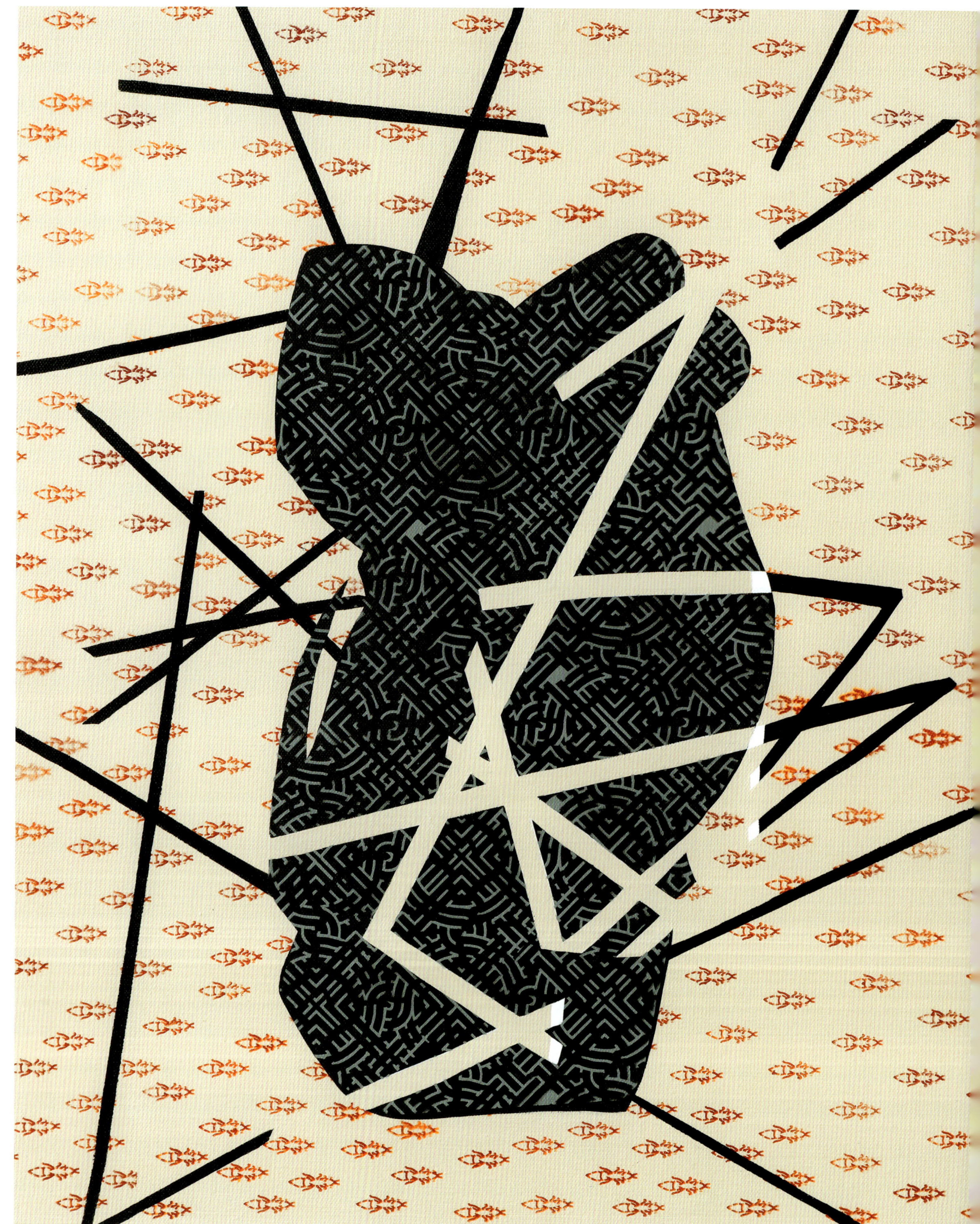

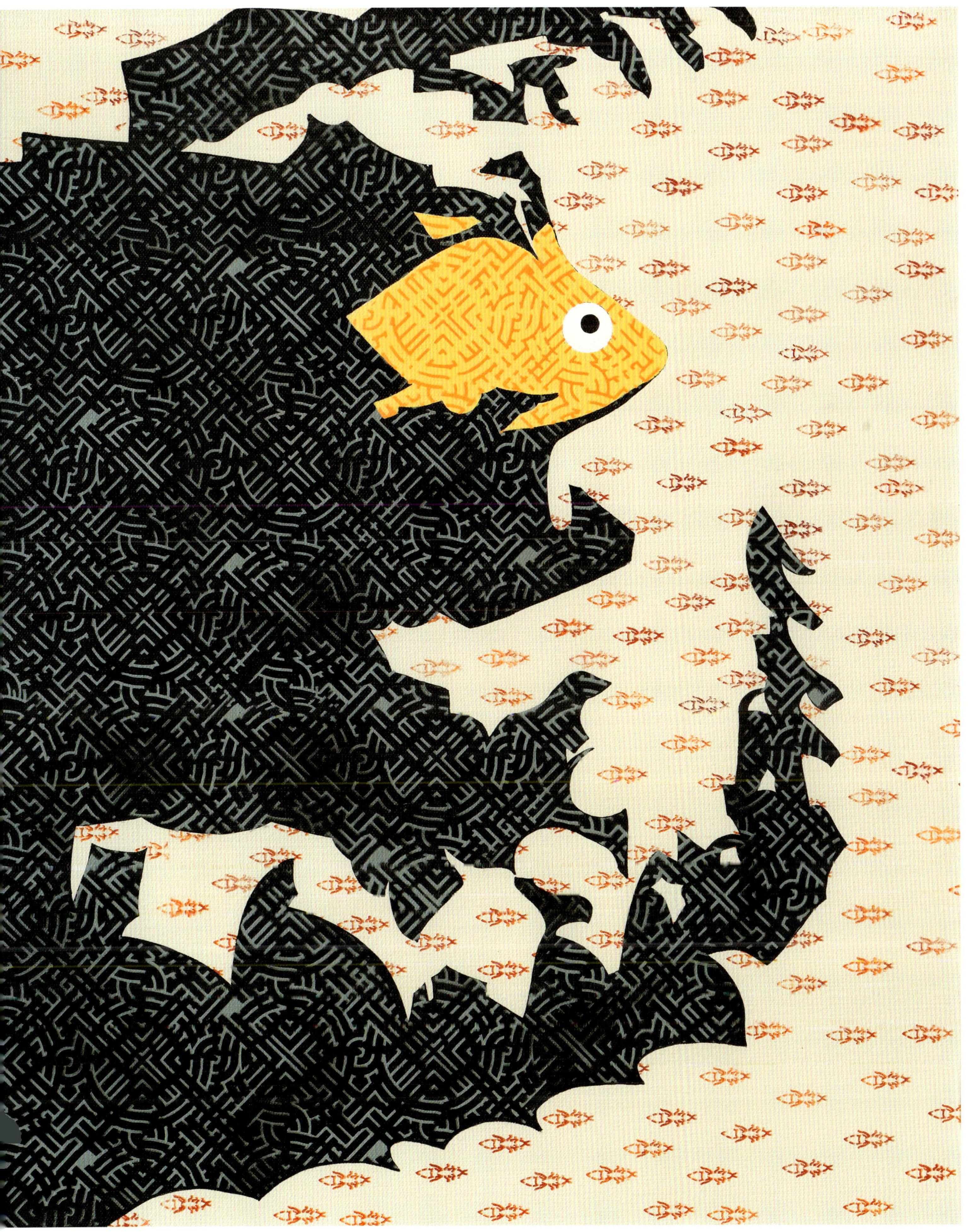

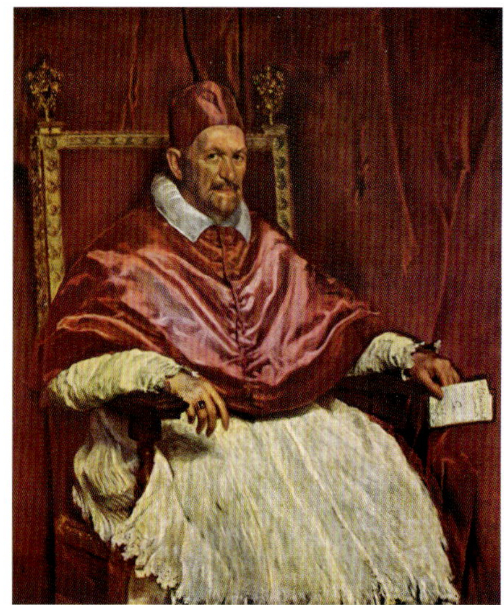

Diego Rodríguez de Silva y Velázquez,
Portrait of Pope Innocent X, 1650
Oil on canvas, 140 x 120 cm
Rome, Galleria Doria Pamphilij

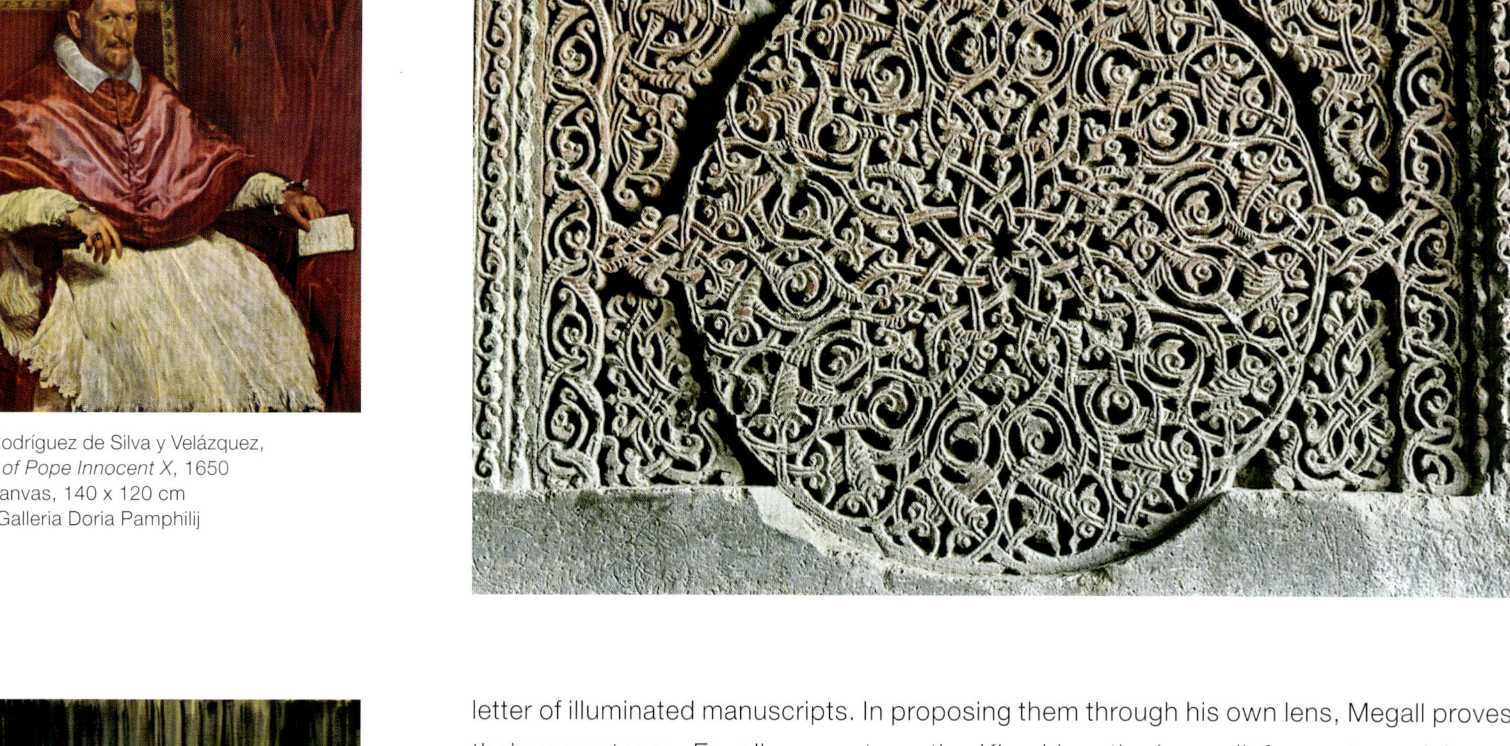

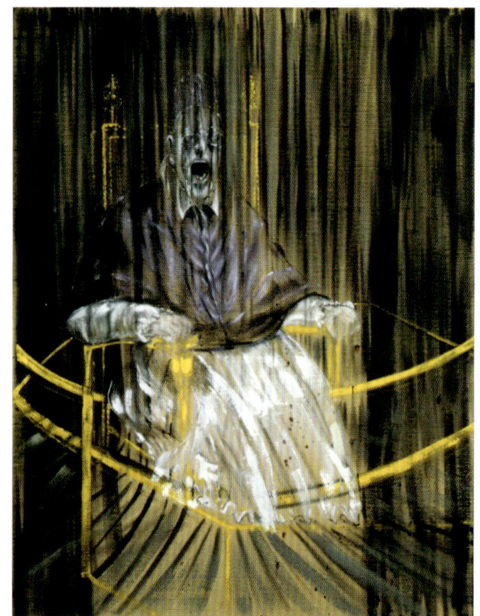

Francis Bacon, Study of *Portrait
of Pope Innocent X* by Velázquez,
1953
Oil on canvas, 153 x 118 cm
Des Moines, Des Moines Art Center,
The Nathan Emory Coffin Collection

Top right
Khachkar, Hovhannavank,
13th century

Facing page
Pope, 2009
Acrylic on canvas, 140 x 118 cm

letter of illuminated manuscripts. In proposing them through his own lens, Megall proves their currentness. Equally current are the *Khachkar*, the bas-reliefs on stone slabs on which are etched crosses with blooming buds at their base. Widely spread throughout Armenia, they symbolically transform an instrument of the passion of Christ into a tree of life. And still, in these paintings Megall recognizes that the ancient iconography depicting evangelical episodes, or symbolic iconography that dates back to medieval lectionaries, are tied to the present.

Born in 1983 in Yerevan, Armenia, Megall belongs to a generation that did not experience first-hand the drama of the Armenian genocide. As a person who never lived through it but only gathered testimonies of the genocidal drama from those dear to him, Megall has focused his attention on the existential dimension of the singular, placing the uniqueness of the individual, raised in a relational environment, in the dealings each individual has with others and with the world, at the forefront of his work. Inevitably, this discourse leads us to the theme of the mask.

In the triptych *Cycles of Psychological States* from 2011, the figure of a woman is shown three times: from the front, in the central panel, and facing the central panel in the two side panels. In the side panels, the woman is wearing a mask decorated in an Armenian style that once again uses the vine shoots that derive from Christian iconography. The figure on the left is about to pick up a black cat with a pink collar, while the one on the right seems pensive as the cat observes her. In Megall's personal symbolism the black cat represents the freedom that we hide with our mask. The animal's collar indicates domestication. The motif of the vine shoots runs along the upper portion of the background of the entire triptych, and constitutes a sort of fabric. In the central panel the mask hangs around the woman's neck and the cat is not present, signifying that there is a moment in life in which we believe we can affirm our freedom without hav-

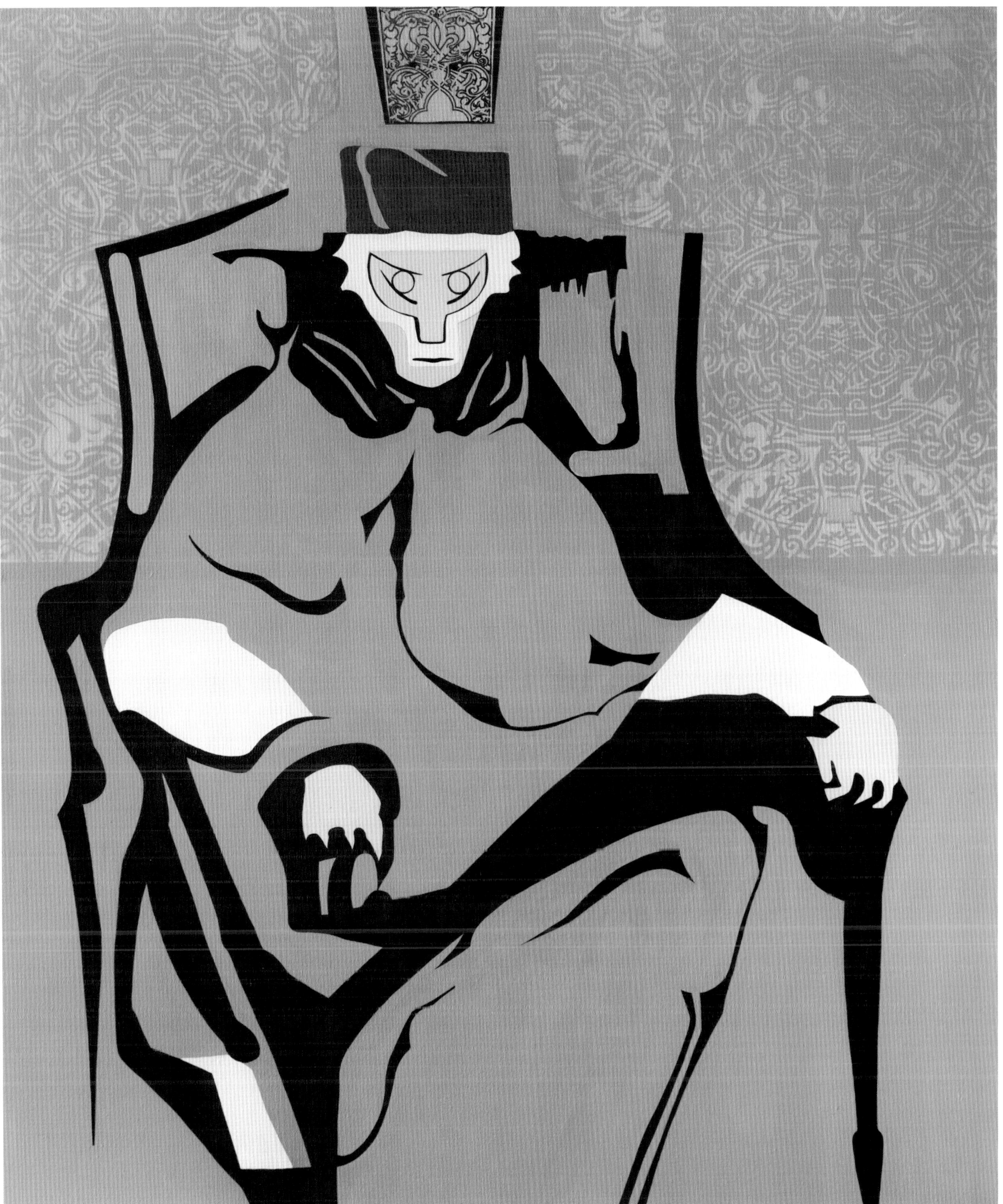

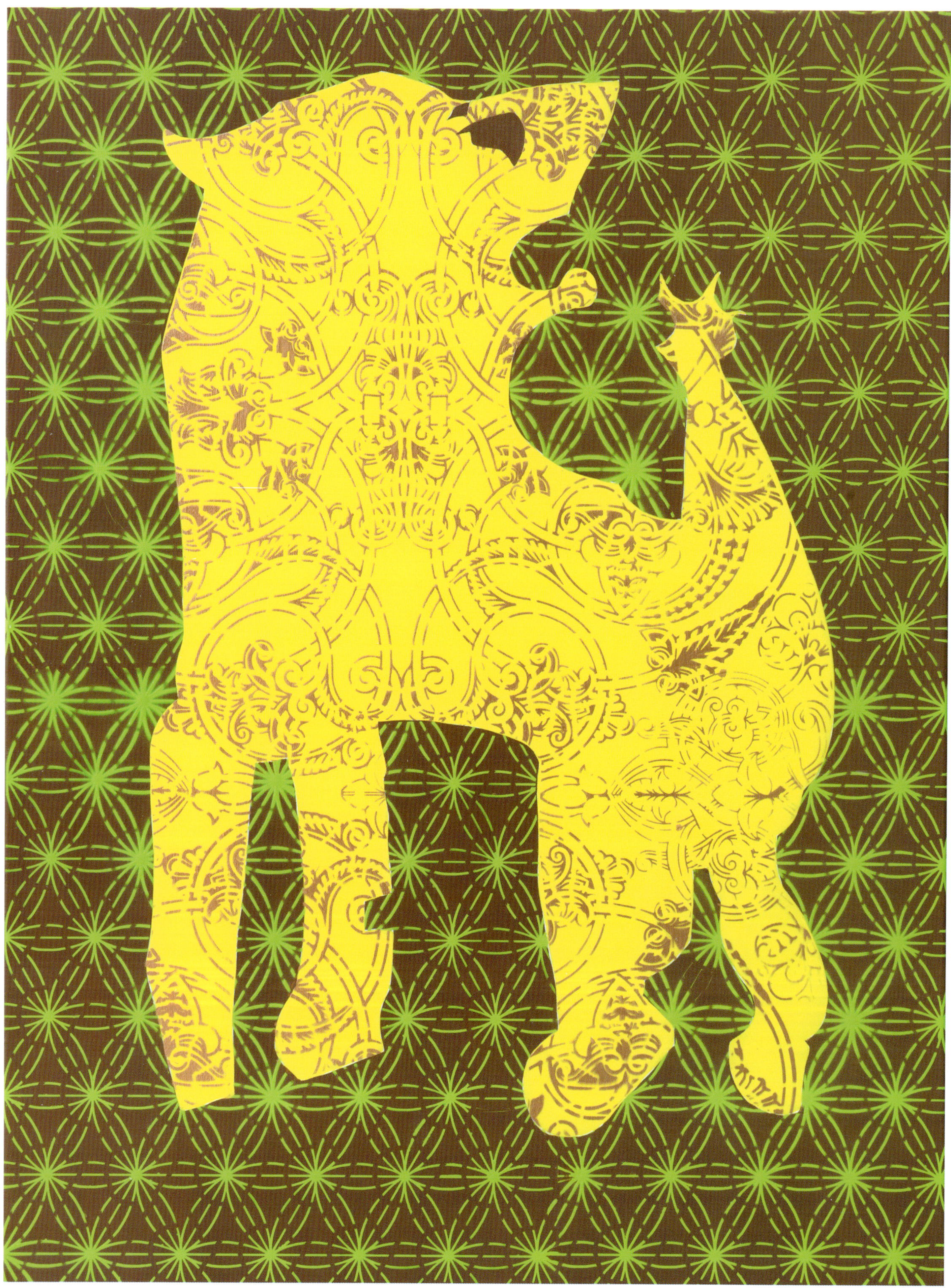

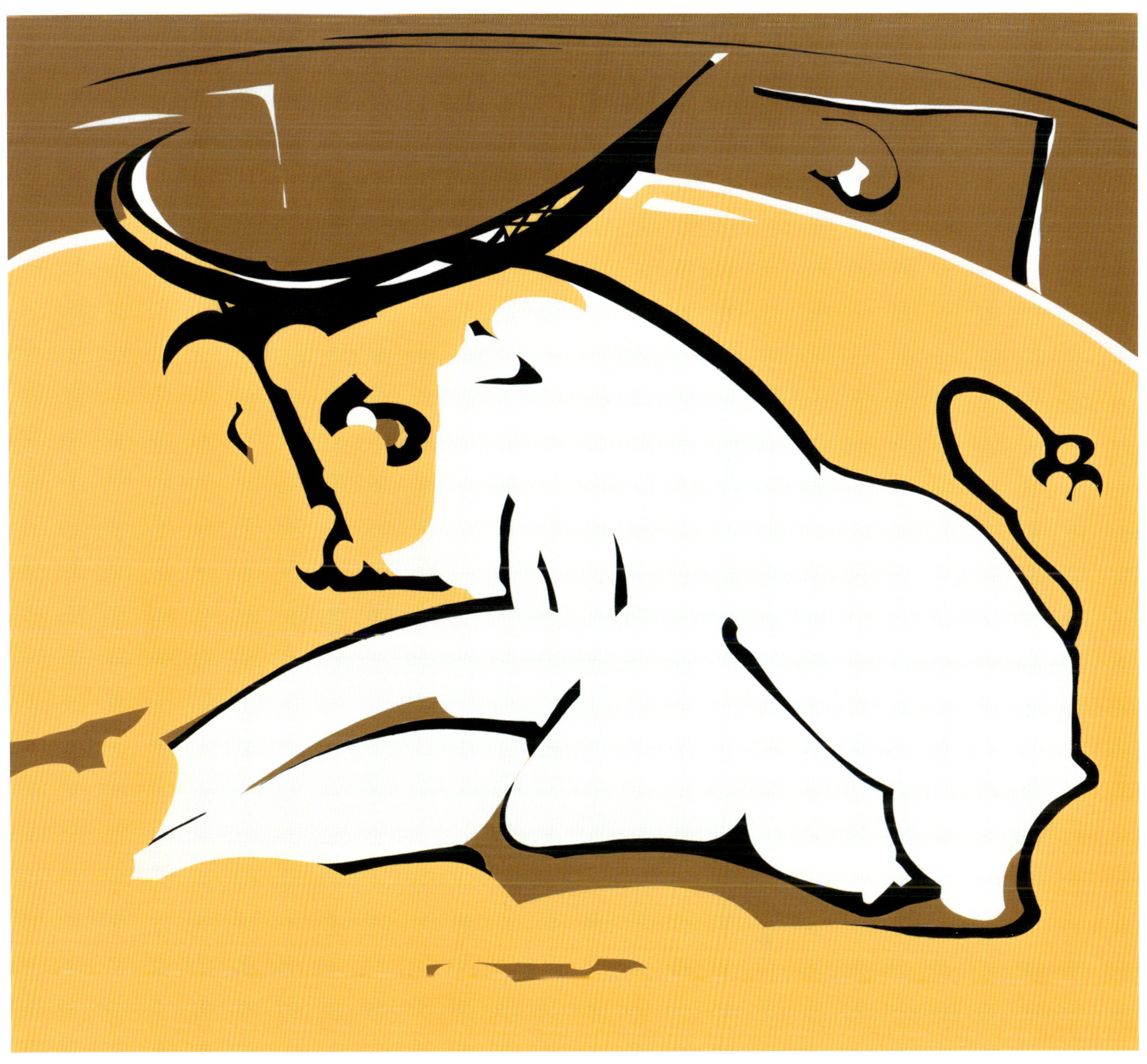

Bull, 2012
Acrylic on canvas, 105 x 115 cm

Facing page
Constellation of *Canis Major*, 2015
Acrylic on canvas, 100 x 75 cm

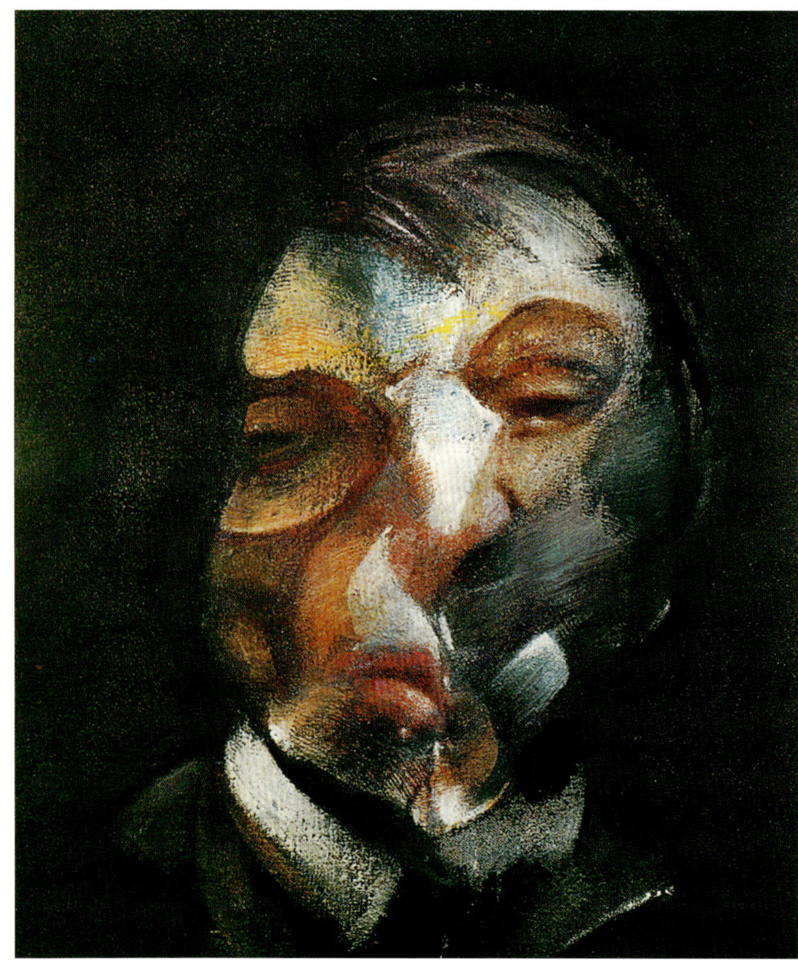
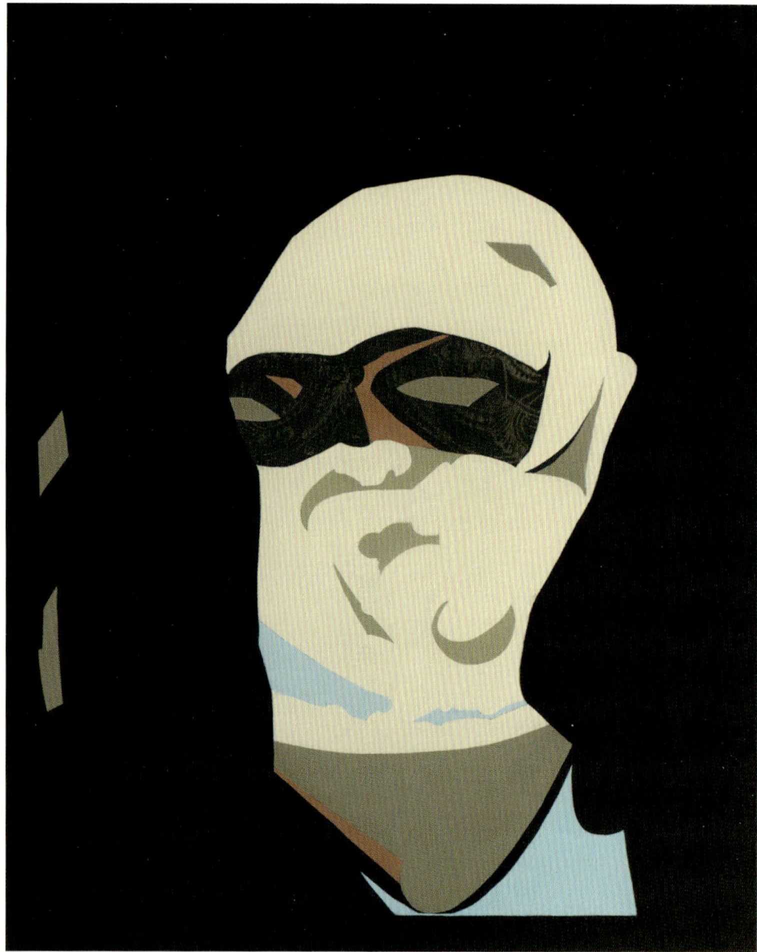

Francis Bacon, *Self-portrait*, 1971
Oil on canvas, 35.5 x 30.5 cm
Paris, Musée national d'art moderne,
Centre Georges Pompidou

Self-portrait, 2013
Acrylic on canvas, 80 x 65 cm

Facing page
The Mask of History, 2015
Acrylic on canvas, 100 x 75 cm

ing to hide it. *Cycles of Psychological States* describes the development of human freedom, from childhood to old age. In the first phase of life depicted by the artist, upbringing seeks to stop the instinctiveness that characterizes infant behavior, dictated, as Freud would say, by the pleasure principle. Thus a sort of social mask is constructed that inhibits freedom. Gradually, as the child grows, Megall says, we see the need to affirm our individuality, even if, through the course of this search we never completely remove our mask; keeping it around our necks, it is ready to be used at certain times, depending on the circumstances. In other words, through his work, Megall shows how the illusion that has fed the idealism of adolescence, during which one dreams of being able to be freed of the social mask, gives in, over time, to a form of skepticism that makes the individual aware of the impossibility of living outside the world of simulation. The work's narrative shows how an acute sense of the tragic that dissolves into bitter irony hides behind the apparent serenity of the pure colors, unsettling in their stamped iciness. Megall's work thus becomes the equivalent of the disenchanted smile of those who observe the tragic contradictions of their own existential condition from a distance. The reference to European existentialism is woven together with the irony of the characters of one of the key figures of twentieth-century European theater, Luigi Pirandello, in whose works the individual continually confronts the need for the social mask and the limits that the mask imposes on life.

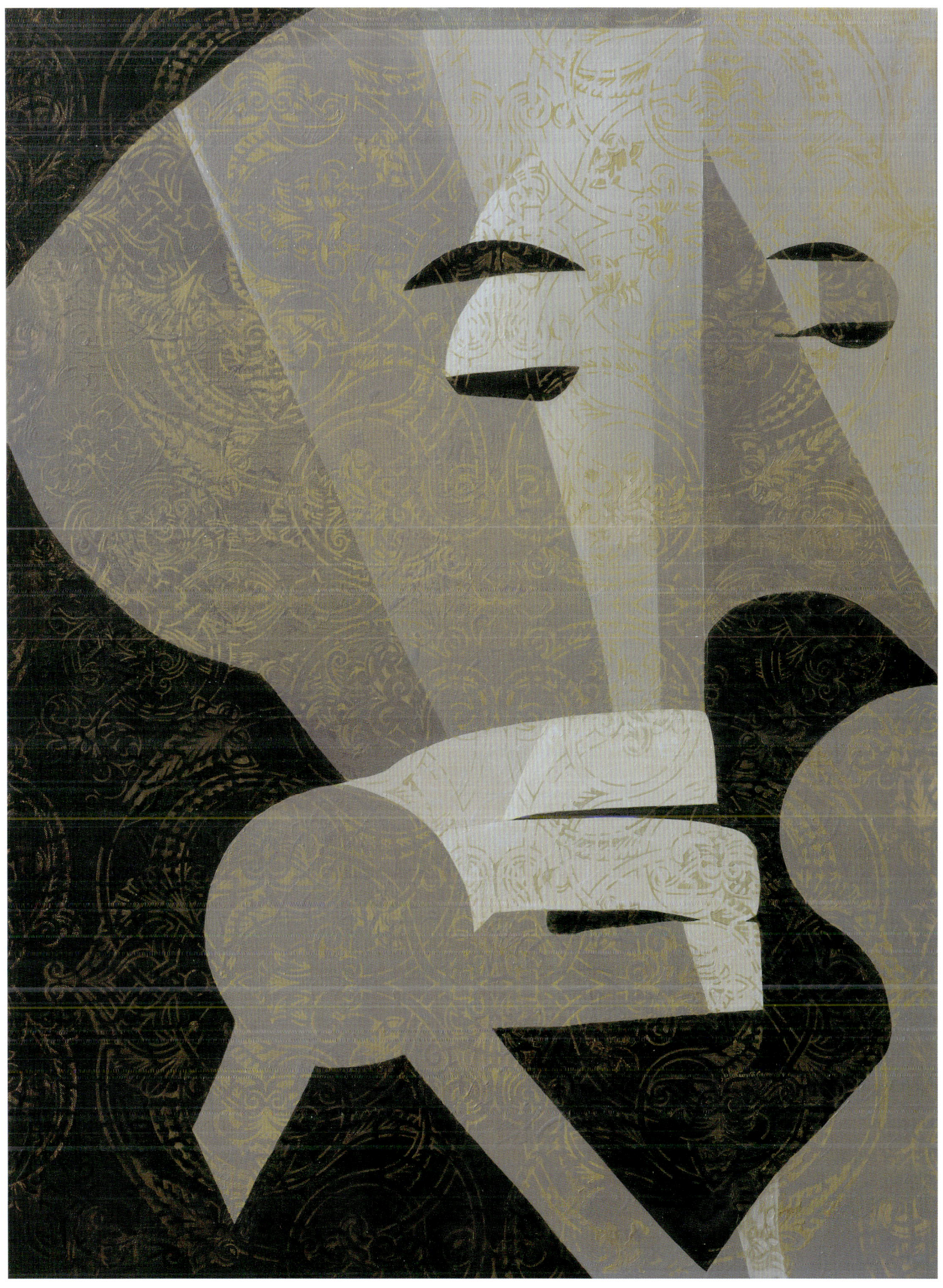

Ecstasy, 2009
Acrylic on canvas, 35 x 28 cm

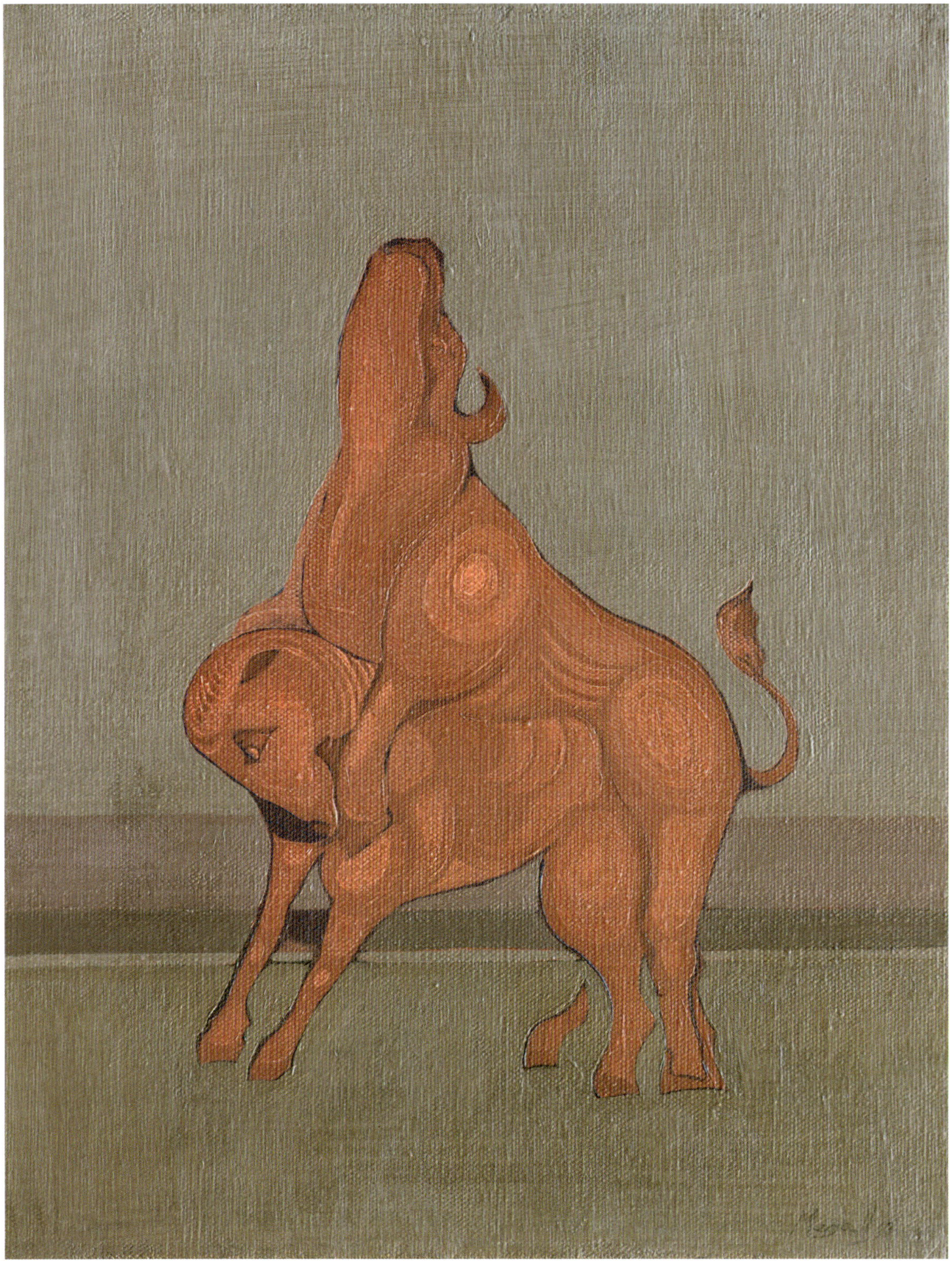

The Hunter and the Panther, 2013
Acrylic on canvas, 140 x 200 cm

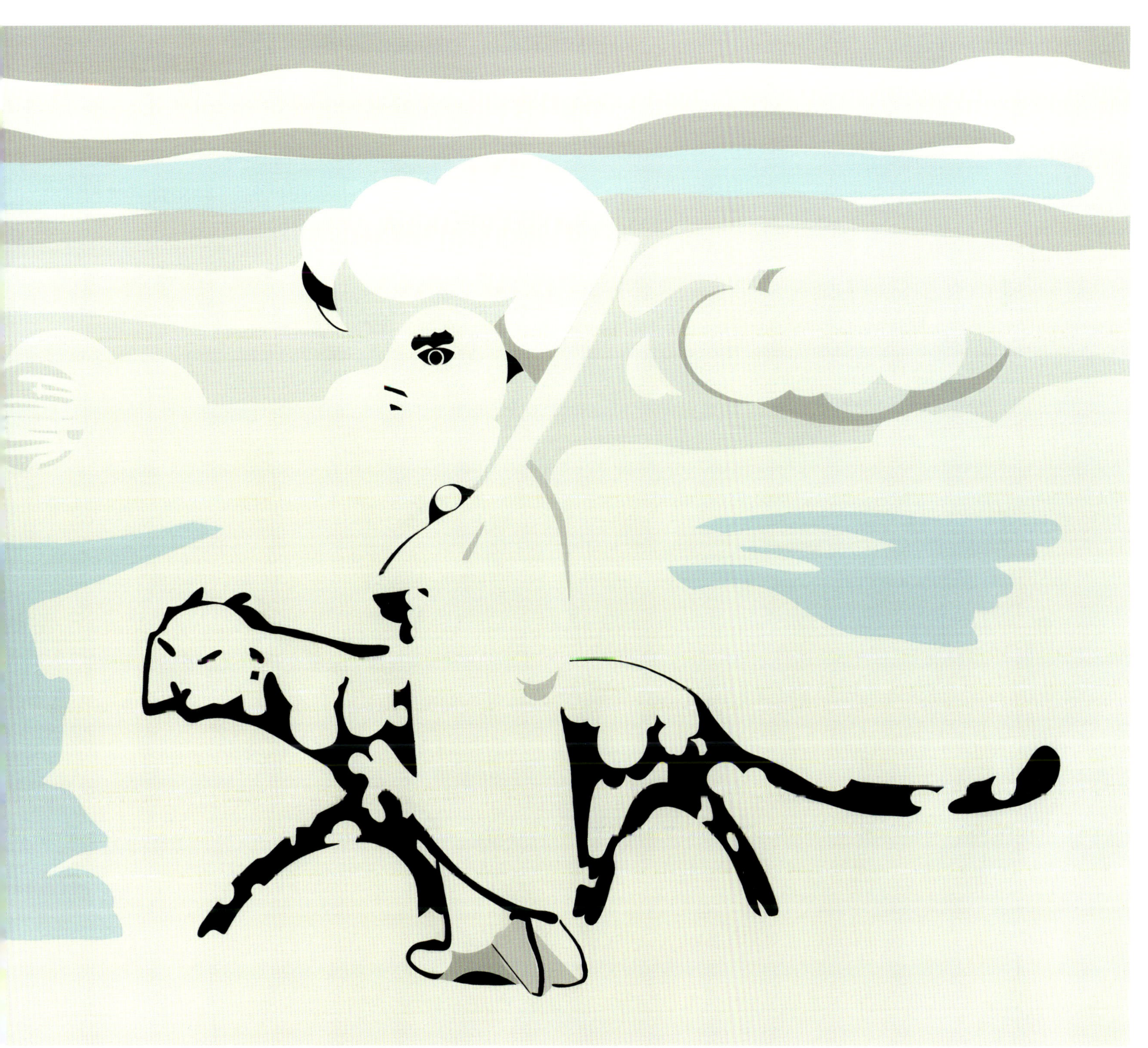

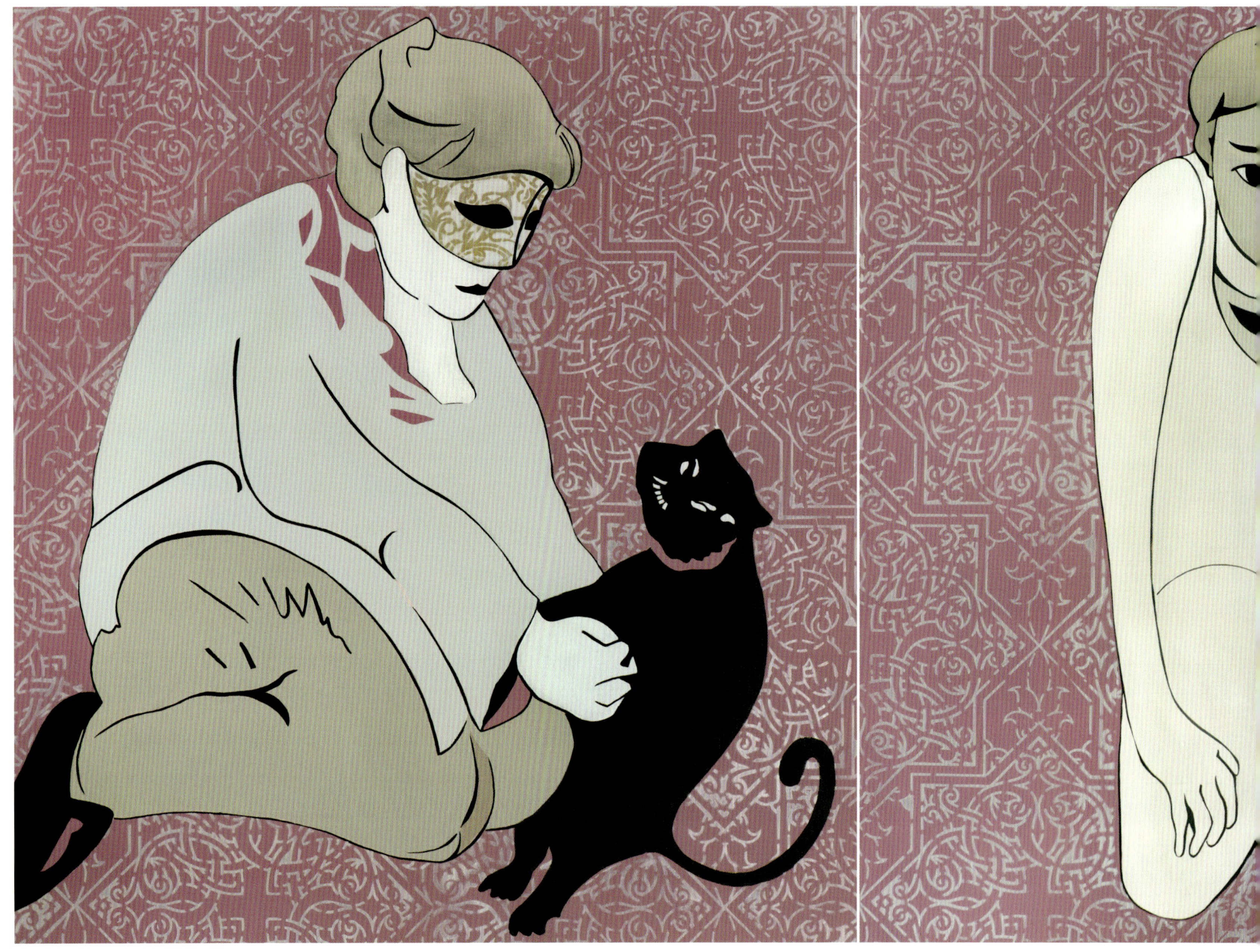

Cycles of Psychological States, 2011
Triptych
Acrylic on canvas, 115 x 105 cm each

The existential theme expressed in *Cycles of Psychological States* returns in the last series of works entitled *The Mask of History*, which was started in early 2015. In these paintings the mask becomes the protagonist, invading the entire space of the painting and completely hiding the wearer. While it has the characteristics of embellished origami with decorations inspired by flora and fauna, it is also reminiscent of a helmet, an object of offense that is hidden in the shadow, camouflaged like an animal ready to attack.

On the formal plane, *Cycles of Psychological States* recalls certain triptychs by Francis Bacon. But while in Bacon the figure and its context are dramatized at the limits of expressionism and the most exasperated tragedy, in Megall the figure and

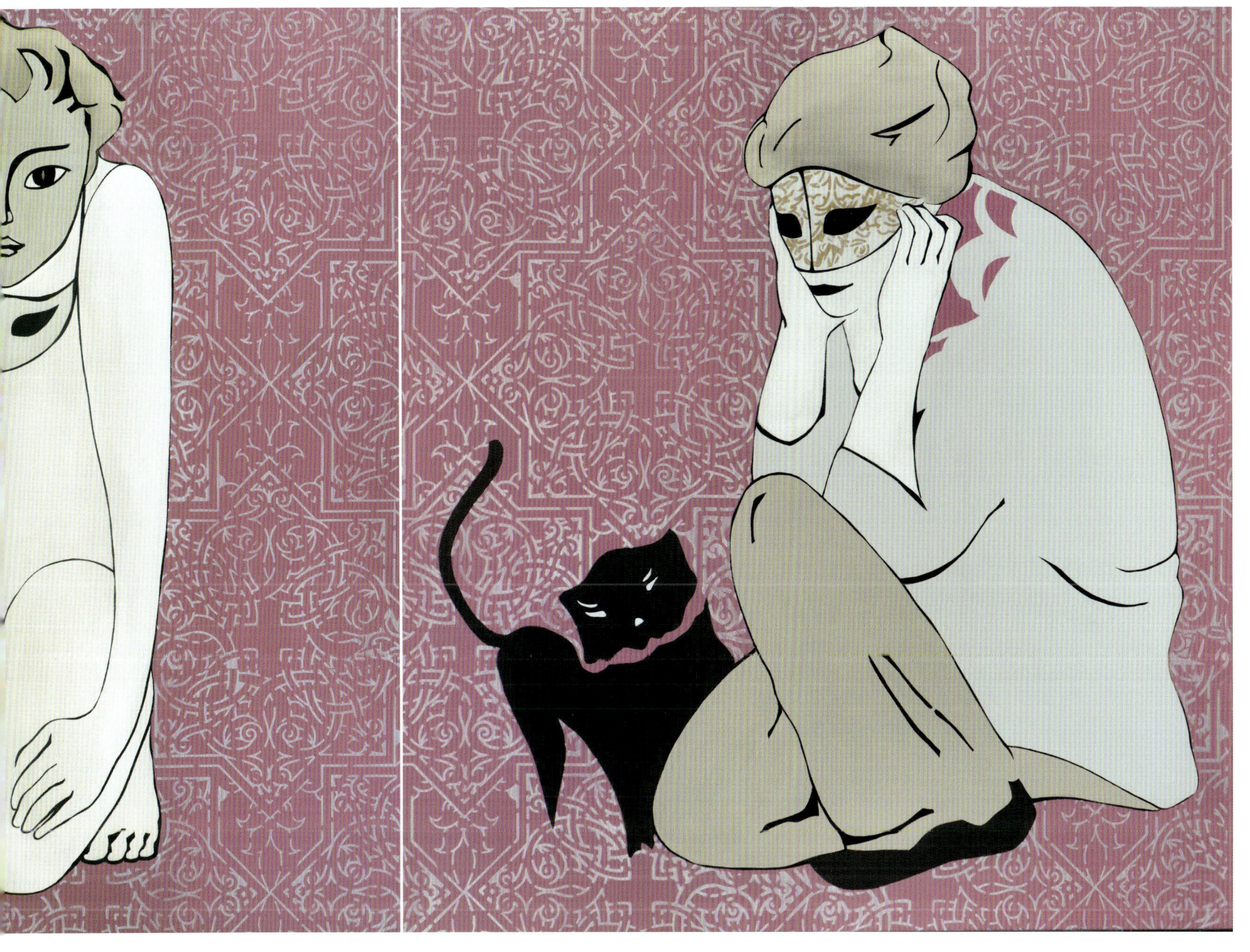

context are characterized by their inexpressiveness, and by the stamped nature of both the drawing and the layers of color. Megall was trained during the years of the telematics revolution, and he belongs to a generation that is accustomed to the flow of images that lives off those brief instants that the web displays on the screen. Contextually, the synthesis that, in art, comes from pop and minimalism is an established given that reaches us even through the stamps of those same commercial logos that pop art appropriated. In Megall, attention to the styles of the present does not exclude the reference to the traditional symbolism of Armenian Christian painting, as is shown by his appreciation of bestiaries, medieval illuminated codices, and the theme of vine shoots prevalent in church decorations.

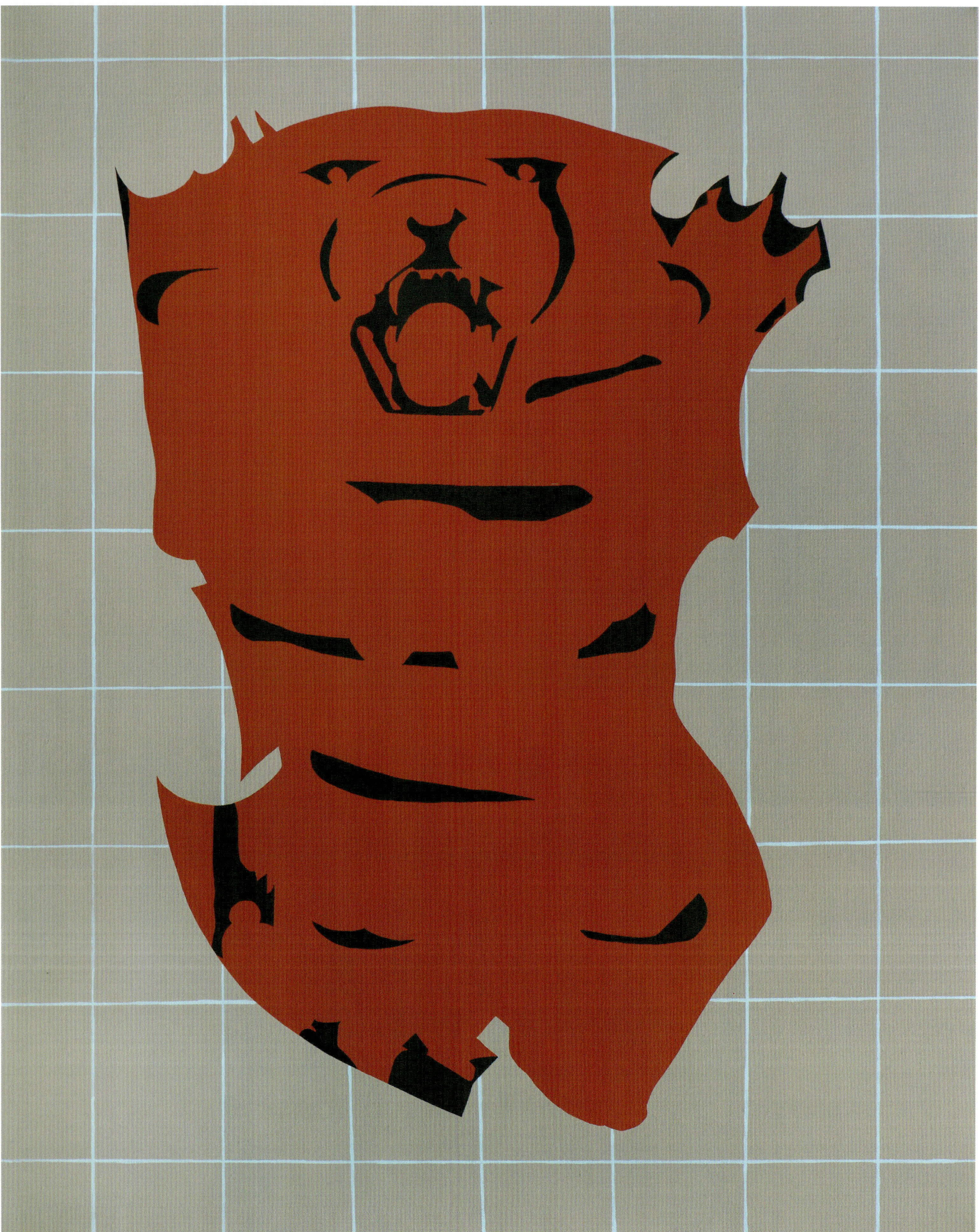

Culture Stems from Attitudes Already Present in Nature

Elio Cappuccio in conversation with Rafael Megall

Elio Cappuccio: In your work, traditional figures of medieval bestiaries are woven together with universal themes, to attain a depiction that deals with the relationship between man and animal.

Rafael Megall: Animals are characterized by behavior that is determined by the survival instinct, whereas man is always faced with choices in which the instinctive dimension represents a constant that, however, must be subjected to the analysis of reason. A rational mediation is present in man that is unknown to animal.

EC: We always have an ambivalent relationship to animals. The animal can be seen as something completely different with respect to man: on the one hand, there is reason, while on the other there is raw instinct. However, from a naturalistic and Darwinian point of view, the animal is a reference to our origin. Just consider, from this Darwinian perspective, how our progenitors are apes. Do you feel closer to this naturalistic, Darwinian perspective or to a perspective that believes we are descendants of Adam?

RM: I am not far from the idea that the existence of an evolutionary perspective guided by a divine principle is possible.

EC: This means that you do not see a clear-cut opposition between nature and culture.

RM: That's right, because culture is born from predispositions that are already present in nature.

EC: In your paintings, you stress the fact that in building relationships with the world, man needs to mask his more irrational impulses. When I saw your *Cycles of Psychological States*, Adriano Tilgher came to mind. He is a little-known Italian philosopher who attentively studied Pirandello's works. Tilgher wrote that in Pirandellian dramas there is a dialectic between life and form: life in its flow overcomes all obstacles, but precisely because of this, society imposes limits on this flow, which would otherwise risk challenging hierarchies and social roles. Do you think choices exist that allow us to radically free ourselves from the mask? Can man do without the mask, or is it a social necessity, something we cannot live without?

RM: When man identifies with the mask that he has chosen to make his own, or that has been imposed on him, he loses all freedom to act. In my paintings, the mask is a metaphor for the roles that are at the heart of every social organization.

Tiger Fell, 2014
Acrylic on canvas, 130 x 105 cm

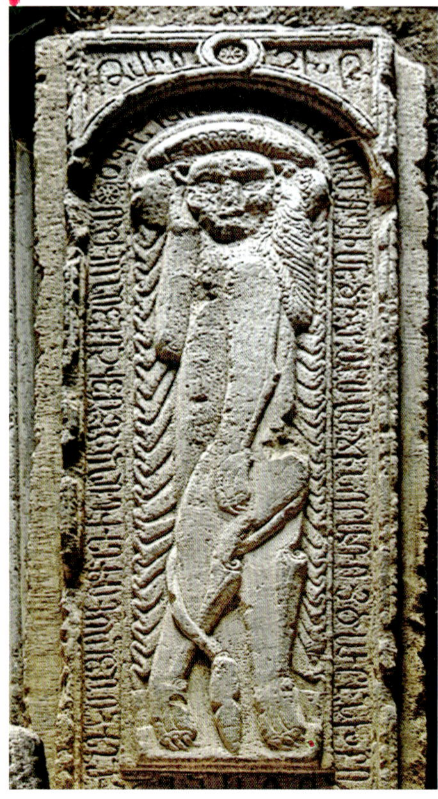

Tomb of Elikum III Orbelian,
Noravank Monastery, 13th century

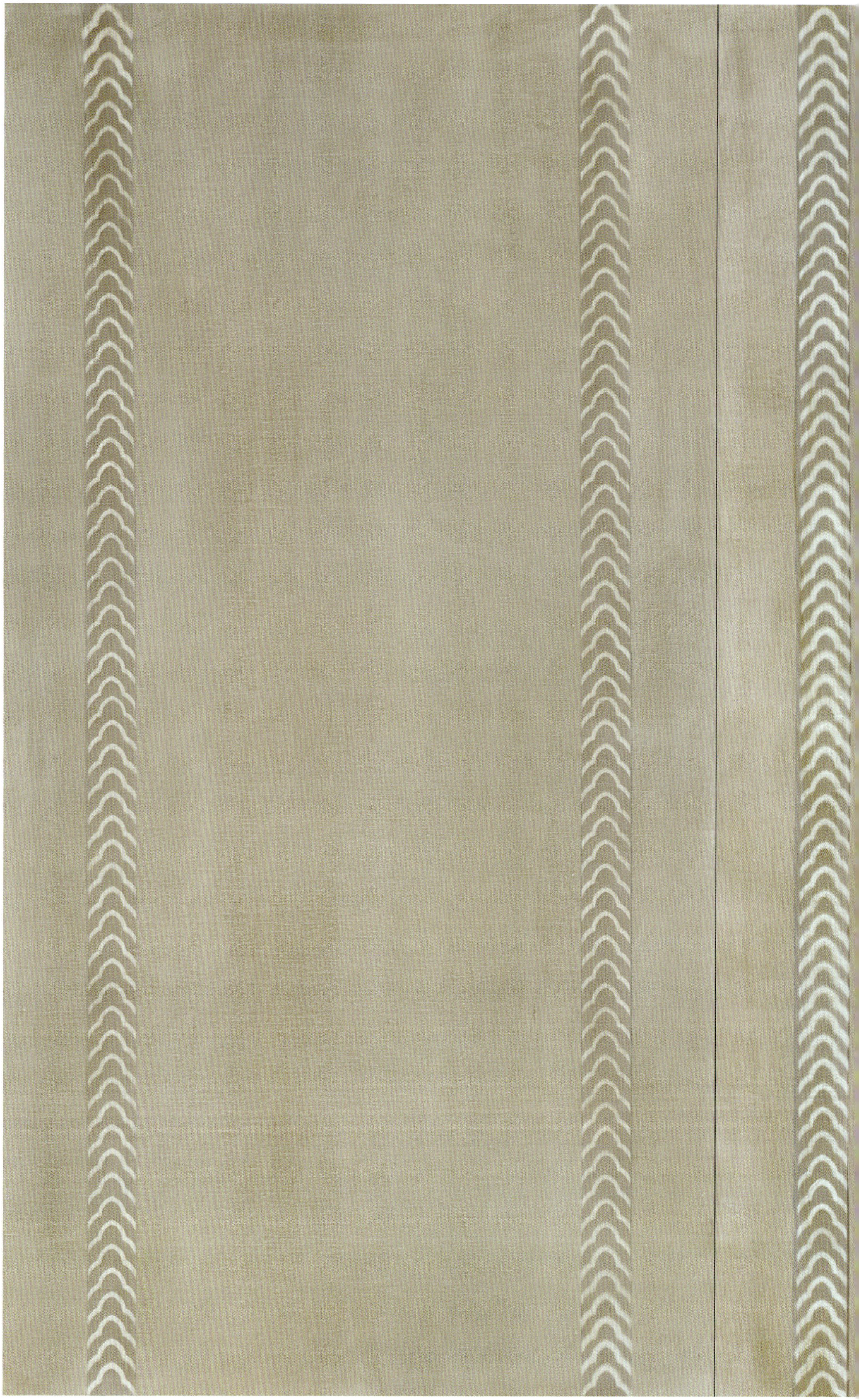

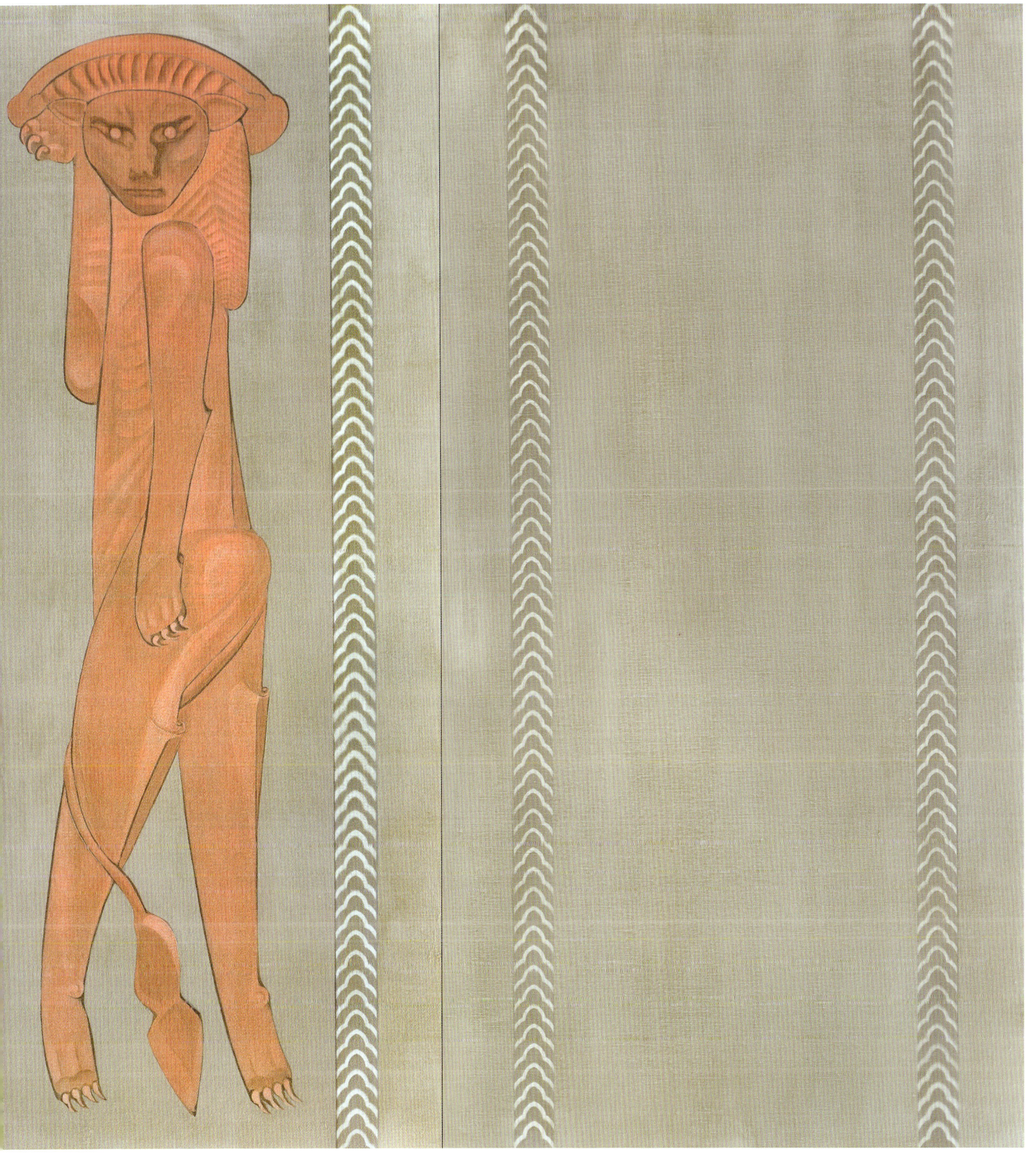

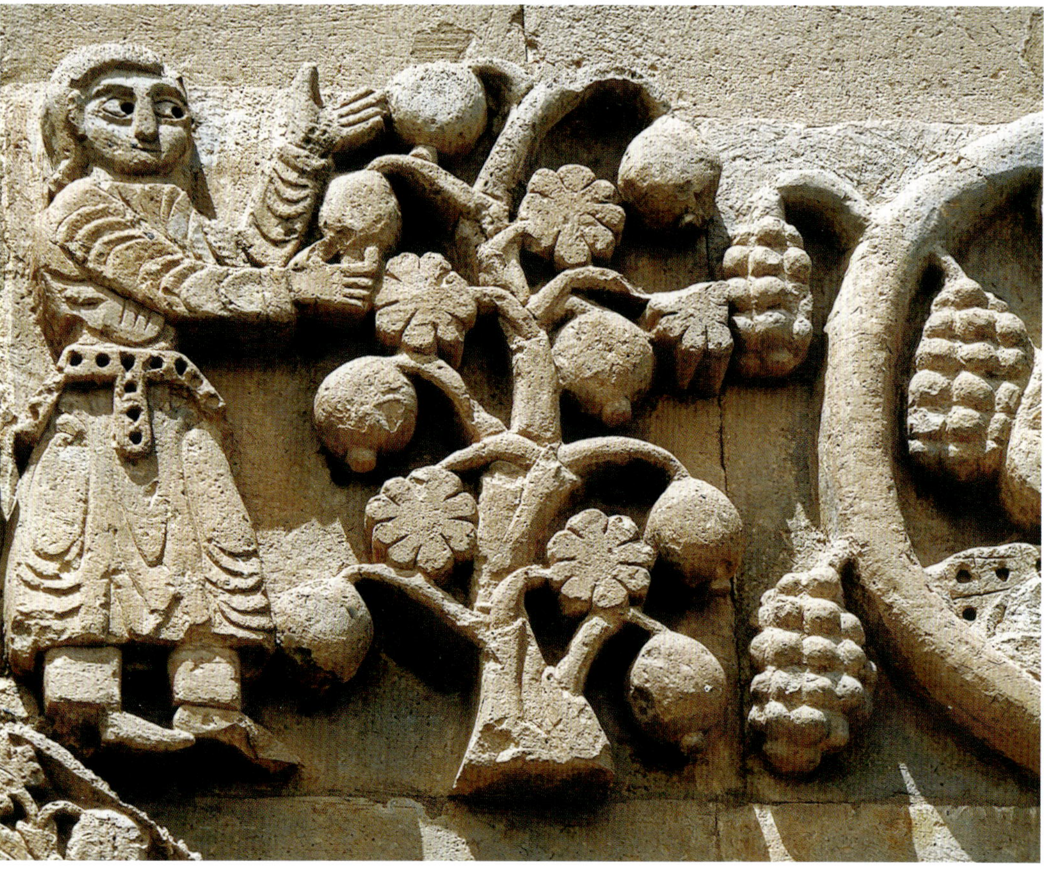

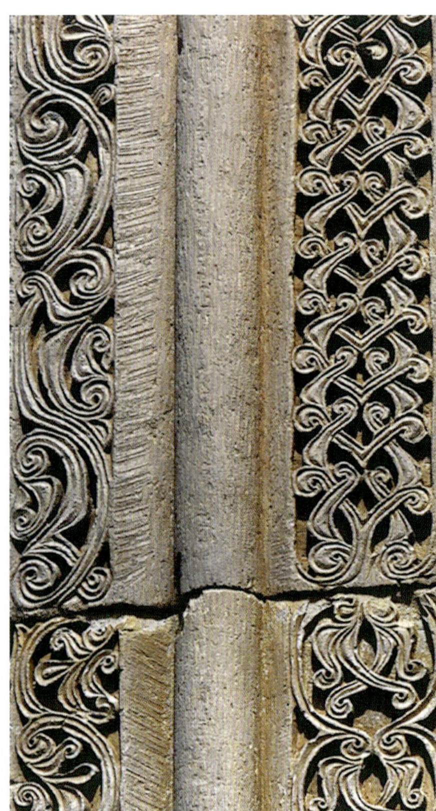

Makaravank Monastery, 1205

EC: What you are saying makes me think of Tilgher's thesis about Pirandello, which I mentioned earlier.

RM: I don't know Tilgher, but I obviously know Pirandello, and I knew about this thesis. There is a painting of mine, *Six Faces, Six Masks*, from 2012, that, while not explicitly referencing *Six Characters in Search of an Author*, certainly brings it to mind. You've made me remember, among other things, that I read a Russian translation of Pirandello's *Six Characters*. The interesting thing is that Pirandello makes meta-theater, and the actors of his characters do not have to trick the spectator. The spectator must understand that he finds himself before actors who are acting: the scene fiction must be clear. In my paintings, something similar happens, in the sense that I don't want to deceive the spectators on an emotional level. I want them to be aware of a situation they all face.

EC: But do you think that we can free ourselves from the mask? Is the answer to freeing ourselves by using it lightly, and being aware of the possibility of occasionally escaping the confines of a character that acts a part?

RM: Freeing oneself from the mask means putting on another one. I ask myself if the soul accepts having a mask. From the point of view of a religious person, everyone must know how to express the best part of himself. But it is unthinkable that showing the best part of yourself is the same as not having a mask. Even when an individual is spontaneous, disinterested, or helpful to his neighbor, he is in some way wearing a mask. But no one can wear just one mask throughout the course of his entire life.

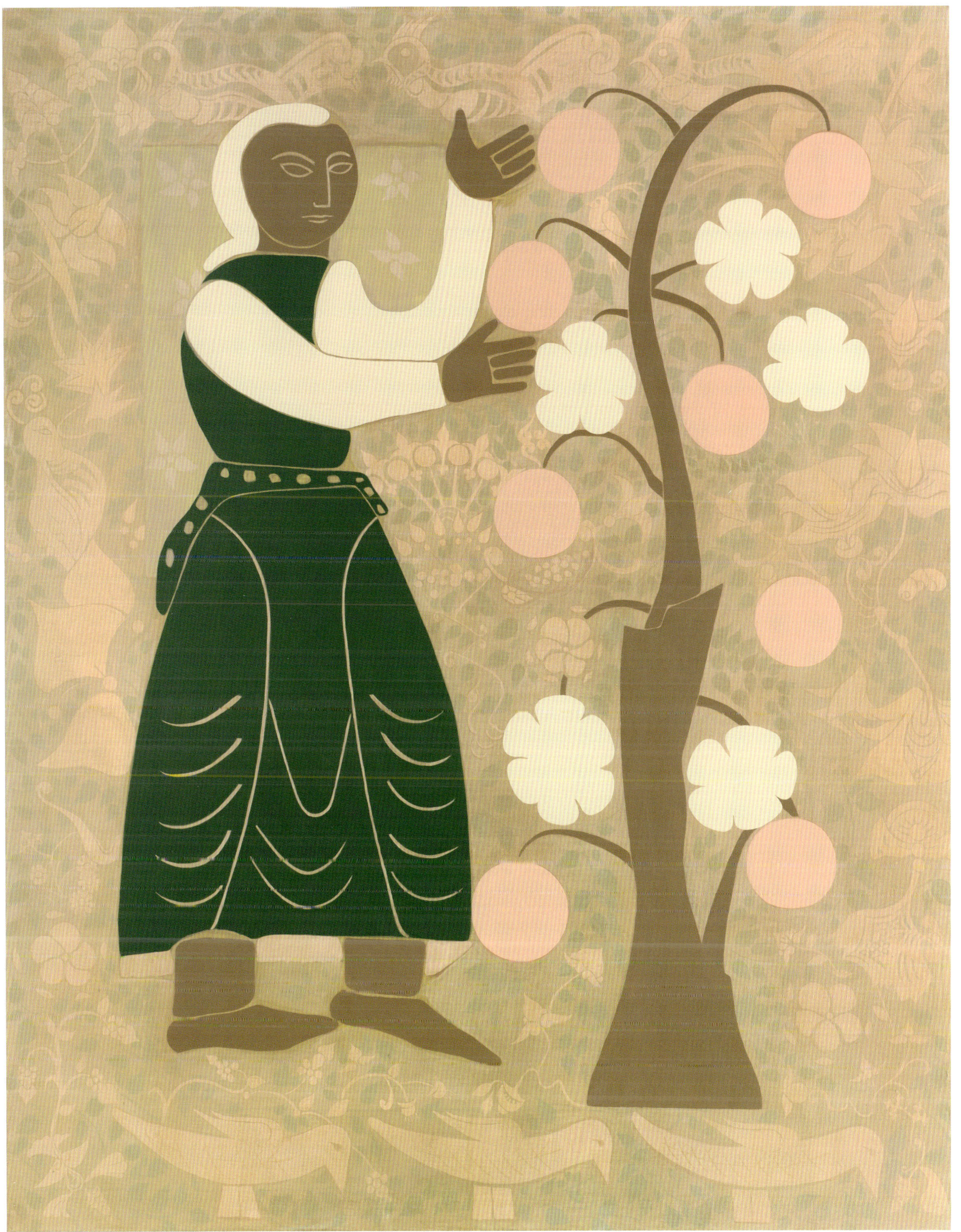

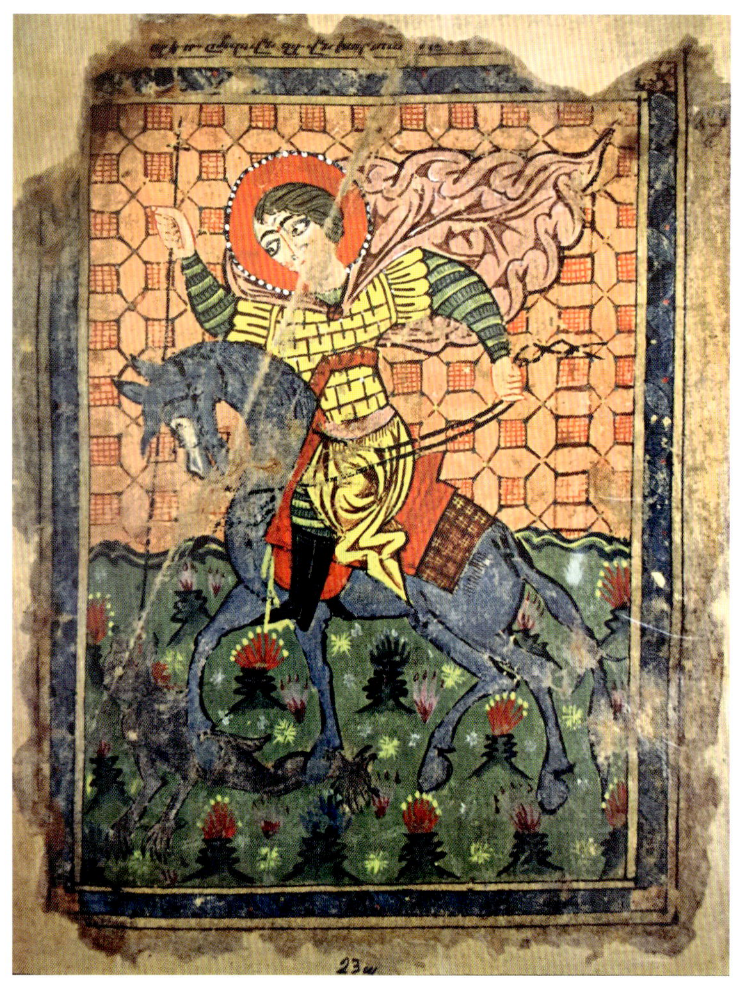

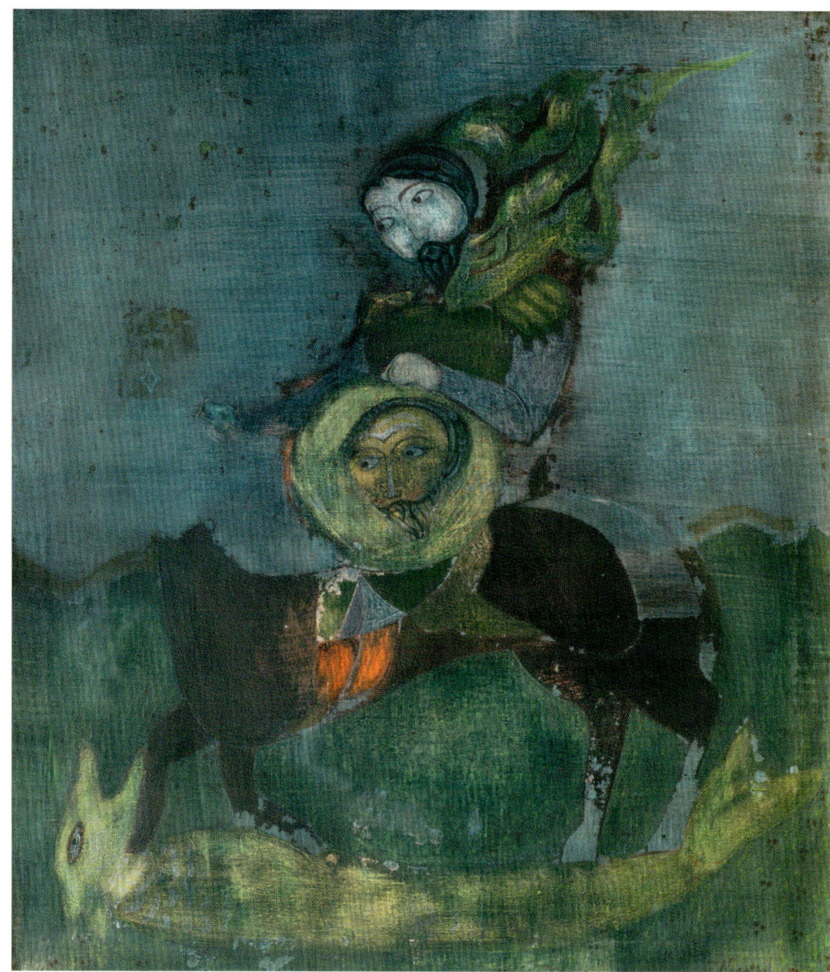

Anonymous painter of Syuniq
Gospel, 14th–15th century,
St. George

St. George, 2012
Acrylic on canvas, 80 x 70 cm

Facing page
St. George, 2009
Acrylic on canvas, 80 x 65 cm

EC: Aside from Pirandello there is another author that we can reference when speaking of your work: the German sociologist Georg Simmel. He sustained that life feeds culture and that the institutionalized forms of knowledge–systems of art, theories on style, artistic or literary trends, etc.–risk blocking the energies that generate culture itself.

RM: This risk is always around the corner, especially when culture becomes academia or pure formalism. This is about the natural order of things. Psychoanalysis has taught us that even the noblest aspects of our existence can be the sublimation of impulses that are anything but noble, and that there is an instinctive part of us that calls to mind our animal side. This consideration leads to the dual role of the presence of the animal in our paintings: on the one hand it refers to medieval bestiaries, while on the other hand it references the ambivalence of human nature. I adore animals. I have two Cane Corso dogs, one of which I got in Italy. When I am home alone with my family I let them run around the garden. I chose them because they are beautiful and courageous, and for their physical appearance. But when people come visit me I lock them up because I don't know what kind of reaction the people who don't know them will have. It all seems so banal, but to me it indicates man's frequently unconscious distrust of animals. These two dogs are often the subjects of my paintings. When I paint at night they come into my studio and watch me, in silence; it's as if they understand what I am doing. I would like to be more extreme in my affirmation: at times their peacefulness as they watch me paint en-

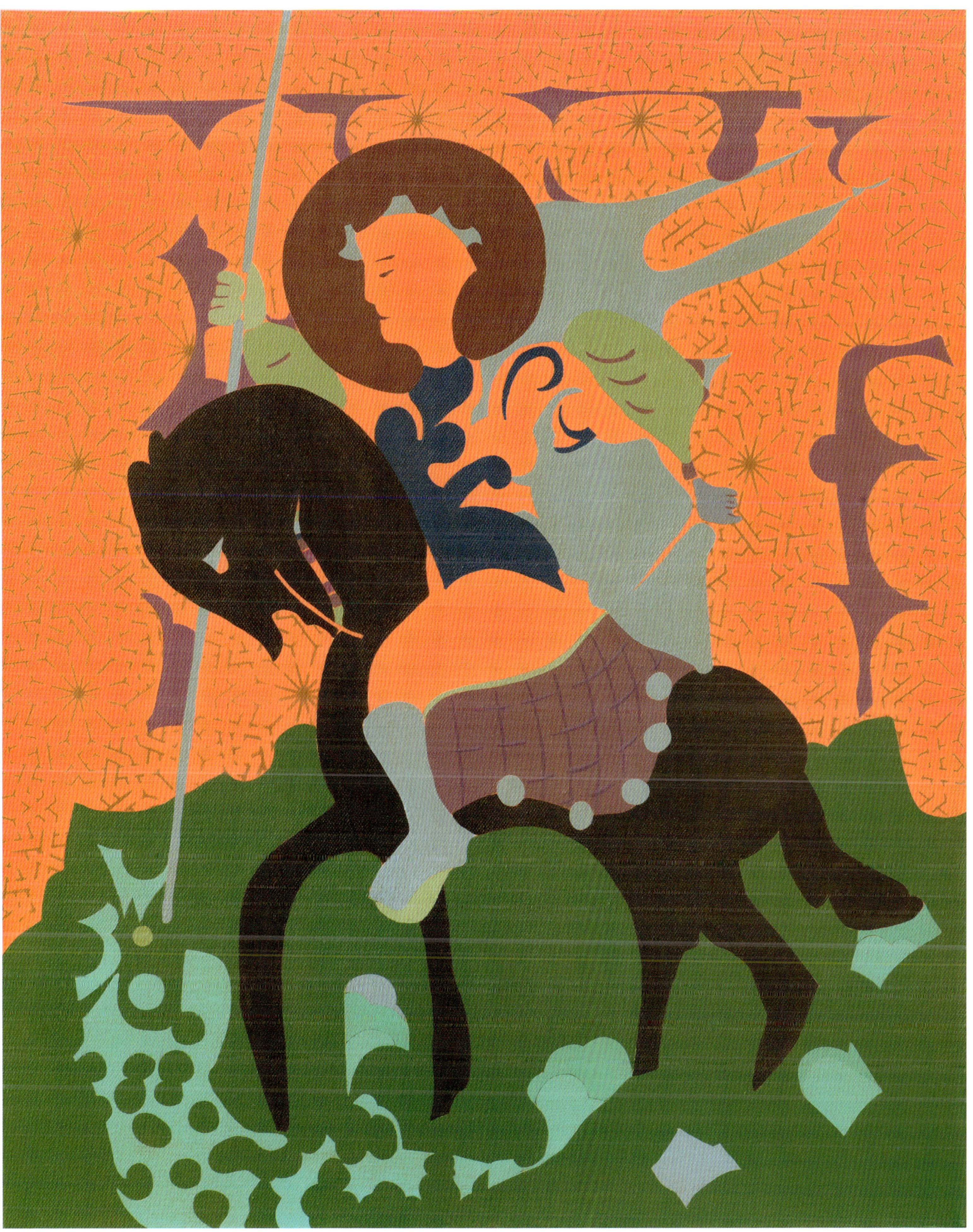

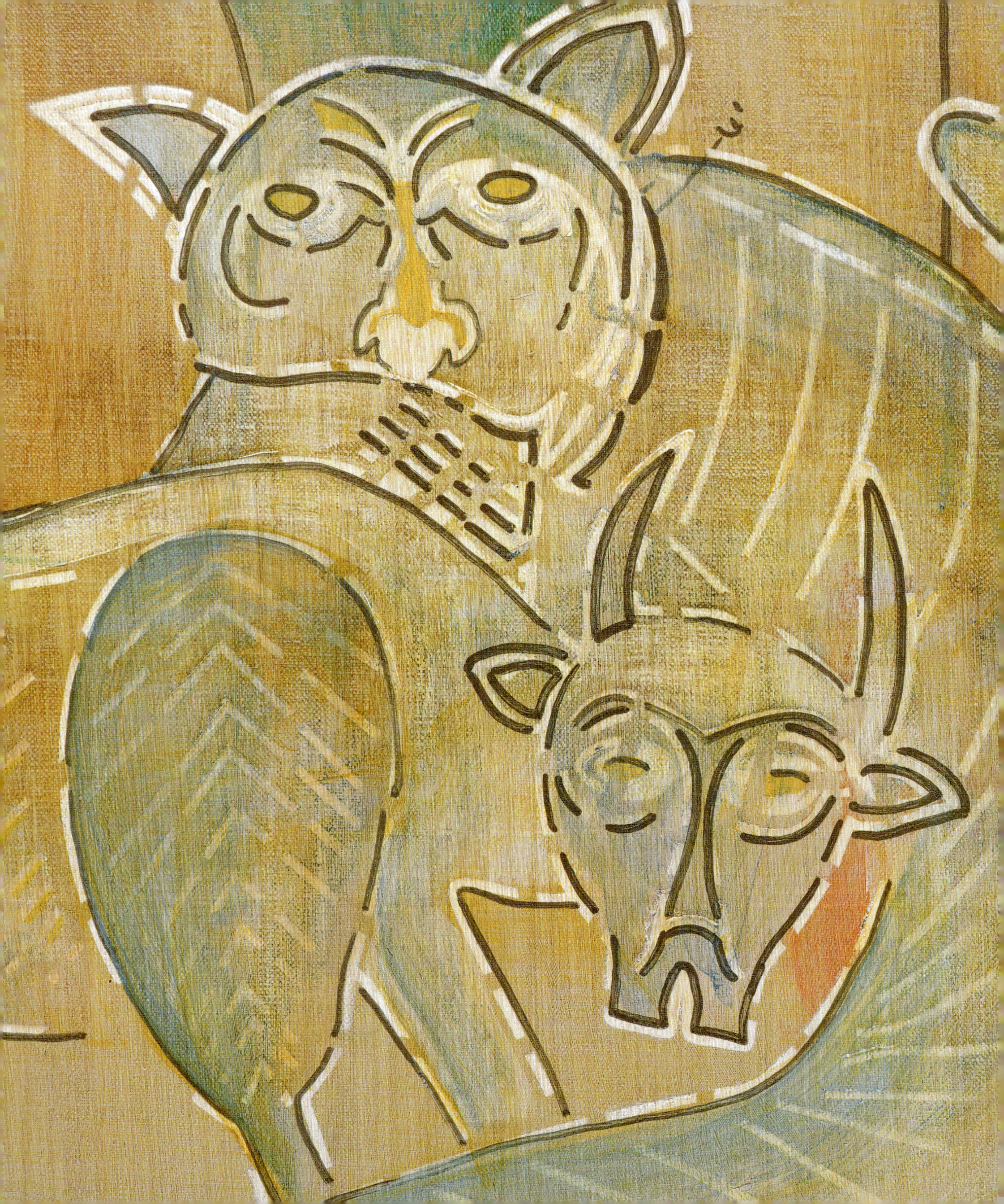

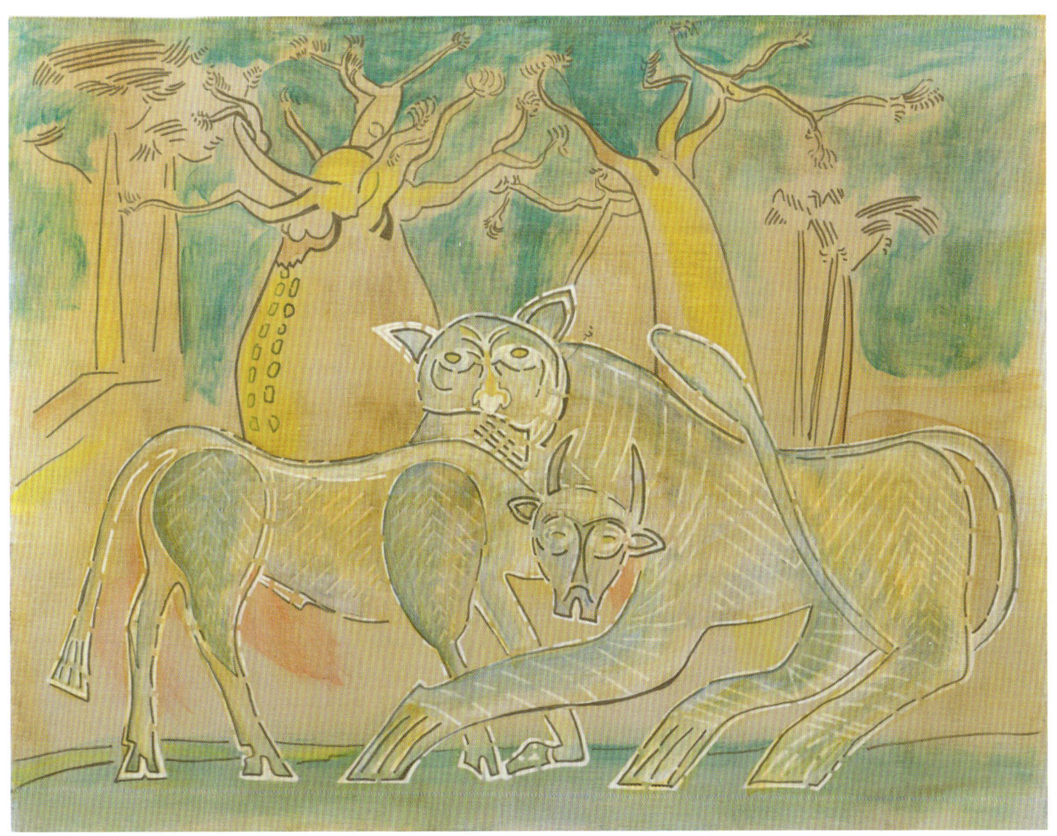

courages me to keep going, because in them I find a dimension that is complimentary to myself. I feel close to the romantics in this relationship with animals and nature.

EC: The relationship with nature is an essential element in the literature and philosophy of German romanticism. Think of Shelling, who saw the absolute in nature and believed that art was key to understanding the dialectic tension at the root of nature itself. Or Schuman's music; in *Waldszenen* he gives voice to the nature of the woods. Or Turner's fading of marine landscapes or the mountains. If I reference Armenia, I have to mention Ivan Aivazovsky and his sea storms. In all these artists the contrast between culture and life seems nonexistent.

RM: Your vision is suggestive and undoubtedly correct. Yes, it is true, on the conceptual level in my work man and nature are two sides of the same coin. This could be a common trait of romanticism. But to be honest, I feel light years away from romanticism, from Turner and from Aivazovsky. Of course, I recognize the greatness of these artists. But it is one thing to recognize the greatness of an artist and it is another to share formal solutions and their thoughts, which are tied to the period they lived in. My painting is more stamp-like. I use spot colors. I am quite far, as you may understand, from the *Sturm und Drang* from which German romanticism was born. The fact you felt the need to bring romanticism up when discussing my work makes me curious.

EC: I spoke of romanticism because you believe that the dual condition and ambivalence of man constitutes the principal dynamic of existence. In everything that you say the dialectic tension between passion and reason, instinct and thought, impulse and

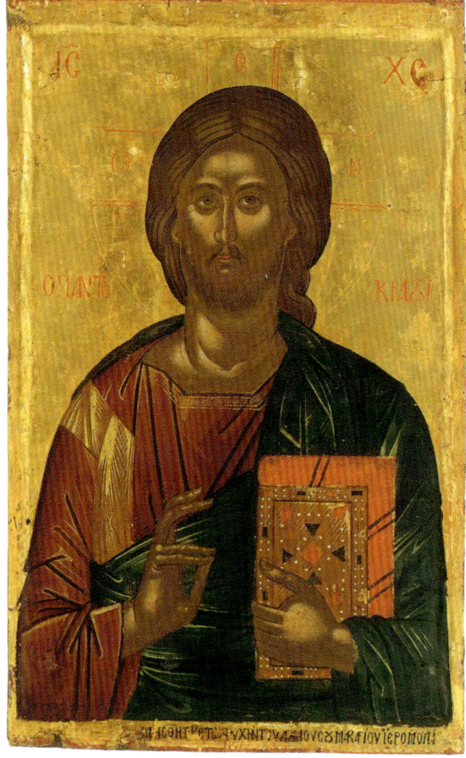

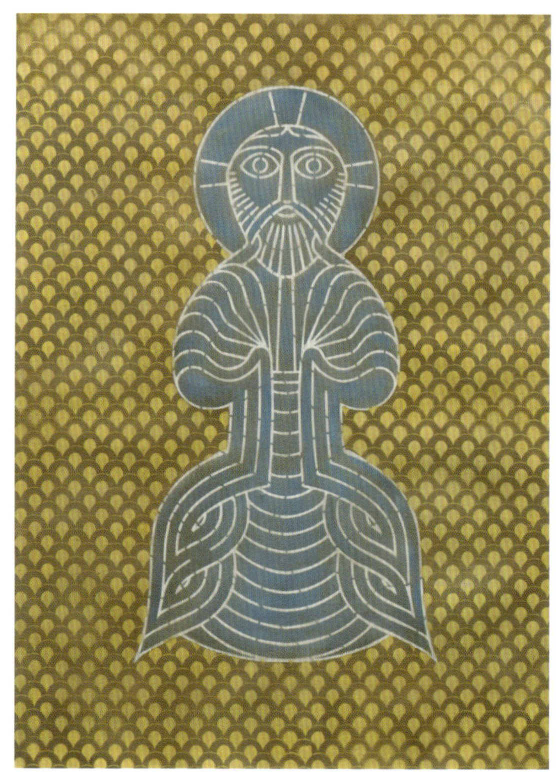

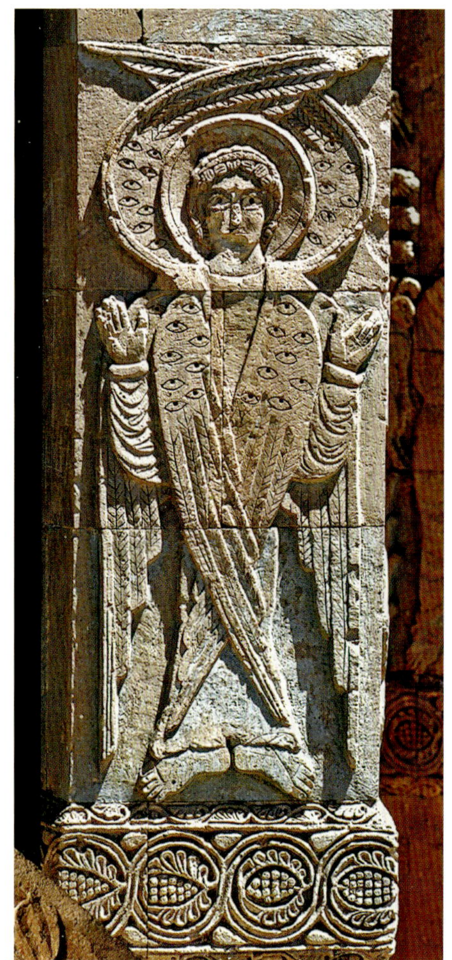

Akhtamar Monastery, 915–921

moral principles emerges. The romantic understanding of nature, especially in Schelling, can be identified in the polarity between nature and spirit, or between the conscious and unconscious. Art, again, according to Schelling, was the only human activity capable of expressing this dialectic. You can't deny that these elements are present in both your work and statements.

RM: I do not disagree, theoretically speaking, with anything you are saying. But I am a painter. I express myself through images. On the level of style, I can't relate to romanticism, but it is also true that I am drawn to looking for the traces of romanticism that are present in symbolism. That's why I feel closer to Vardges Surenyants than I do to Ivan Aivazovsky, if we stay within the bounds of the Armenian art you referenced. It is also true, however, that at times I feel the need to paint in a way that is different from the style that characterizes my spot color paintings. Sometimes I use a more expressionist style, which, in some ways, evokes Parisian abstraction of the 1950s because of the softness of color, or the postmodern painting of the 1980s. Every time I change my style to make one of these paintings I feel reinvigorated, ready to return to what I consider "my painting." I am referring to my paintings with the stamped style and layers of solid color.

EC: Your thoughts on solid, non-expressionist color make me think of the two-dimensionality of icons.

RM: I construct my image differently. My works are always developed on different perspective planes.

EC: That's true, but it is also true that you don't perceive sculptural plasticity in your figures. And it is just as true that you have painted icons and sacred images even if you covered them in textures reminiscent of ancient Armenian adornments.

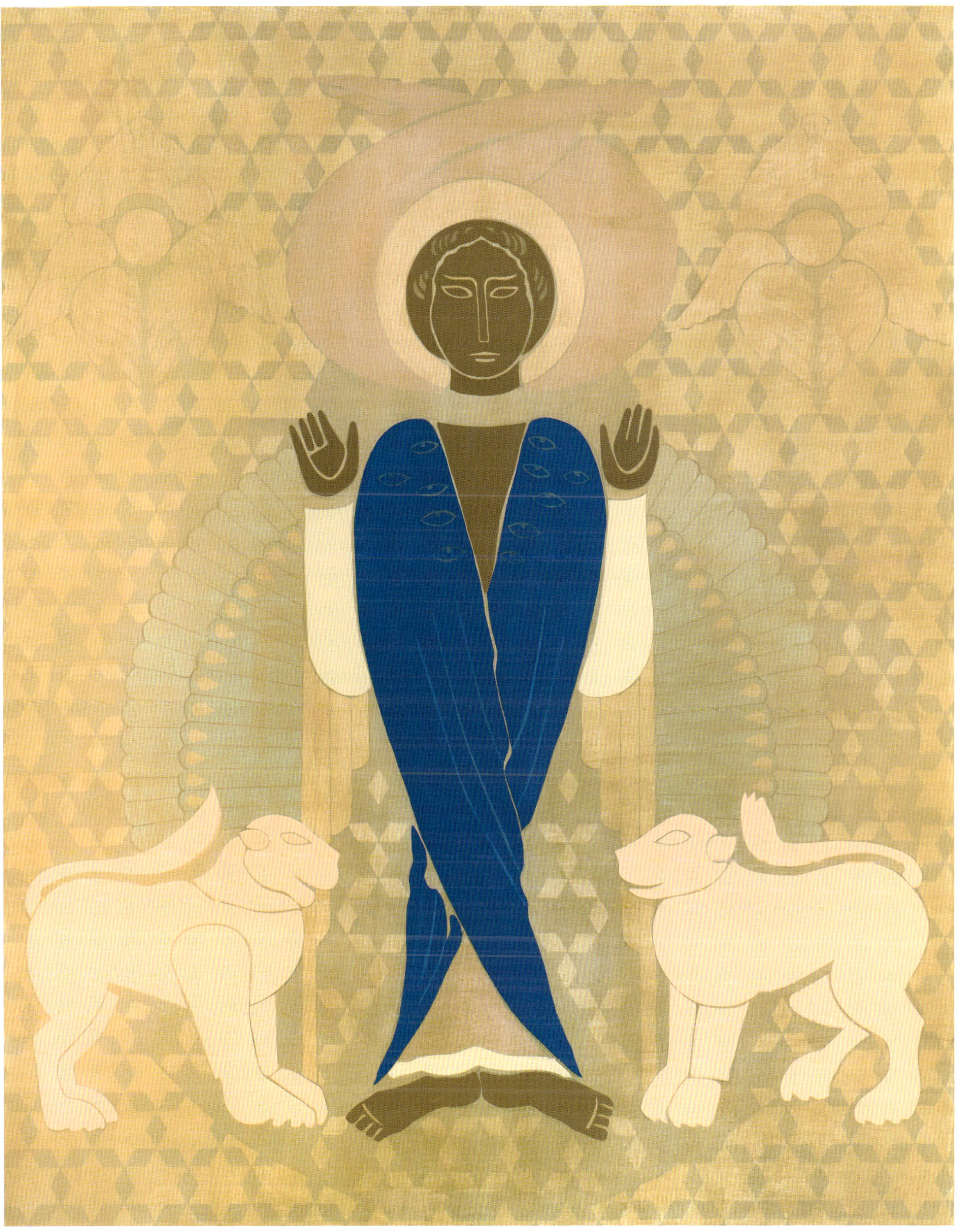

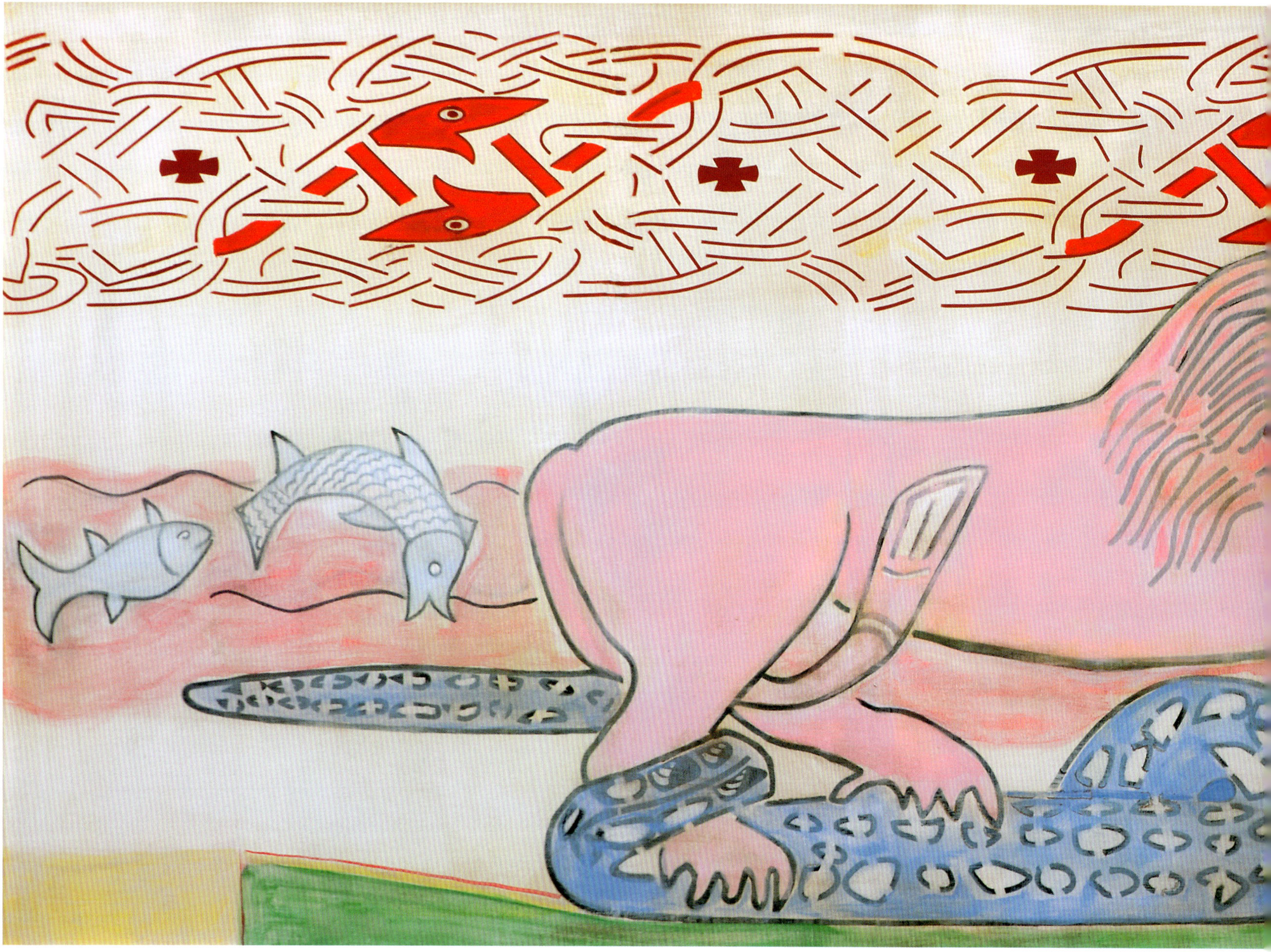

Struggle, 2009
Acrylic on canvas, 85 x 230 cm

Ishkan Church, 7th century

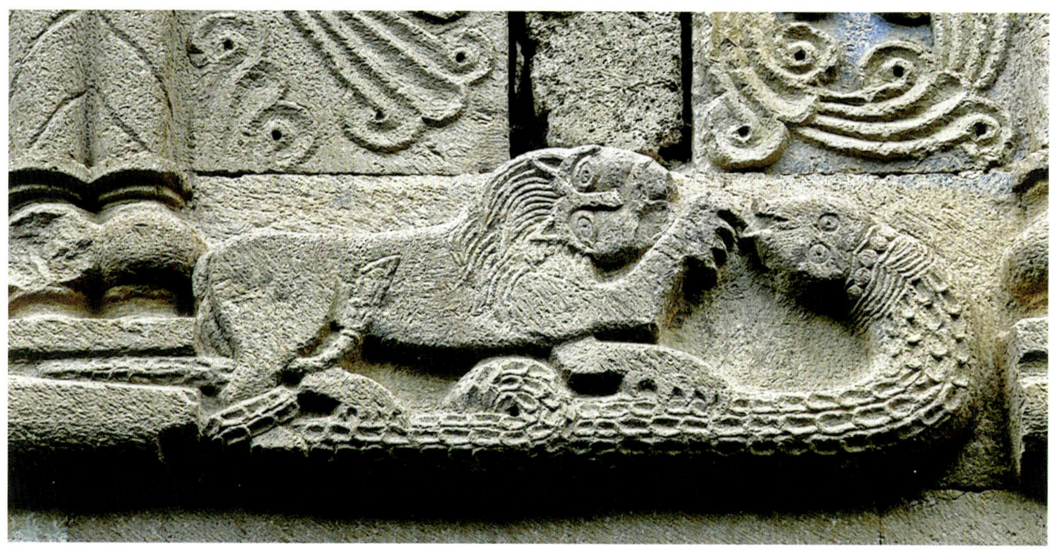

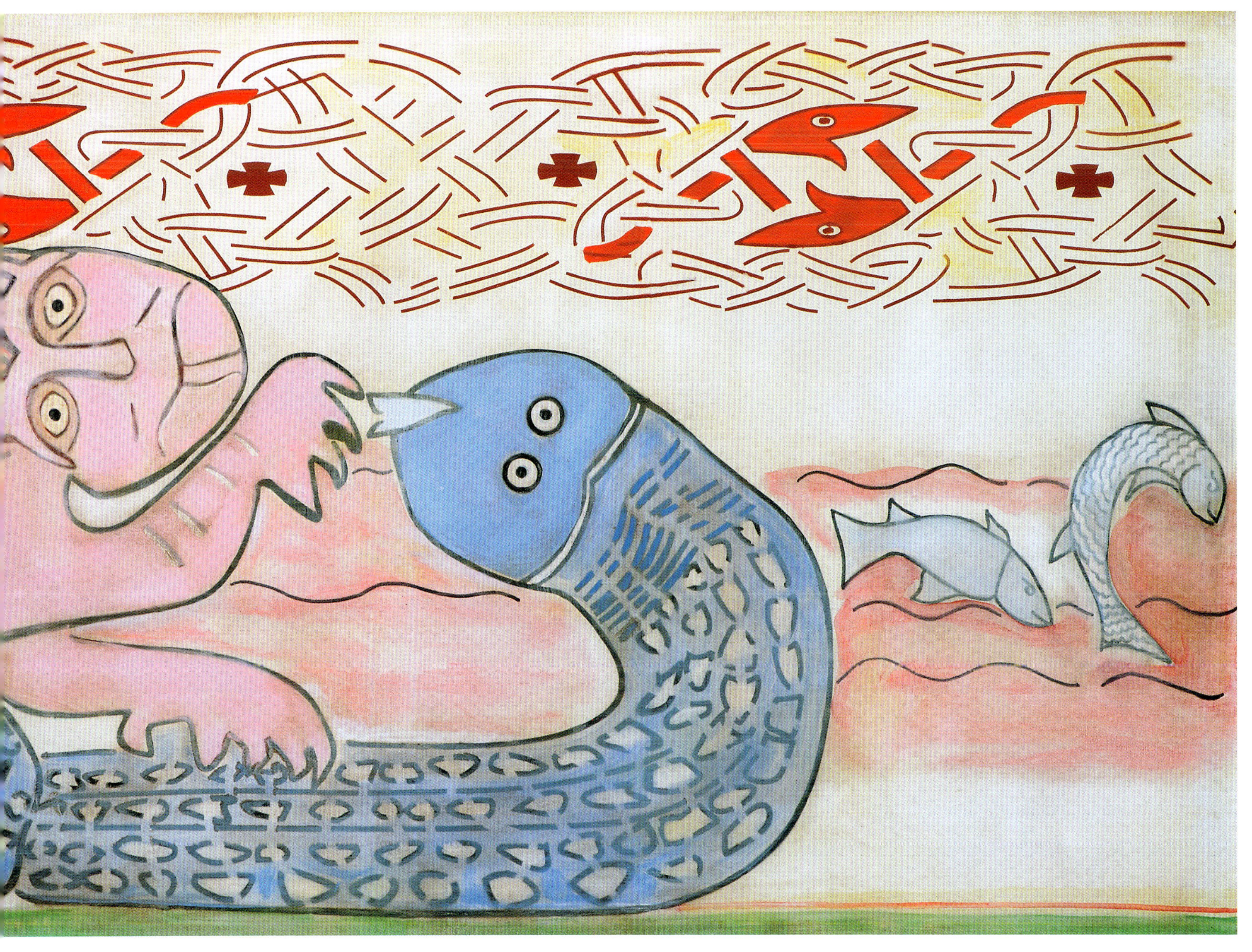

RM: What have you understood of these works?

EC: I try [*laughs*]. For iconographers, painting was like praying, and icons can be considered a visual prayer. They refuted the plasticity of the figures, precisely because it emphasized their physicality, while the body had to be transfigured in spiritual terms. It is clear to me that you have not painted your religious-theme paintings with this intention. The duality that you deal with in these works between the corporeal and the spiritual is not addressed in theological terms.
RM: My intention is linguistic, not theological.

EC: Exactly. But it is also true that you repeat the image as if it were a module, and this happens with sacred icons as well.
RM: That is a suggestive thesis. I know quite well that interpretations can contain as-

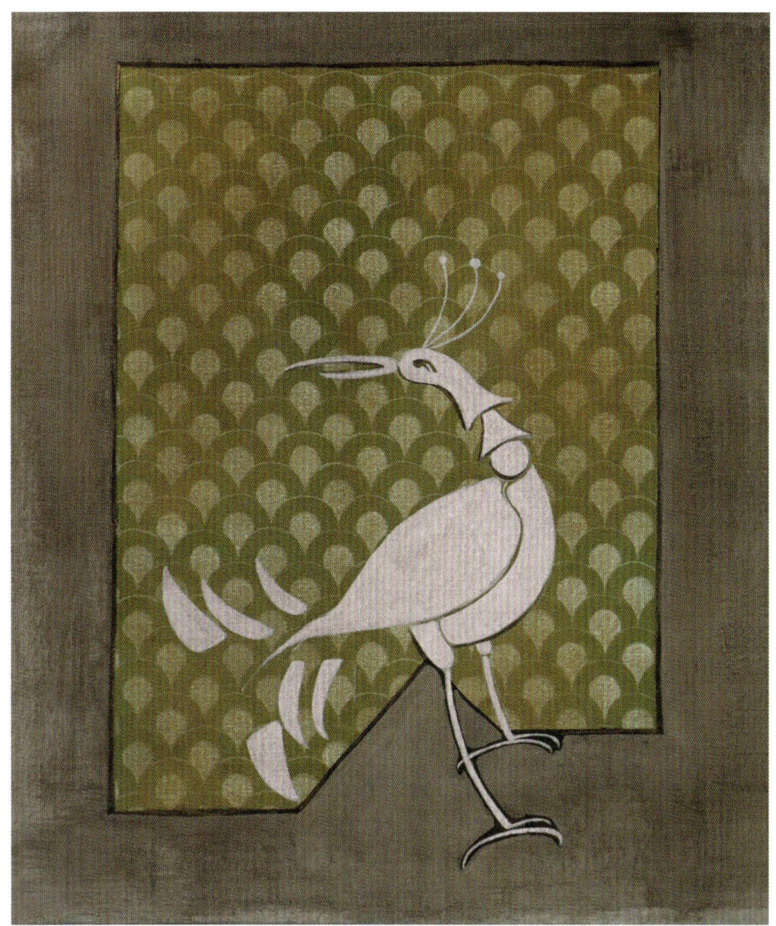

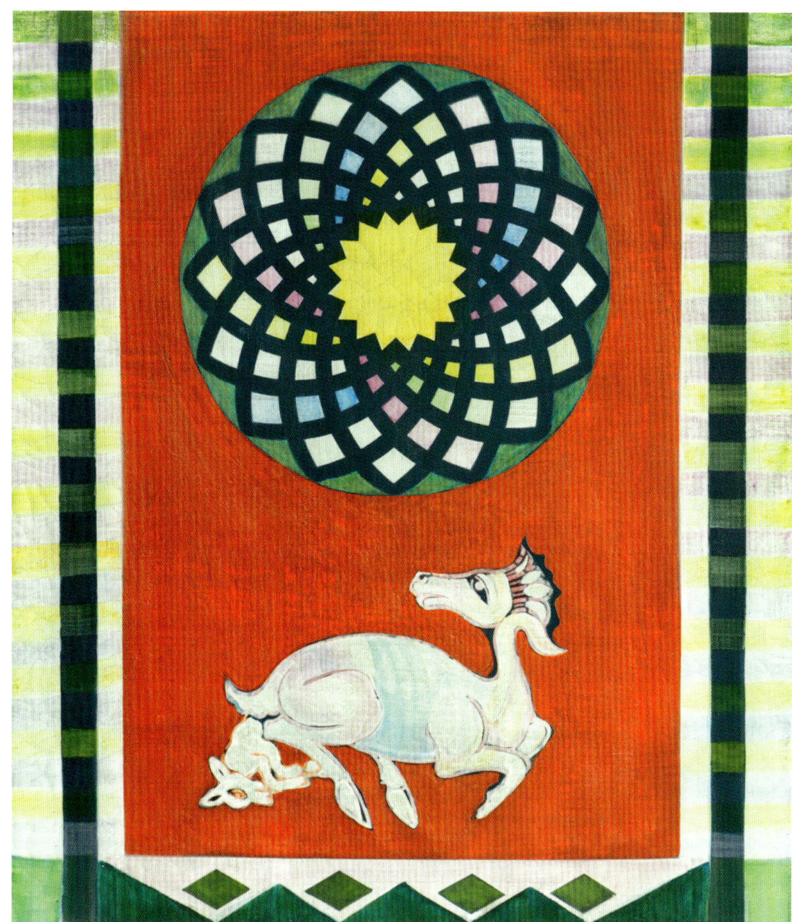

Peacock, 2009
Acrylic on canvas, 70 x 60 cm

Christmas, 2009
Acrylic on canvas, 80.5 x 70.5 cm

Facing page
Washing of the Feet, 2009
Acrylic on canvas, 70 x 60 cm

pects of the works that are unknown to the author. But it is also true that my work has a secular essence, even if it draws upon the Christian iconographic tradition.

EC: I agree, but it stands to reason that the choices of an artist are never only of a formal nature.

RM: You give more importance to concepts, to what the work implies instead of its formal aspect.

EC: I recognize this is my own personal limit that stems from my philosophical upbringing, but it also comes from the fact that, in dealing with contemporary works in which the conceptual element is increasingly more relevant, I sustain that the contents are no less important than the form. Sometimes, to the contrary, they seem to take center stage with respect to the forms themselves. In 1994, I interviewed Arthur C. Danto, who at the time was collaborating with *tema celeste*, the magazine directed by Demetrio Paparoni of which I was the deputy editor for some time. Danto was constantly in the magazine, and he never missed an opportunity to reaffirm that artists, from Duchamp onwards, had brought about the Hegelian prophecy of the death of art.

RM: Content is fundamental for me. But continue with the death of art . . .

EC: Hegel wrote that in art the spiritual content, and therefore the concept, would gradually prevail over the perceivable form. Consequently, art, intended as the form inter-

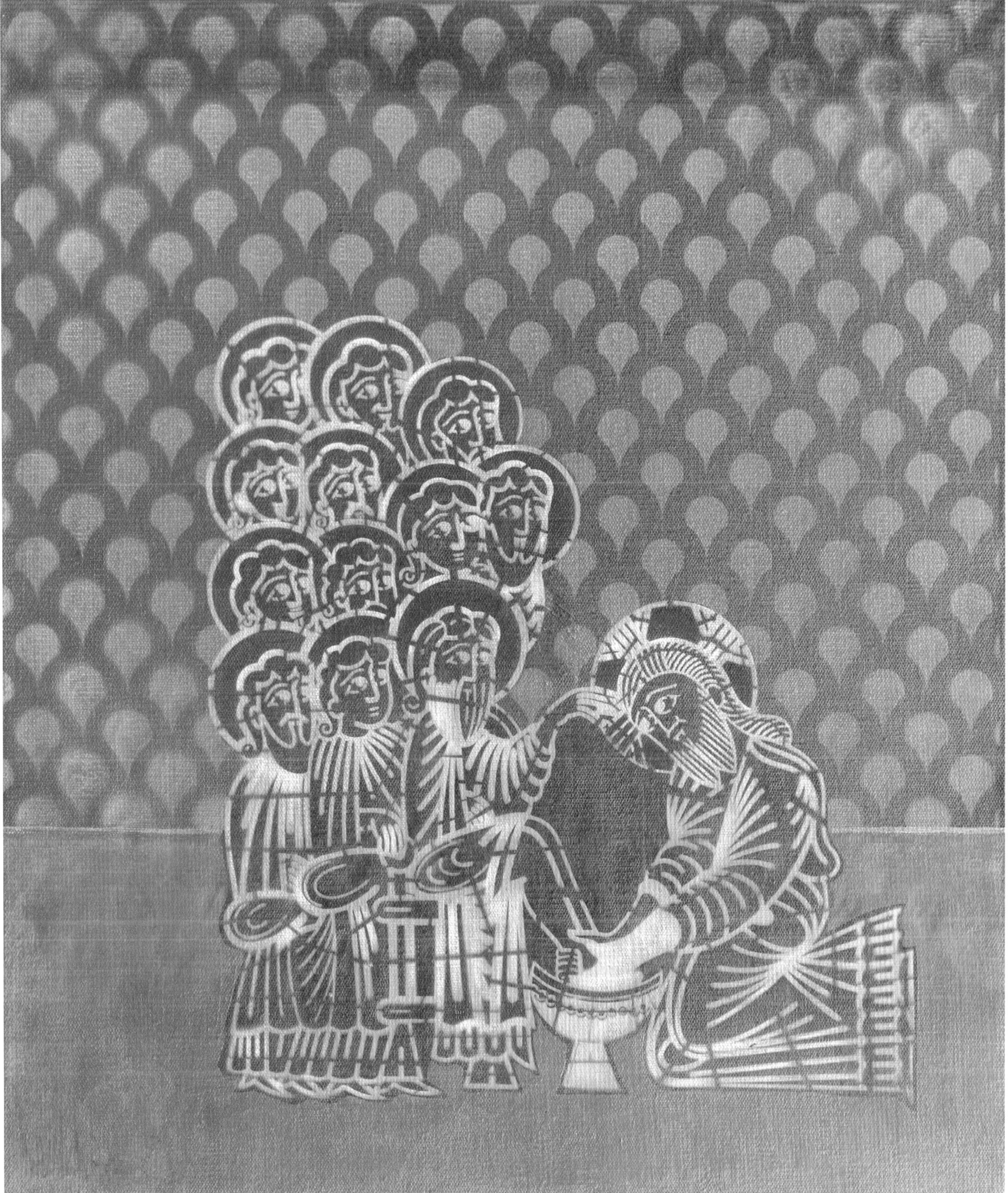

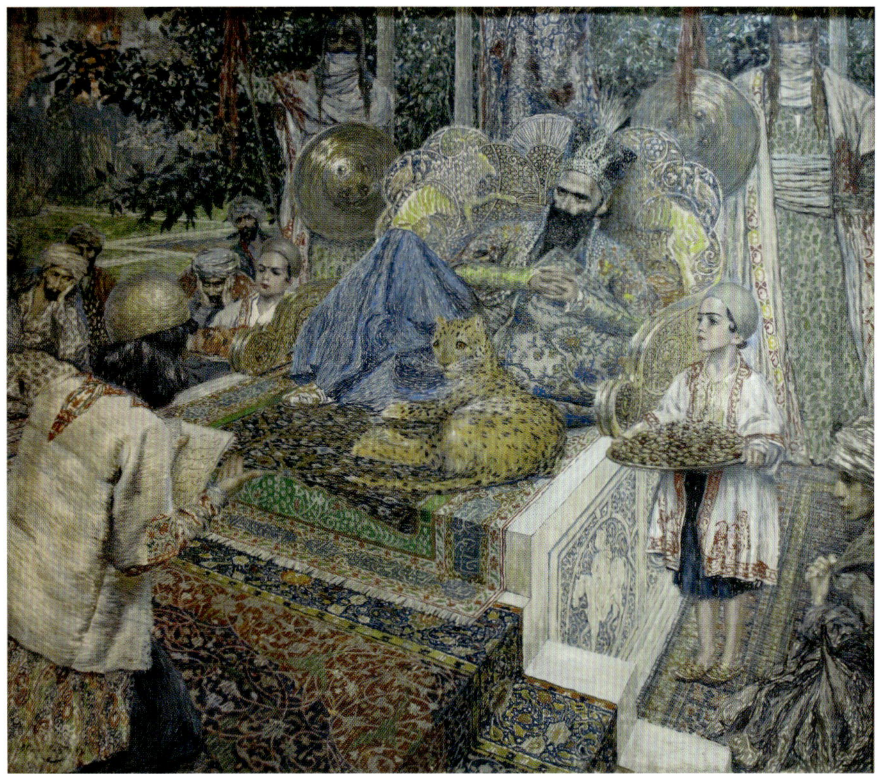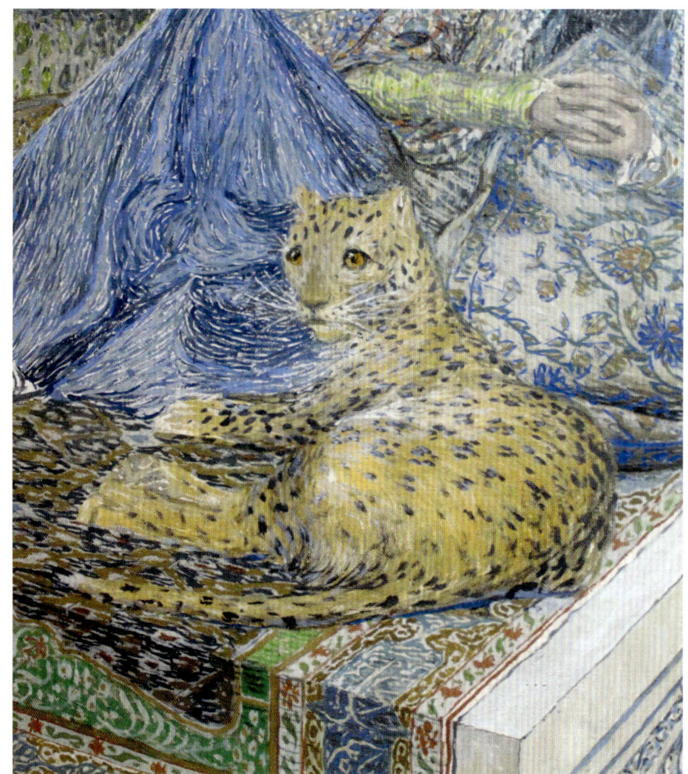

Vardges Surenyants, *Ferdowsi
Reads "Shahnameh" (Book of Kings)
to Mahmud of Ghazna*, 1913
Oil on canvas, 132.6 x 152 cm
Yerevan, National Gallery of Armenia

preted by the eye, would be substituted by concepts that are understood through thought. Thus they would shift from the perceivable to the intelligible. The death of art does not mean, therefore, that art would no longer have a reason to exist, but that it would pass, as Duchamp would say, from the retinal dimension to the conceptual one.

RM: Of course. It's undeniable that people who use a paintbrush must deal with the conceptual change that the historic avant-garde brought about in art. But it is also undeniable that art is free by nature and affirms, in one way or another, the plurality of styles. This plurality belongs to the stylistic choices of each artist as well; they can simultaneously be abstract, figurative, conceptual, or anything the artist wants. Do you think that the artist is asked to be coherent?

EC: In the late modern era, asking an artist to be coherent on a formal level does not make sense. Even on the conceptual plane something similar is happening today, because of the end of the ideologies that contrasted one another throughout the twentieth century. Ulrich Beck wrote that we are in the age of the "and," meant as a conjunction as opposed to the "or" which indicates an opposition. For him the age of the "either, or" has surrendered to the age of the "and, and." An example of this dynamic comes from the fact that today communist states base their economy on the same market laws as capitalist societies. In art something similar happened, you admitted it yourself a little while ago when you affirmed that you can be abstract, figurative, and conceptual all at once. Going back to icons, it is living in the age of the "and, and" that allows you to use the icon without adhering to its theological aesthetic.

RM: You know what . . . I can relate to what you said.

Facing page
Jaguar, 2014
Acrylic on canvas, 155 x 120 cm

Pages 40-41
Plasticine Toys, 2015, detail

August 2014. Thank you to Sona Avagyan for acting as interpreter during these conversations.

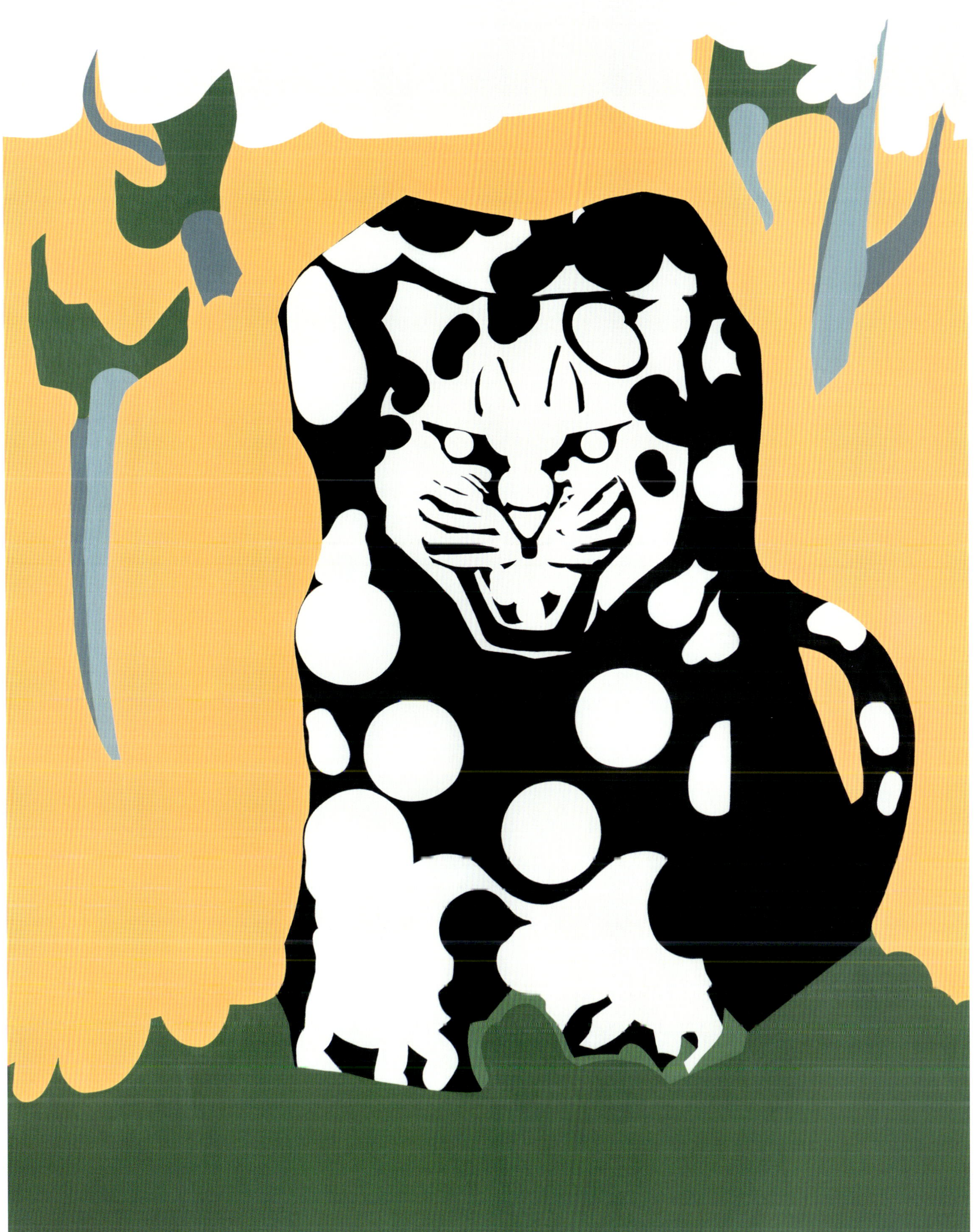

WORKS

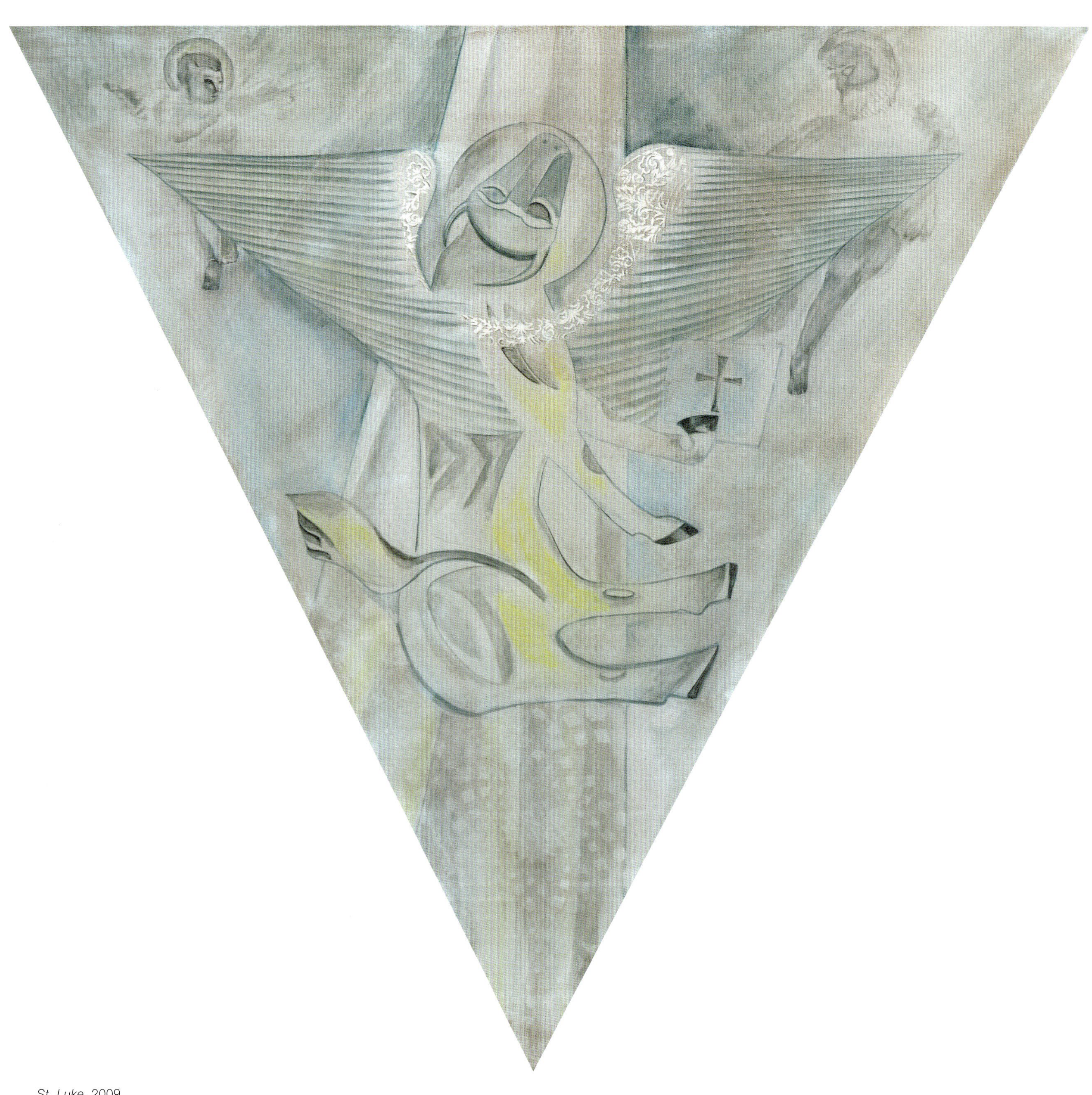

St. Luke, 2009
Acrylic on canvas, 188.5 x 190.5 cm

Prey No. 1, 2000
Acrylic on canvas, 90 x 80 cm

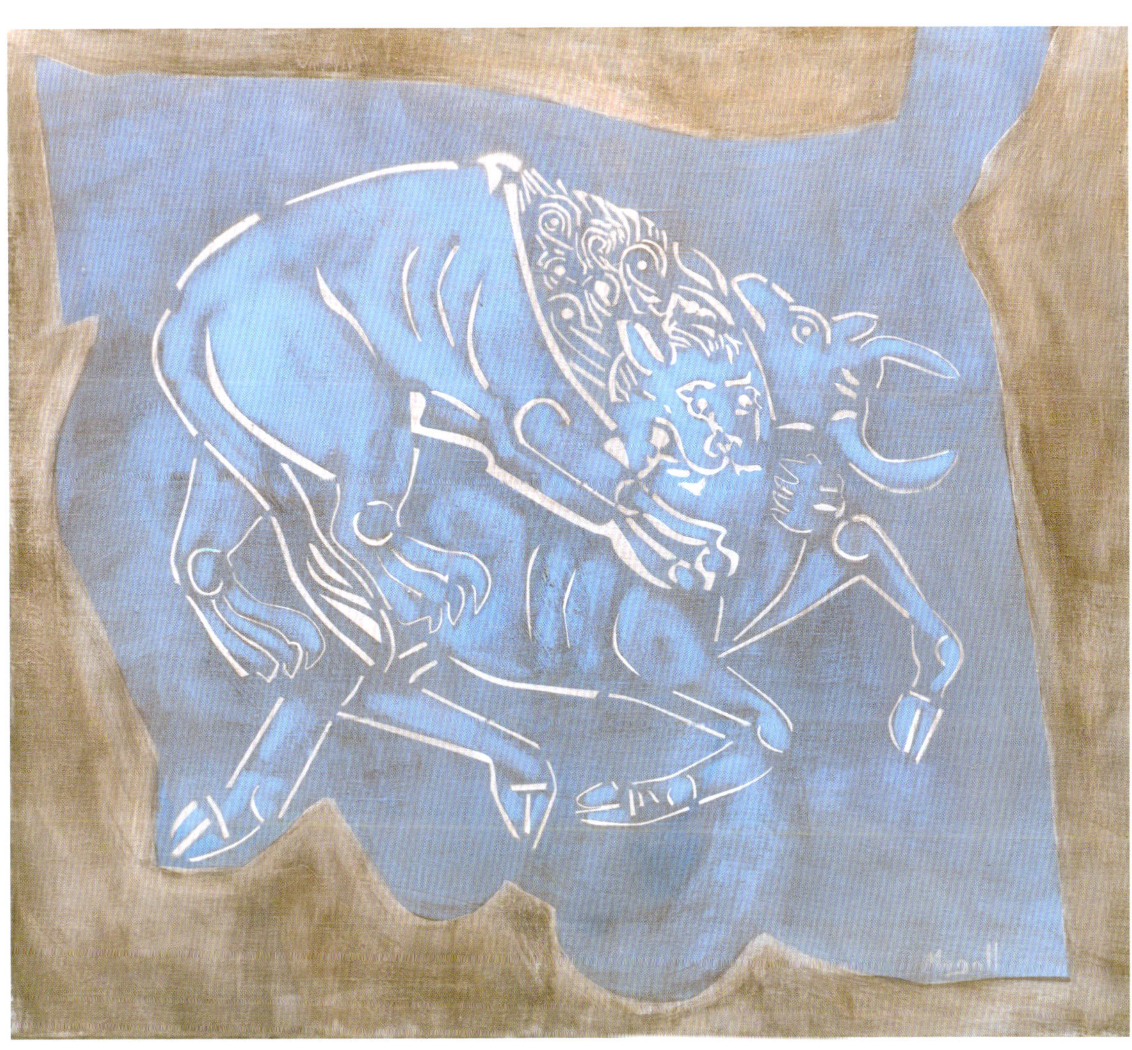

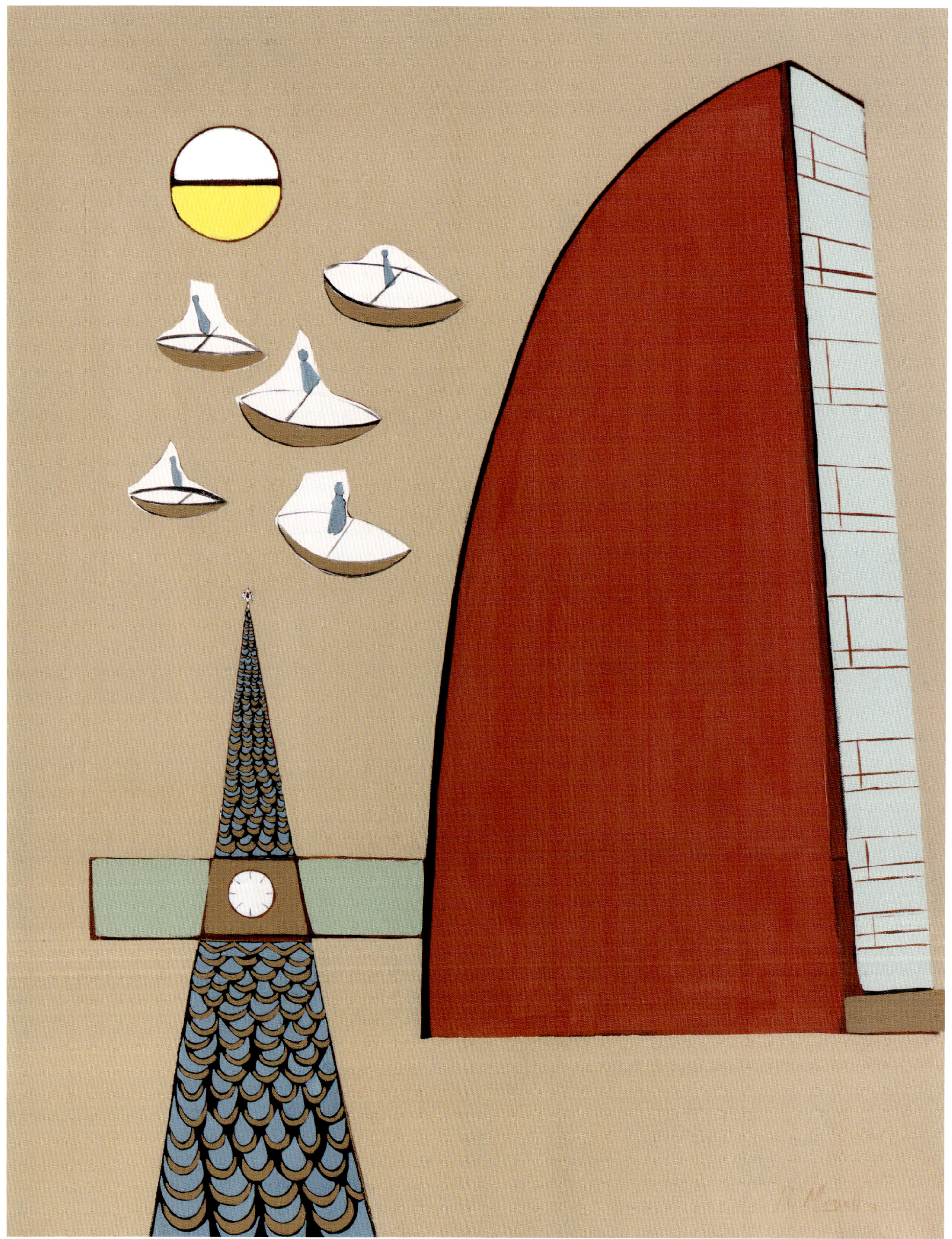

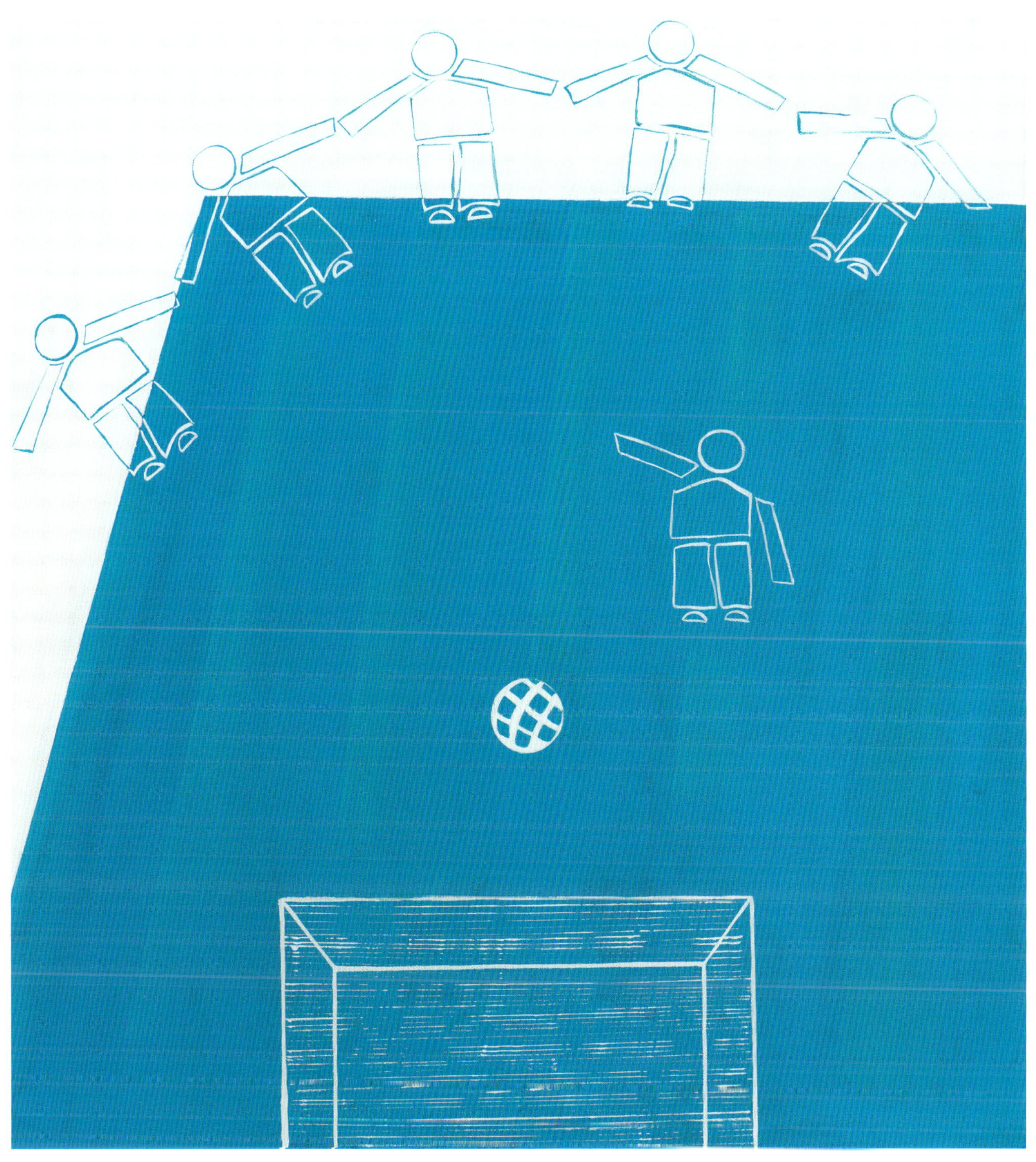

Football Players, 2010
Acrylic on canvas, 115 x 105 cm

Facing page
Dubai, 2010
Acrylic on canvas, 115 x 90 cm

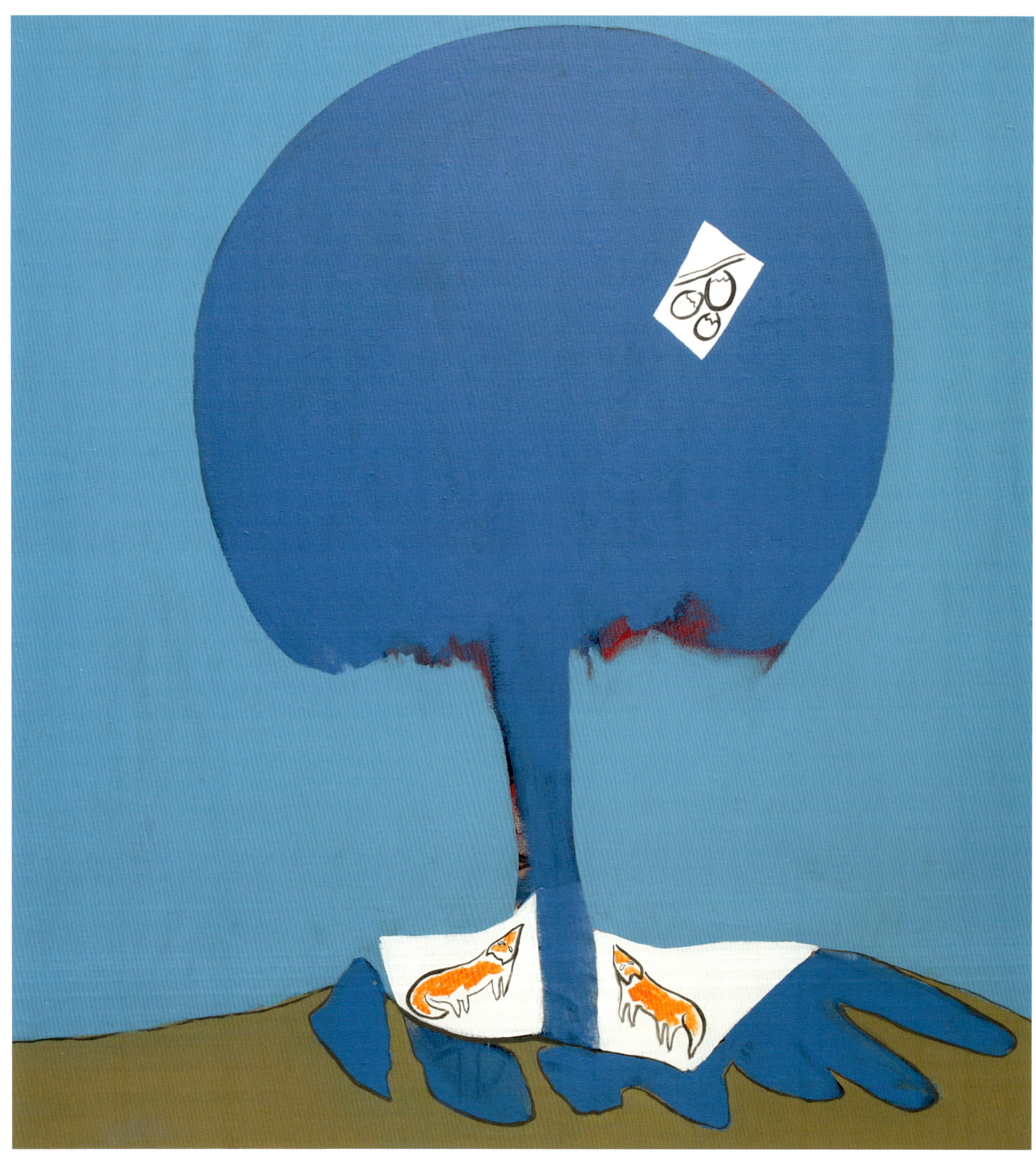

Mirage, 2010
Acrylic on canvas, 115 x 105 cm

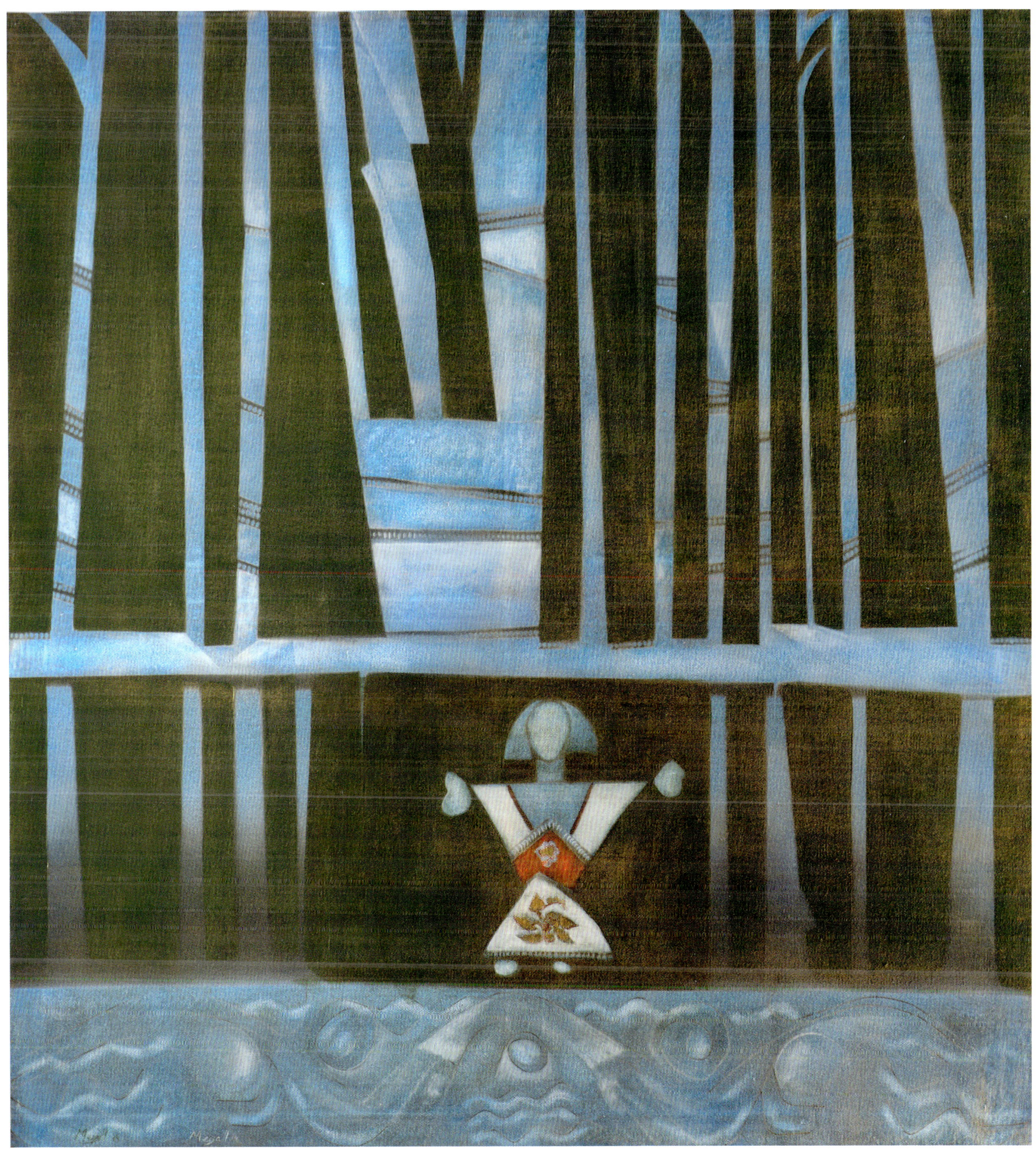

In Russian Forest, 2010
Acrylic on canvas, 115 x 90 cm

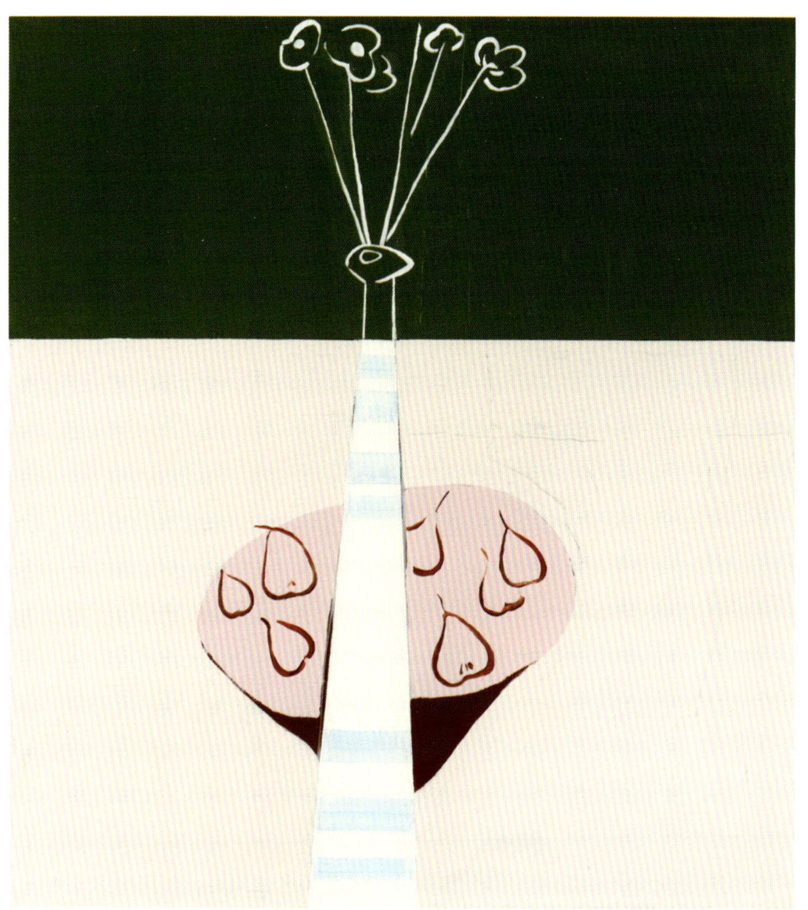

Still Life with Pears, 2010
Acrylic on canvas, 115 x 105 cm

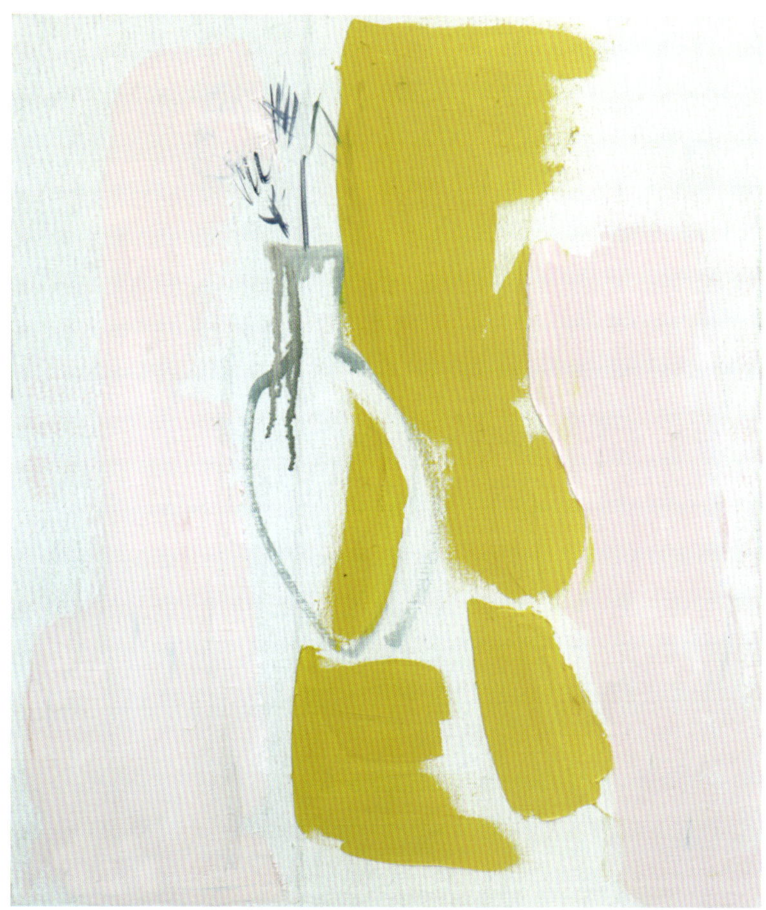

Still Life with Flowerpot, 2012
Oil on canvas, 70 x 60 cm

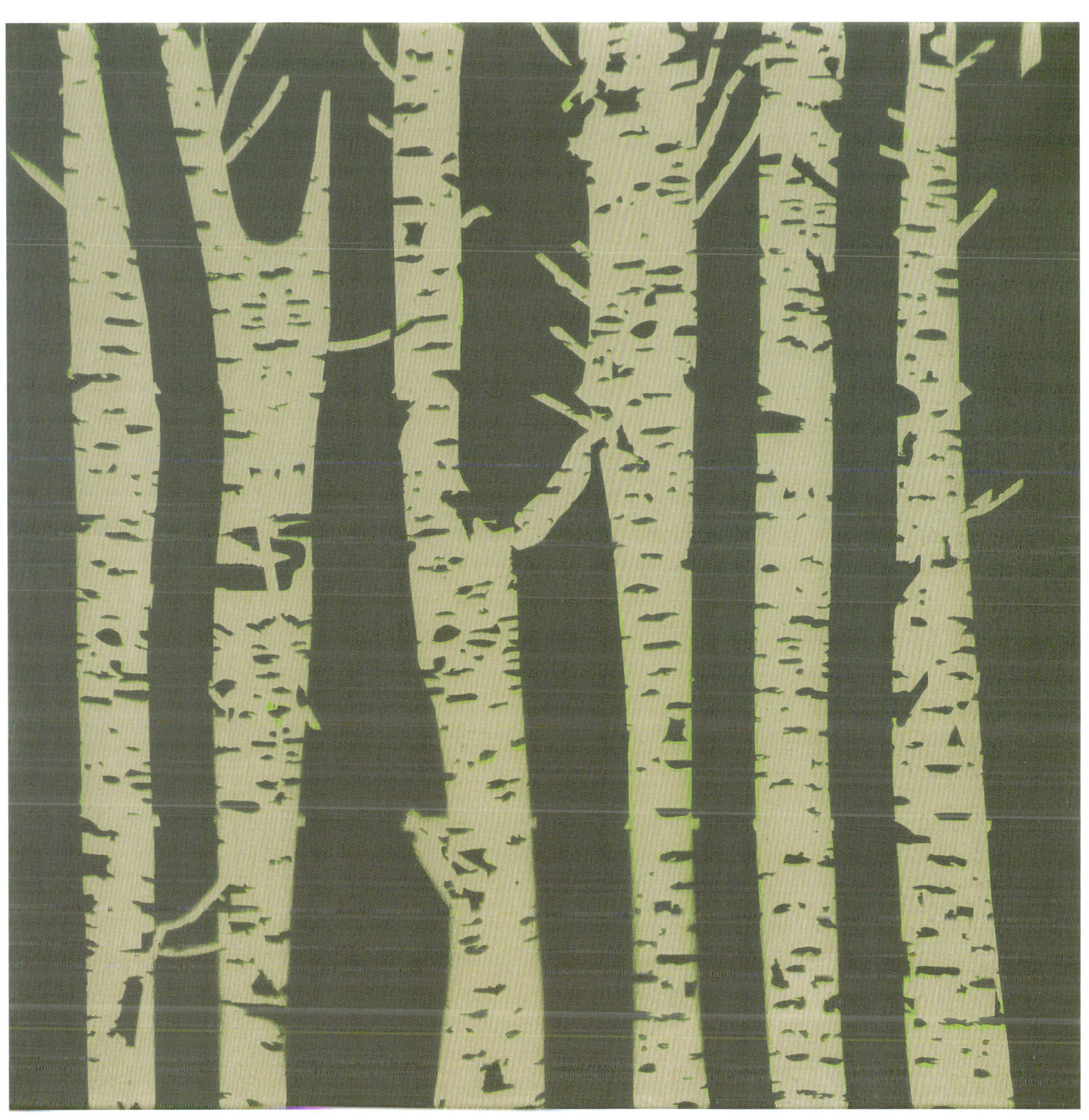

The Birches, 2011
Acrylic on canvas, 45 x 45 cm

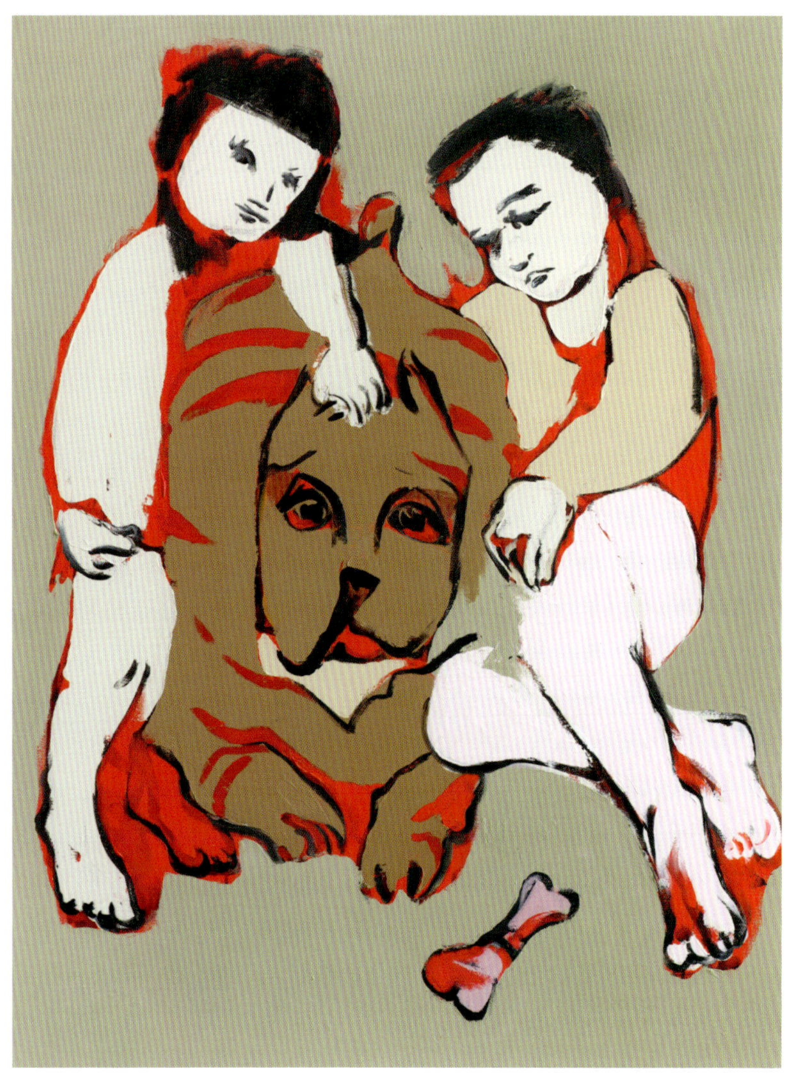

Adon with Children, 2010
Acrylic on canvas, 115 x 90 cm

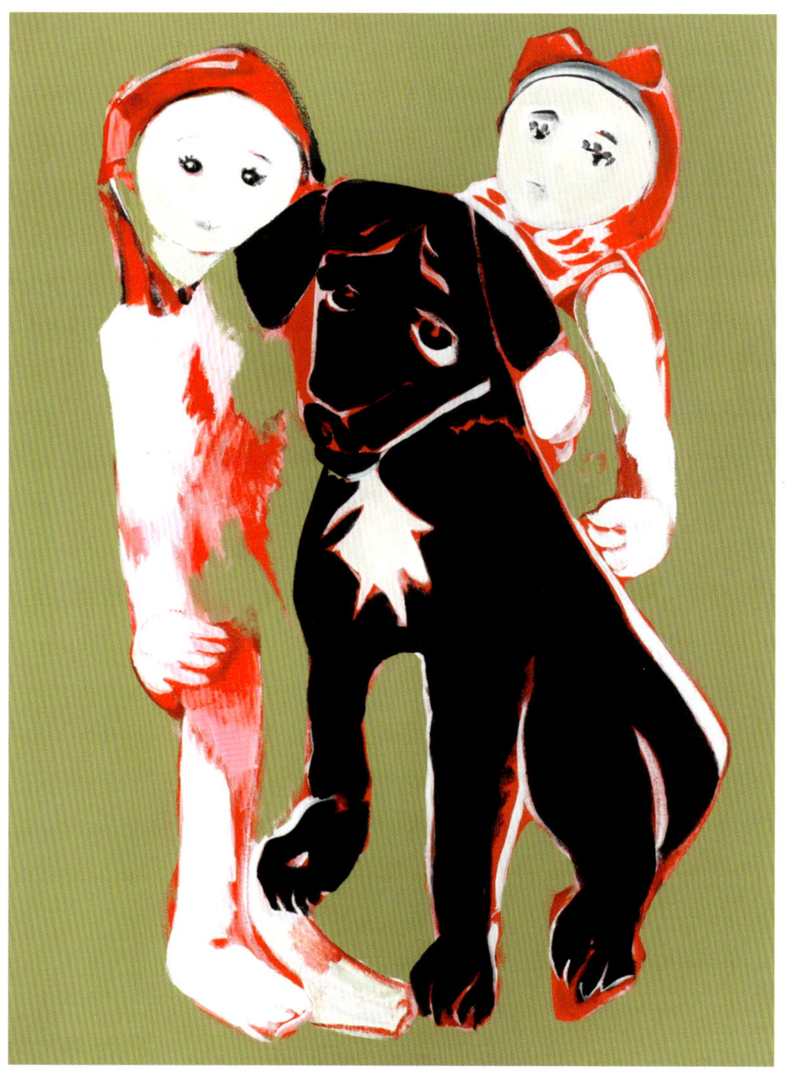

Study for *Koko with Girls*, 2010
Acrylic on canvas, 120 x 90 cm

Facing page
Koko with Girls, 2010
Acrylic on canvas, 120 x 90 cm

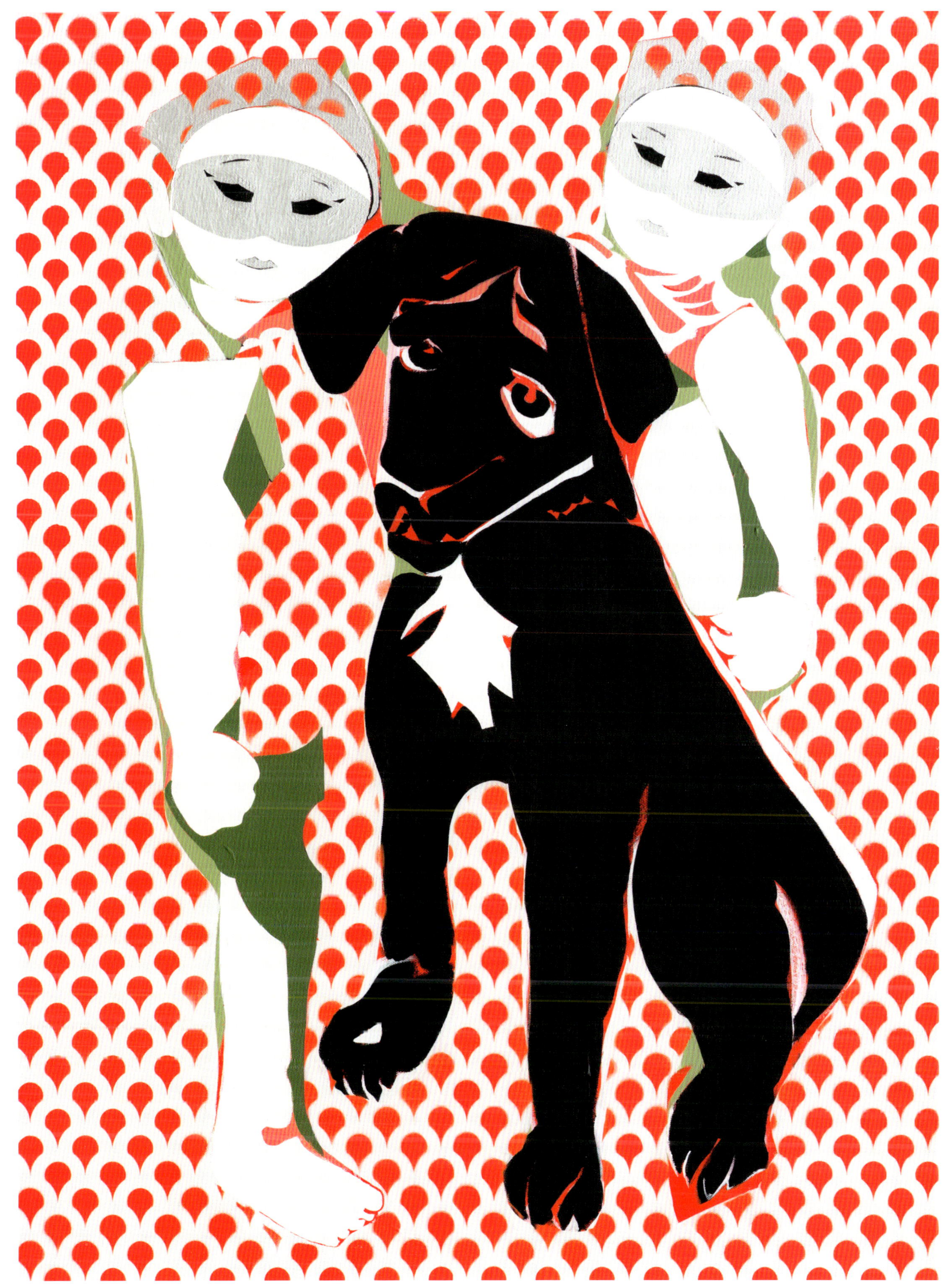

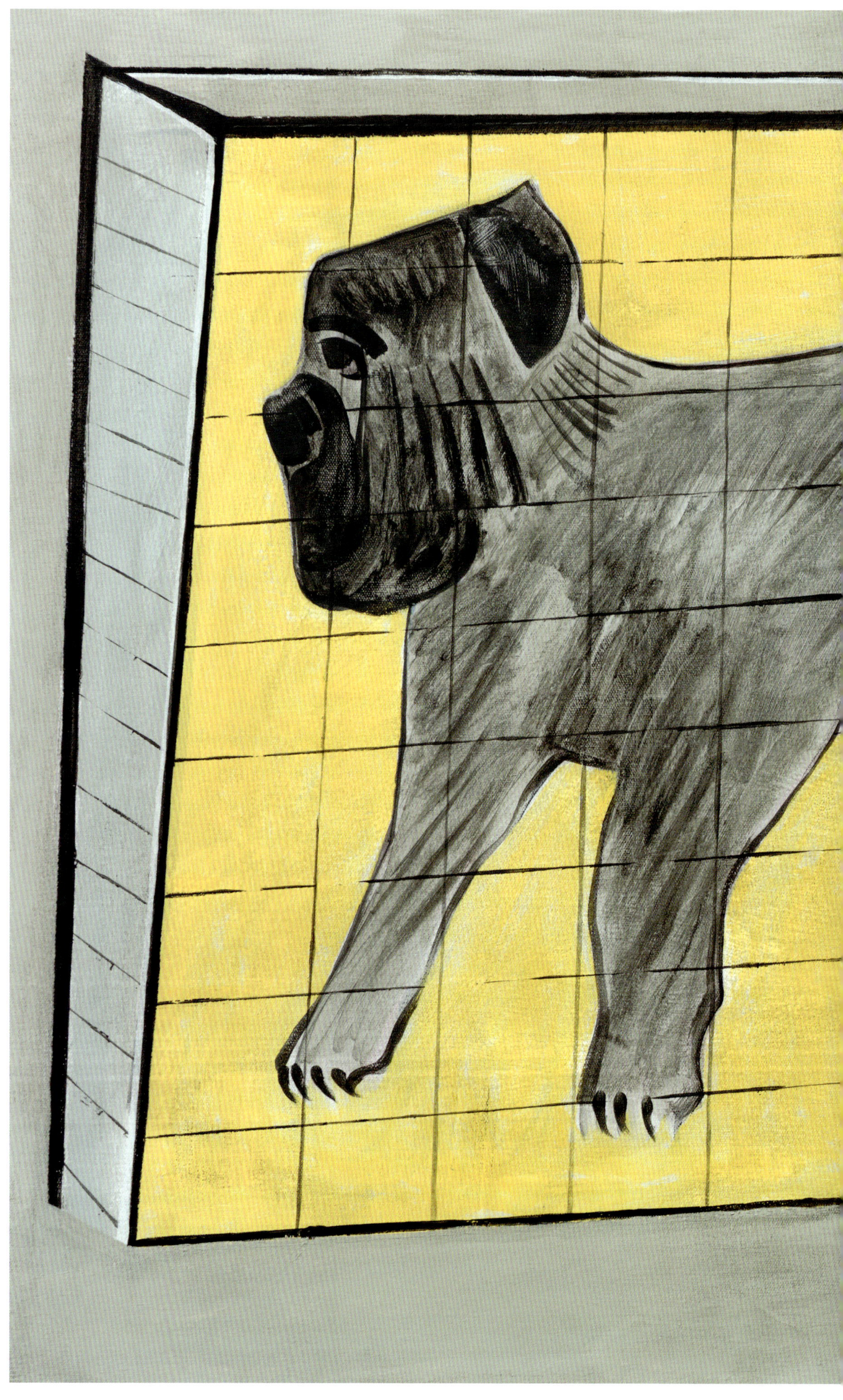

Pages 54–55
Horses, 2011
Acrylic on canvas, 77 x 144 cm

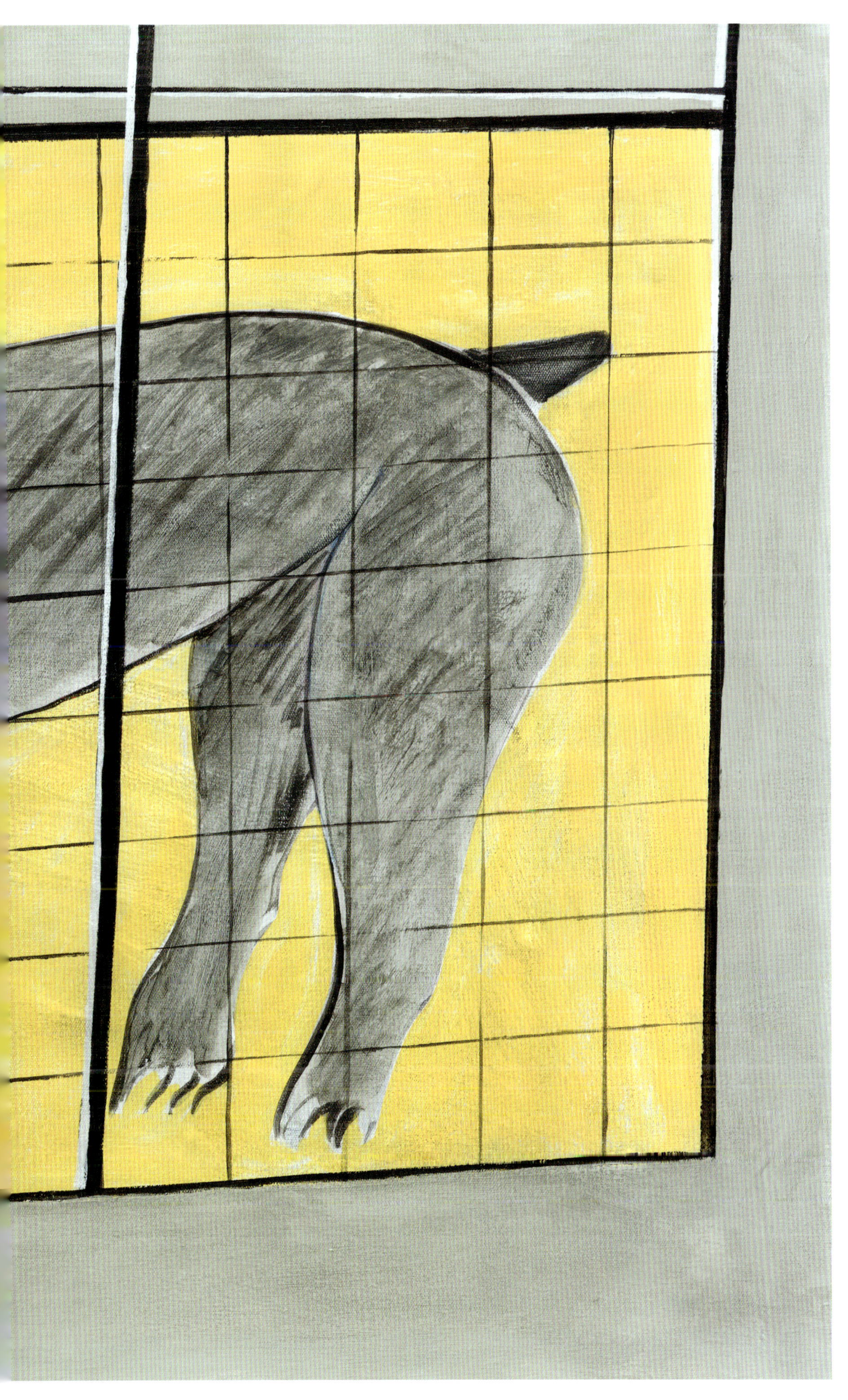

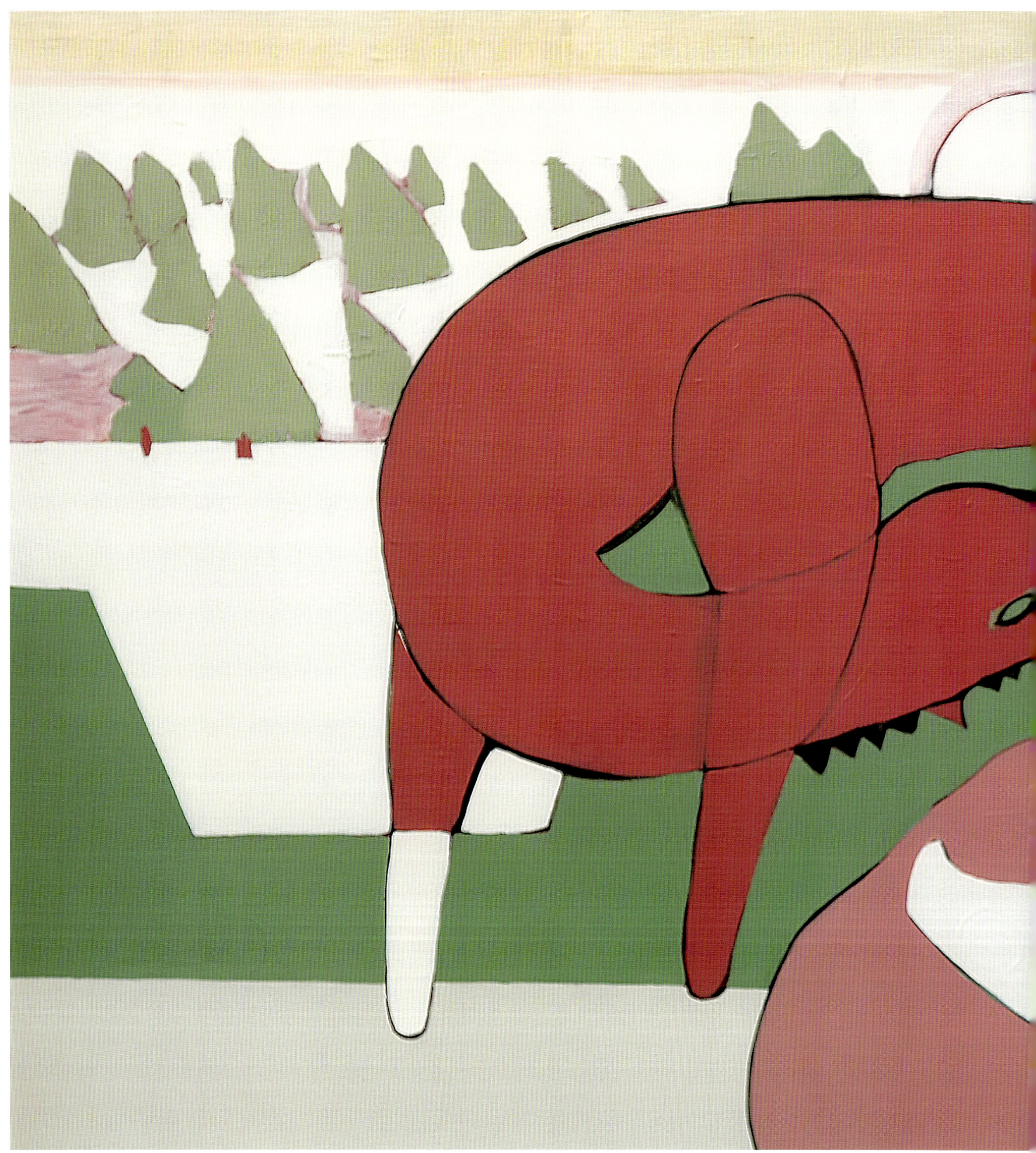

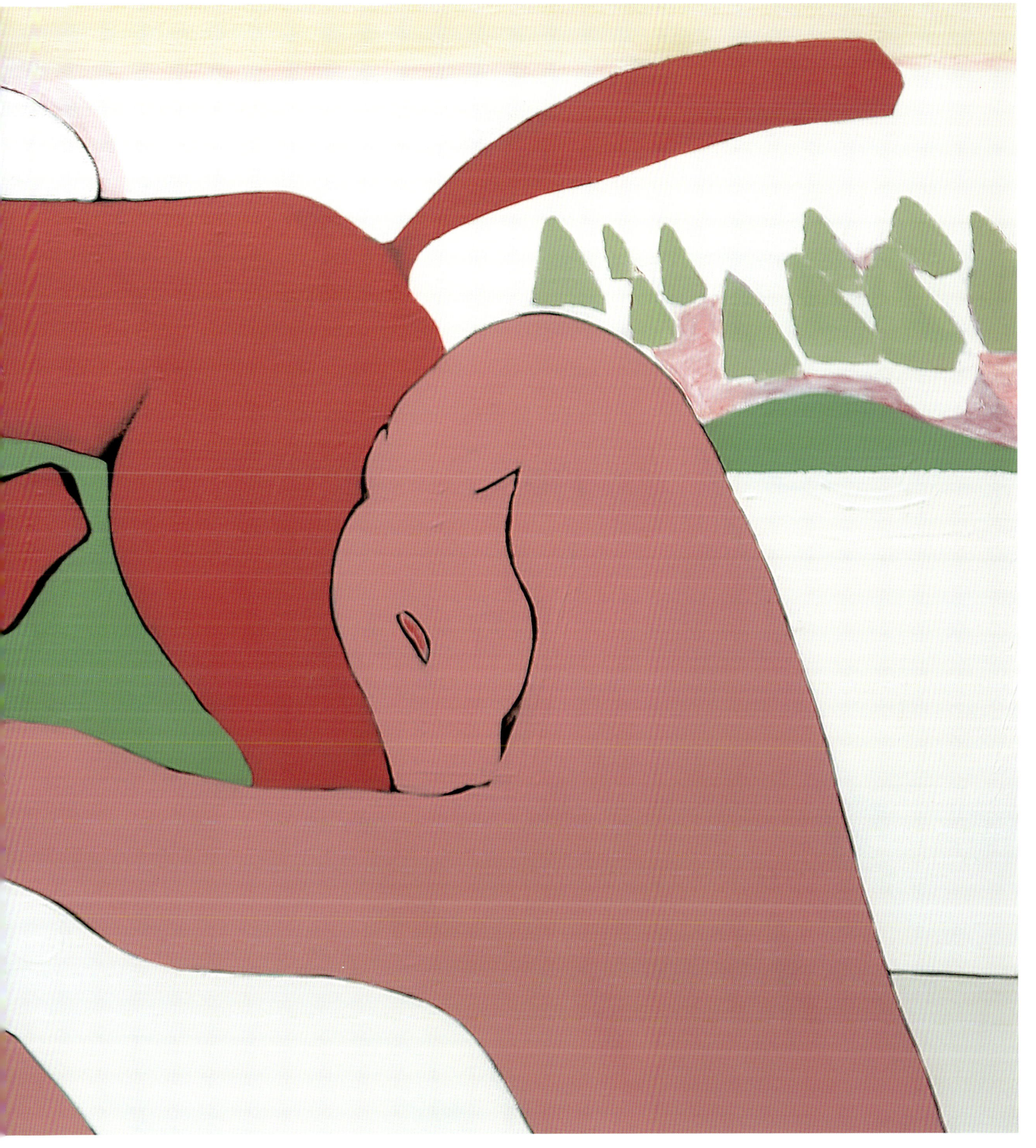

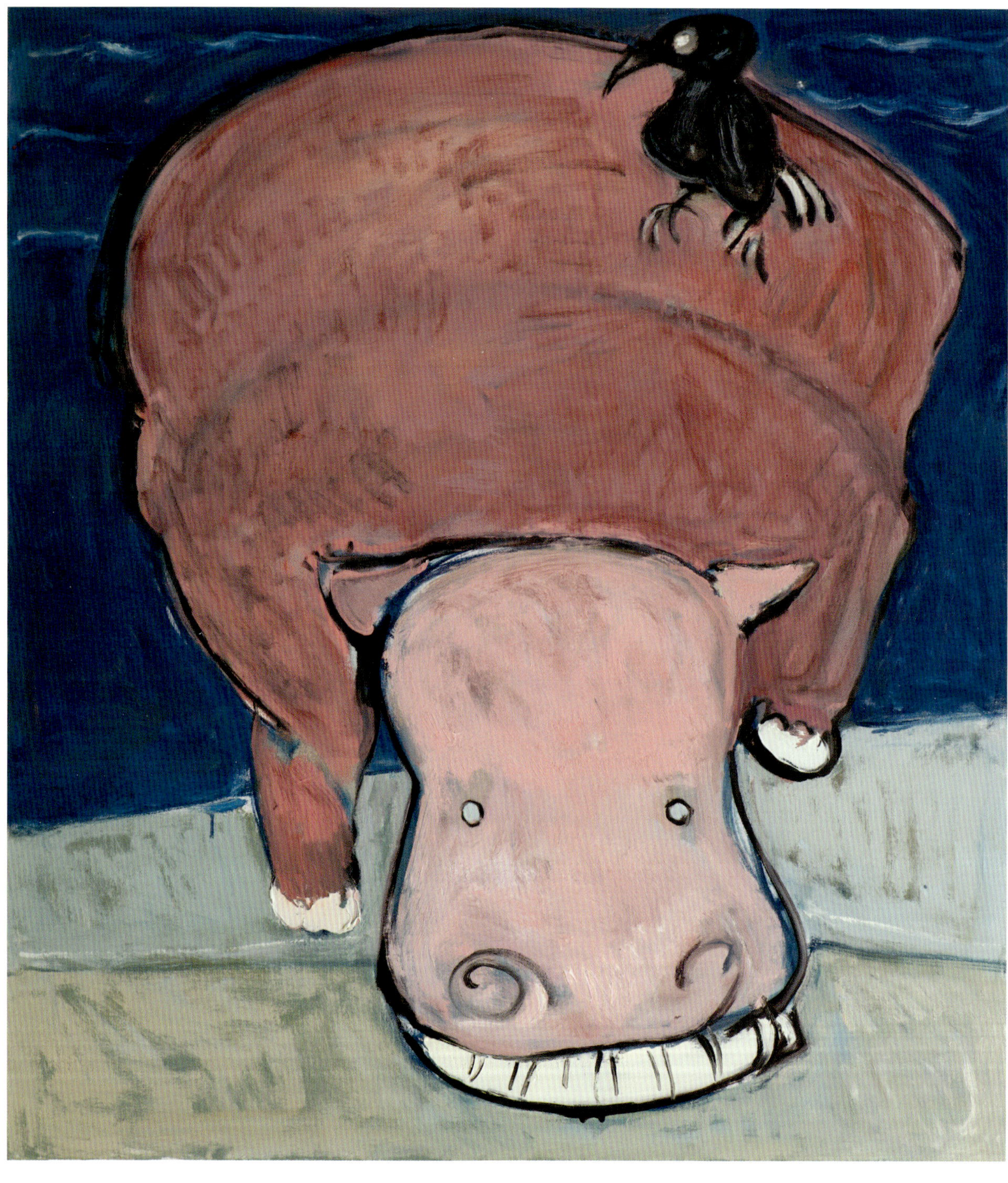

Pink Hippopotamus, 2011
Oil on canvas, 125 x 110 cm

Facing page
Mask, 2011
Acrylic on canvas, 180 x 130 cm

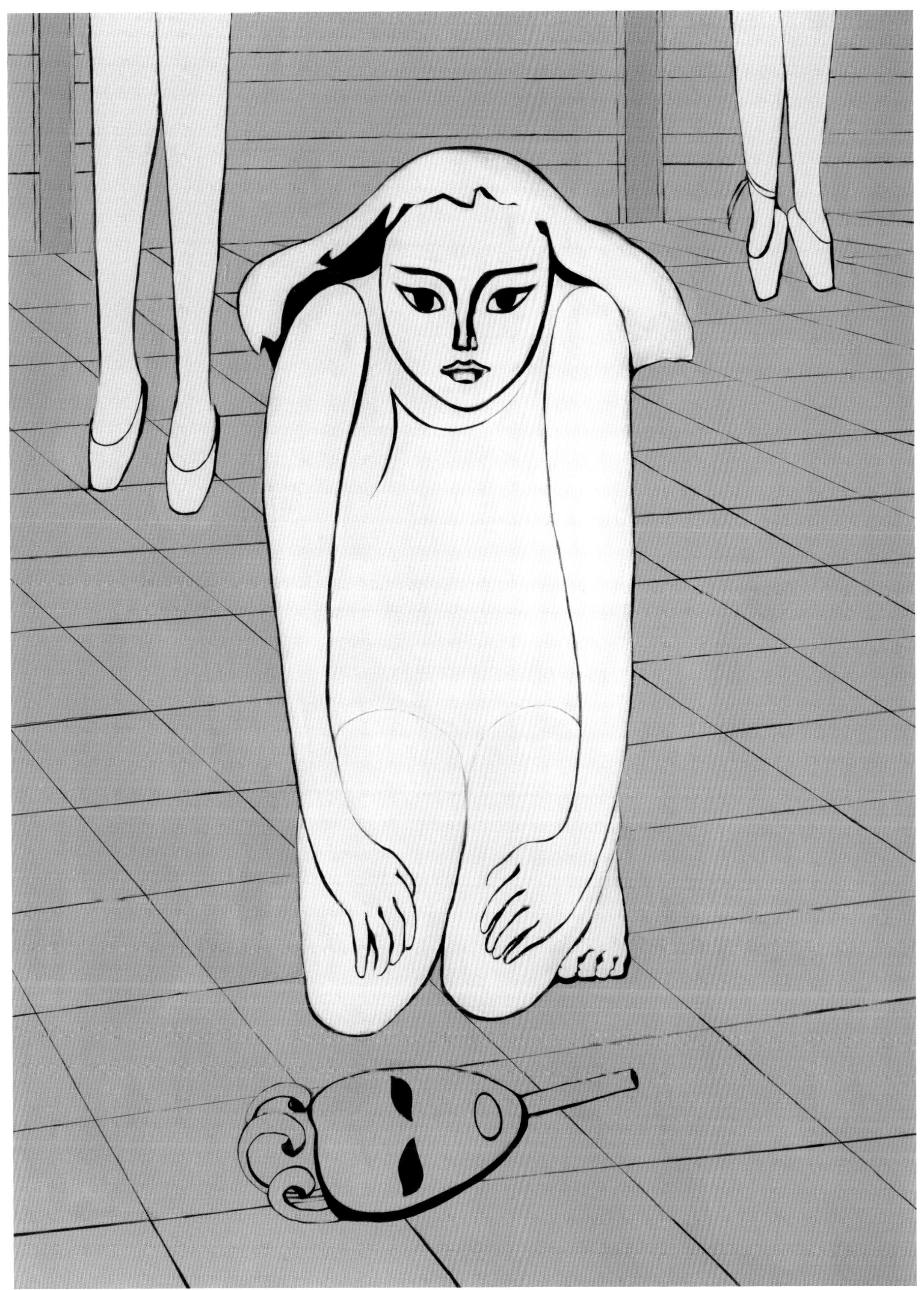

Grief, 2012
Acrylic on canvas, 80 x 65 cm

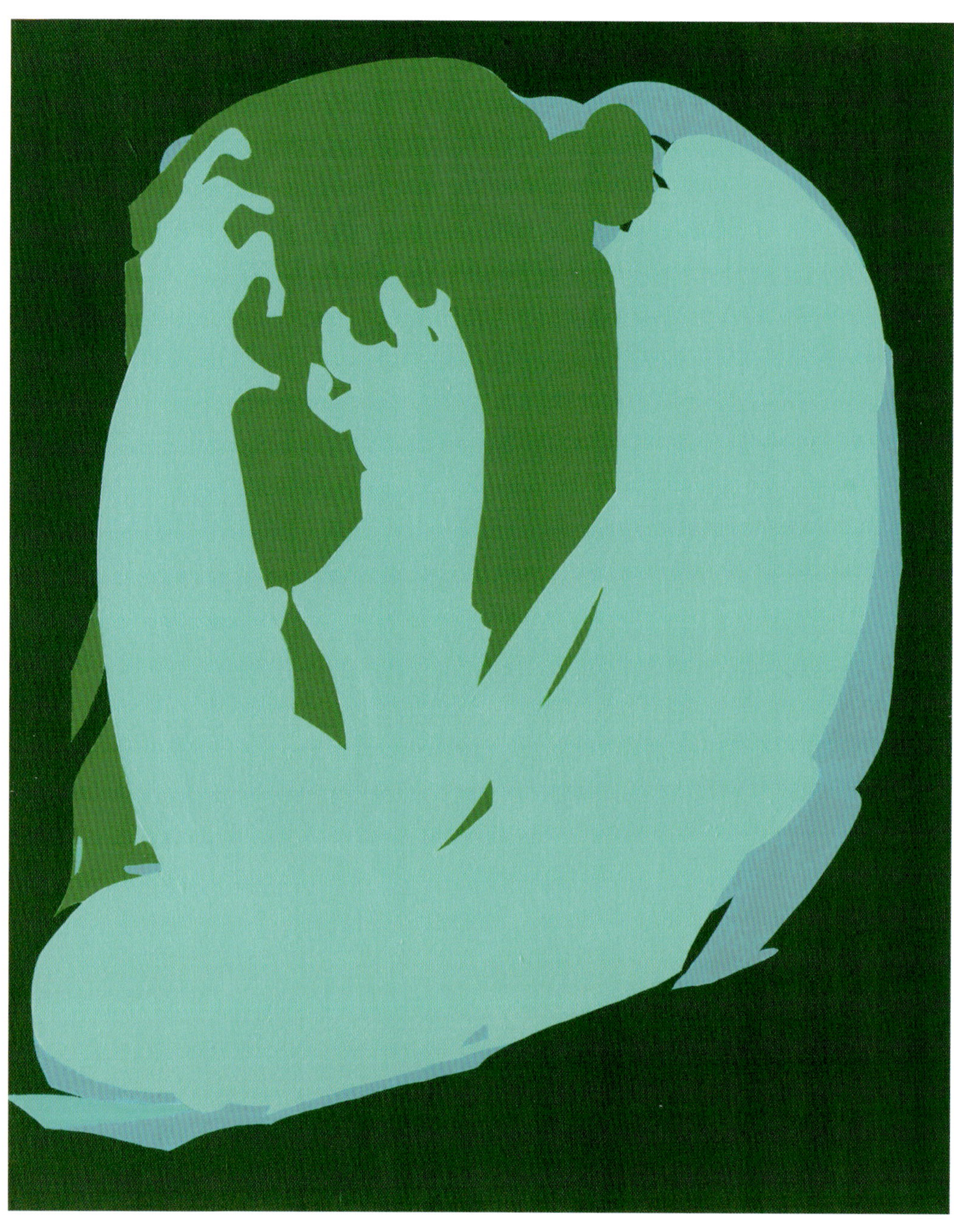

Facing page
Mother, 2012
Acrylic on canvas, 115 x 105 cm

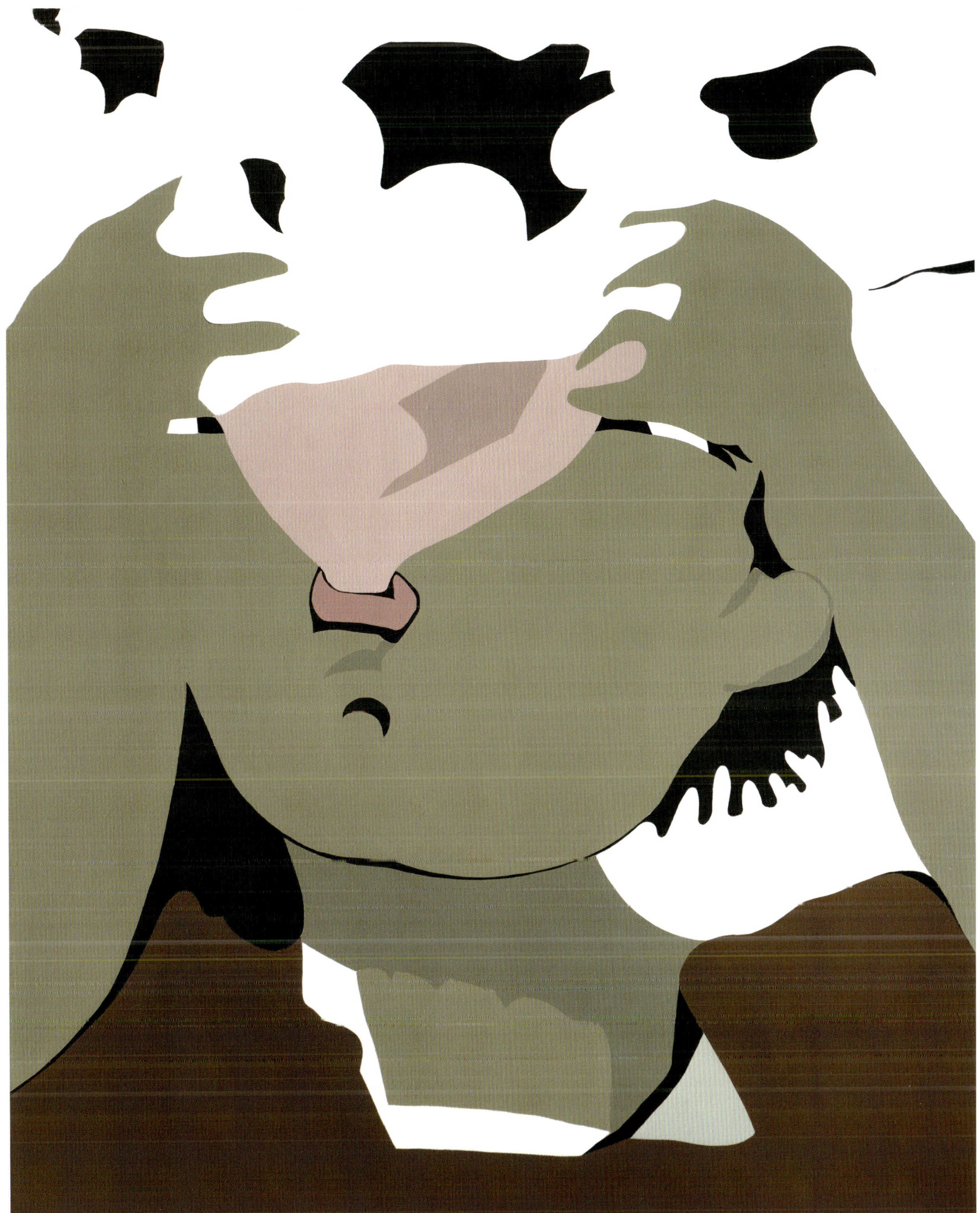

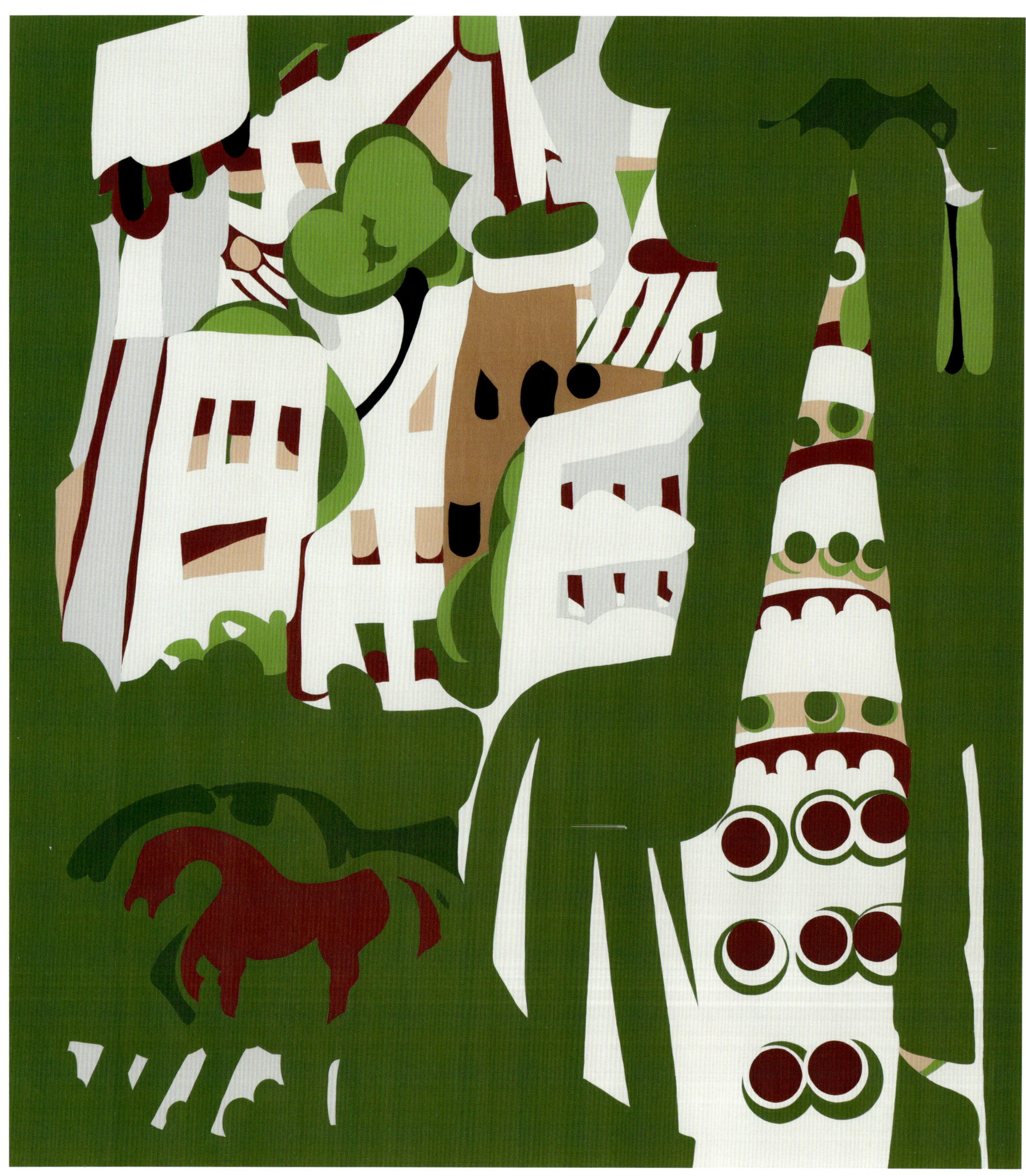

Suburb, 2012
Acrylic on canvas, 125 x 112 cm

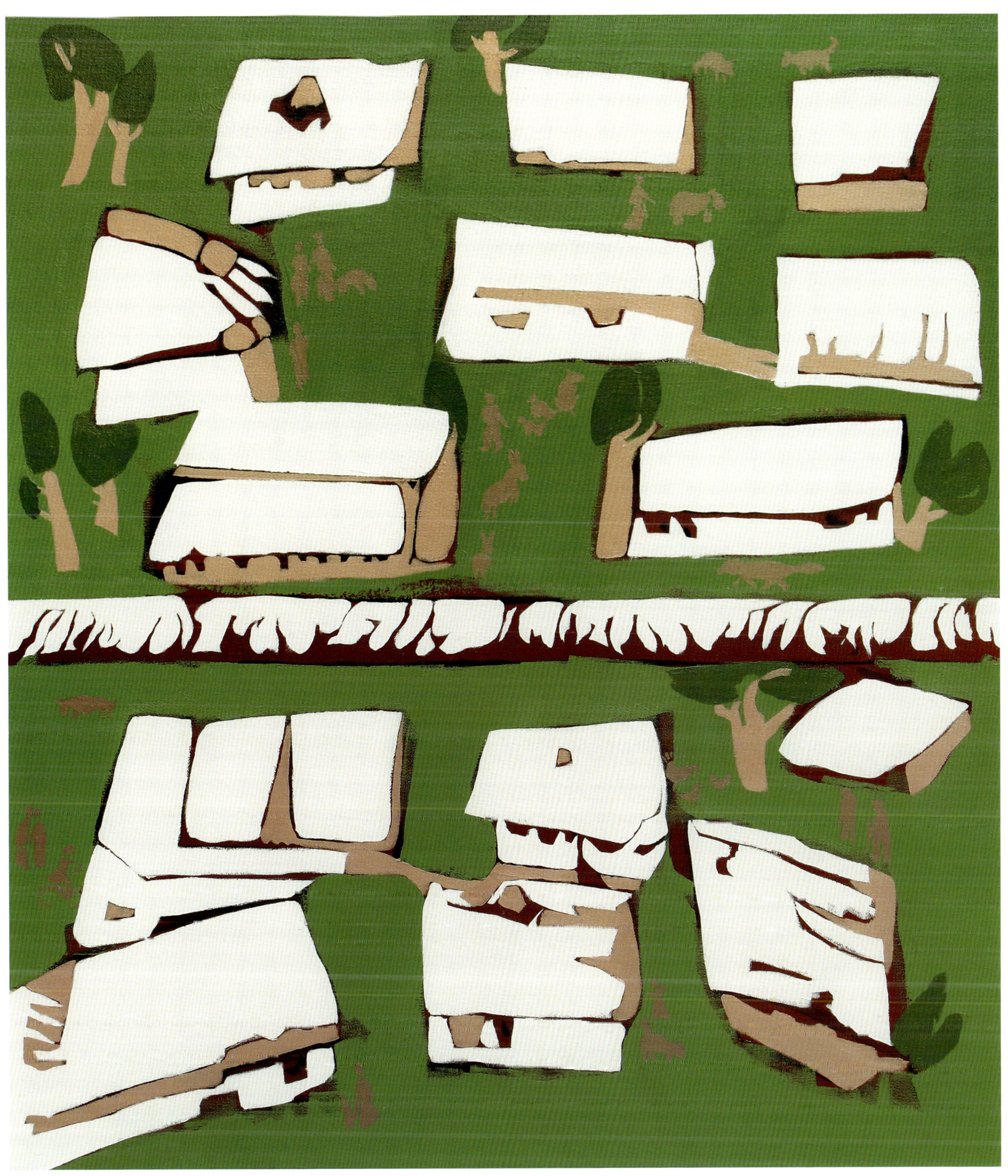

Two Villages, 2012
Acrylic on canvas, 125 x 110 cm

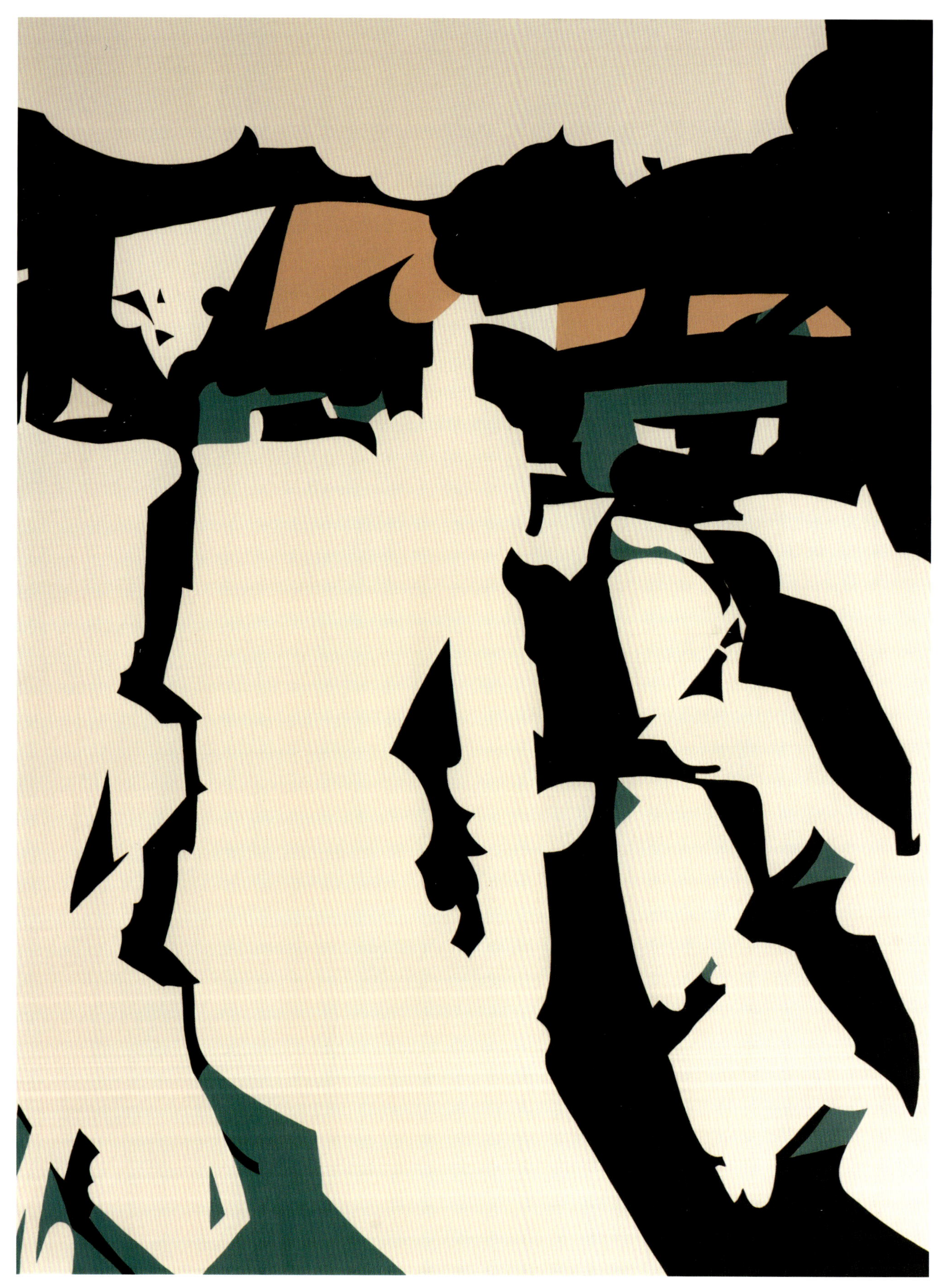

Shadows, 2012
Acrylic on canvas, 100 x 75 cm

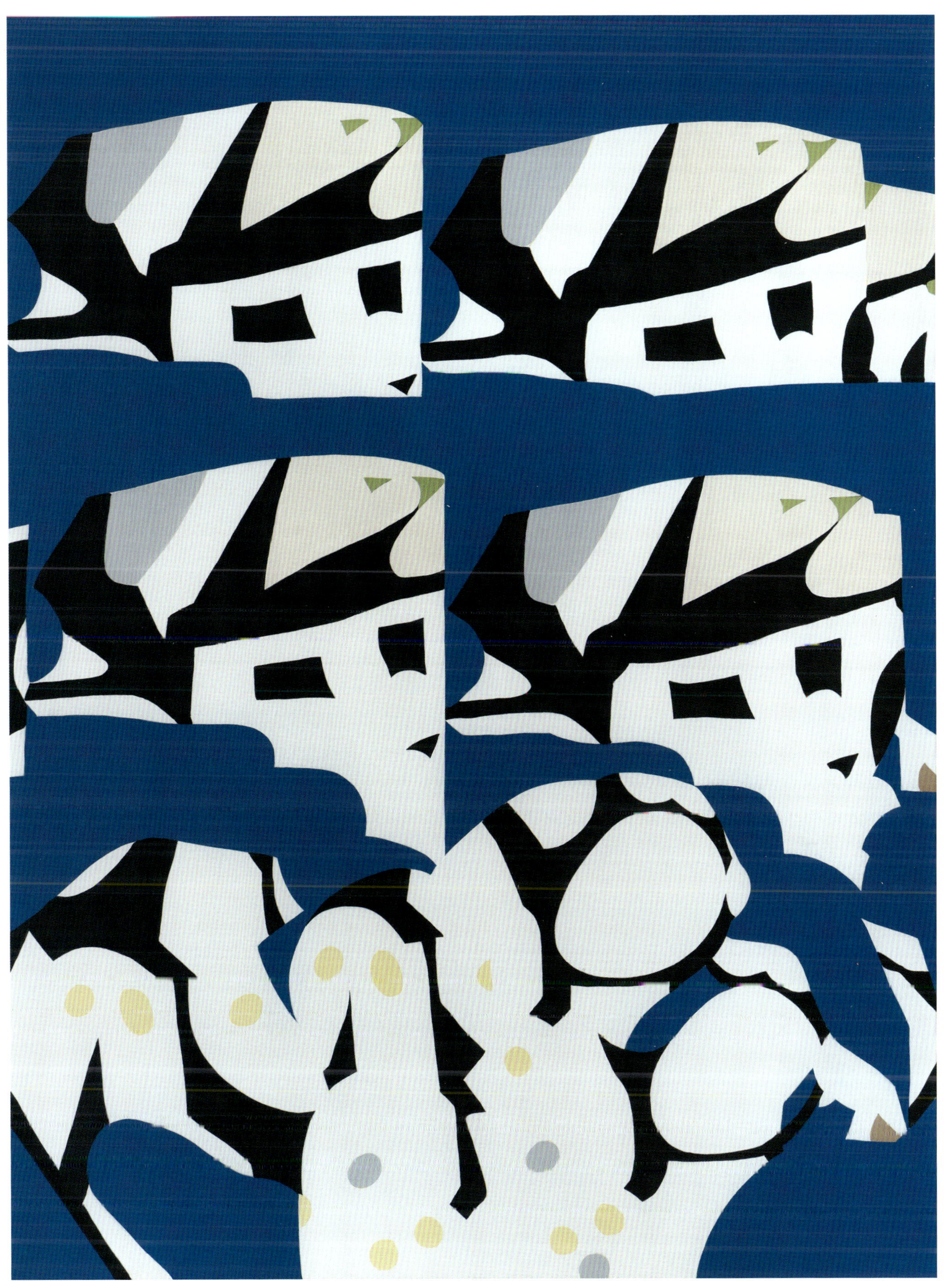

Twins, 2012
Acrylic on canvas, 100 x 75 cm

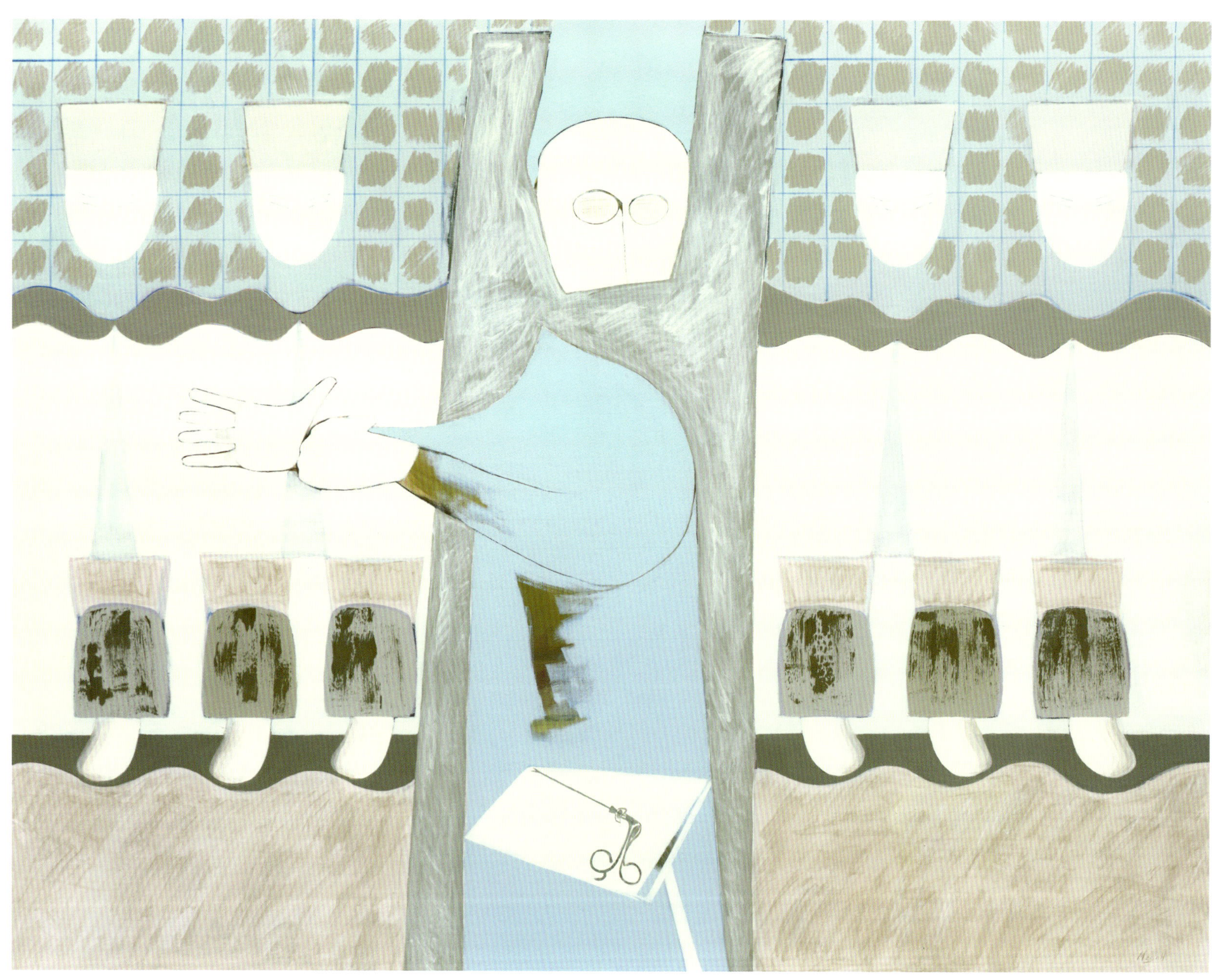

Doctor, 2012
Acrylic on canvas, 183 x 235 cm

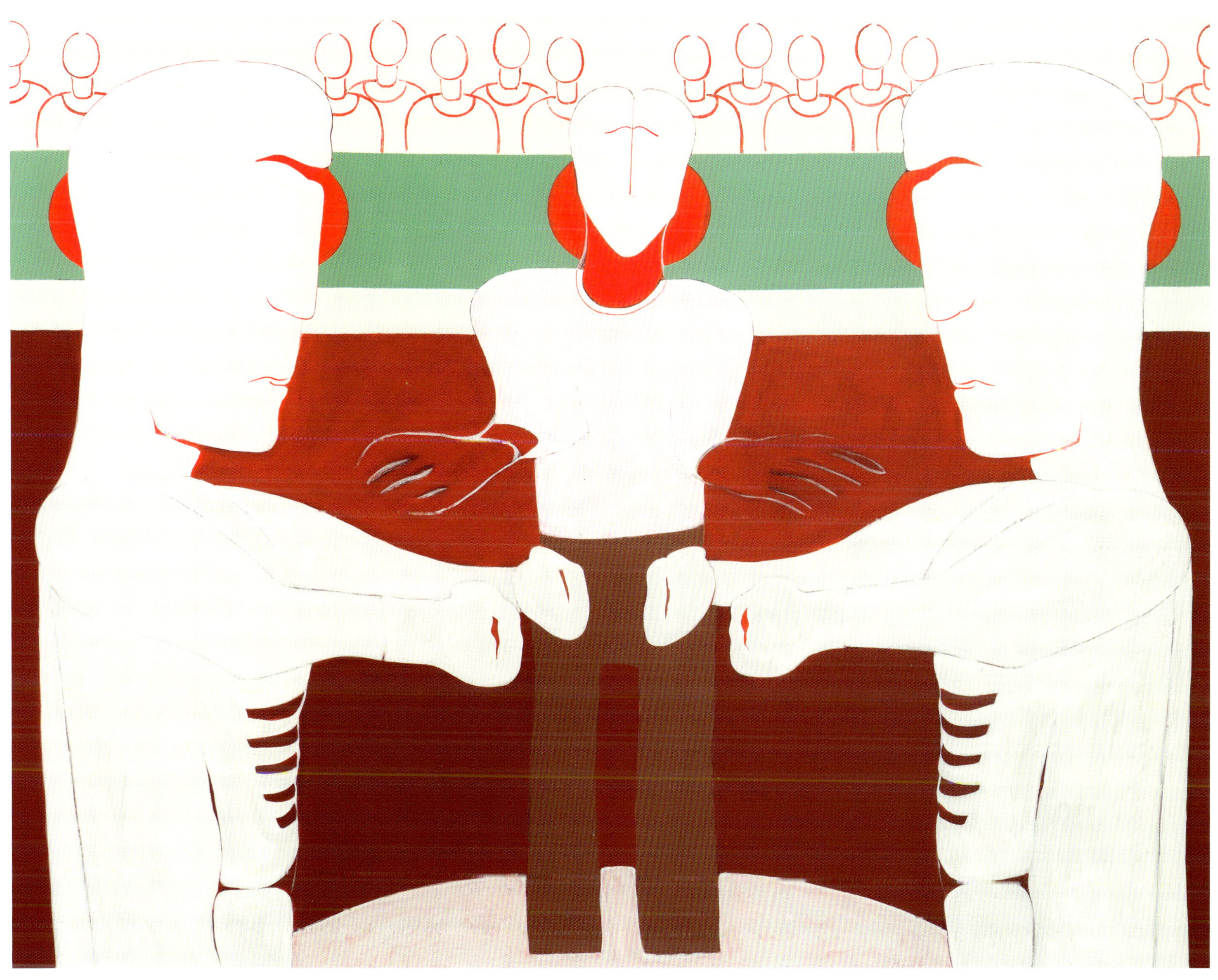

Boxing School, 2012
Acrylic on canvas, 183 x 235 cm

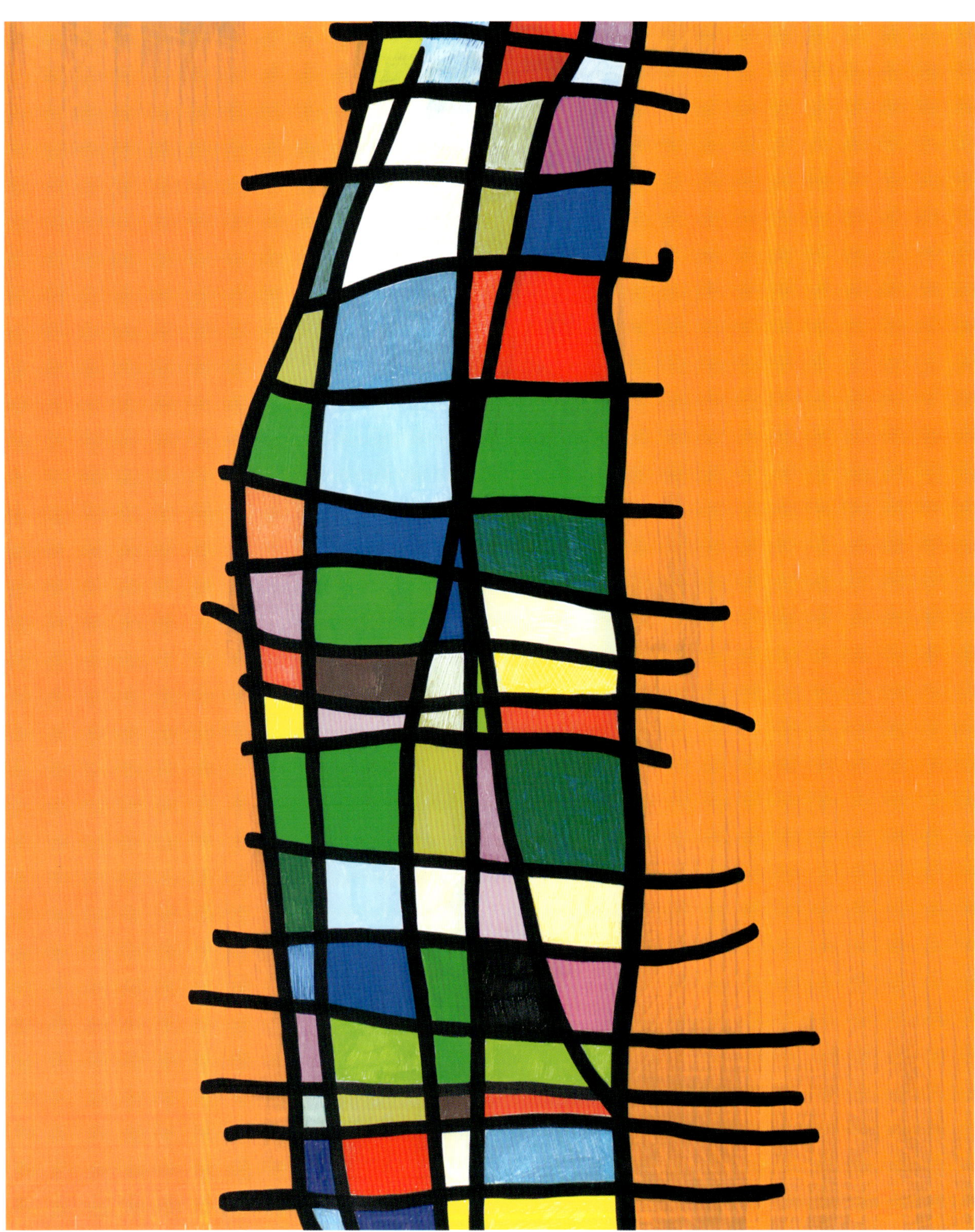

Tower, 2015
Acrylic on canvas, 135 x 110 cm

Facing page
Deposition, 2014
Acrylic on canvas, 180 x 140 cm

Pages 68–73
Cycle of works on the Holy Shroud, 2012
Acrylic on paper, 76 x 56 cm each

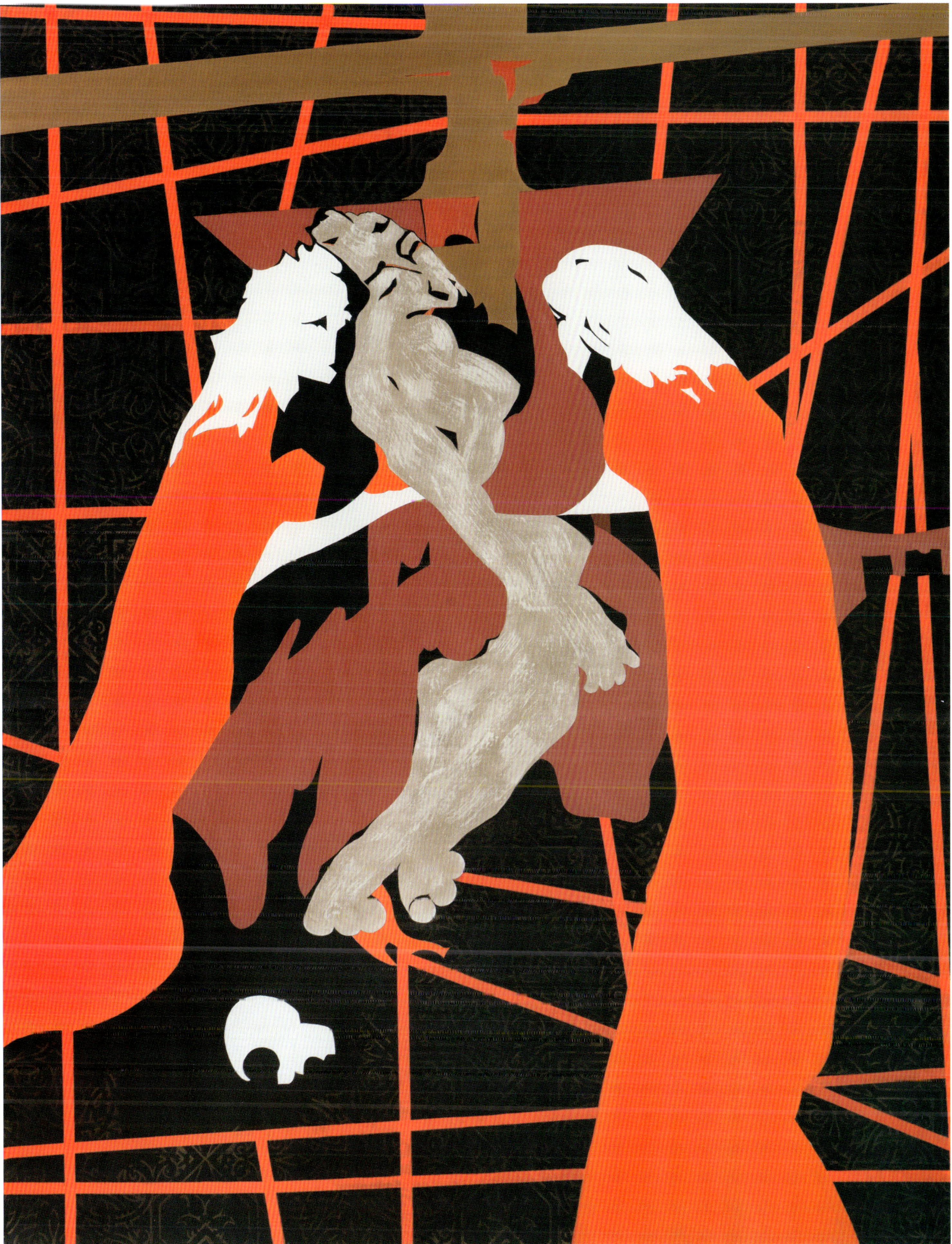

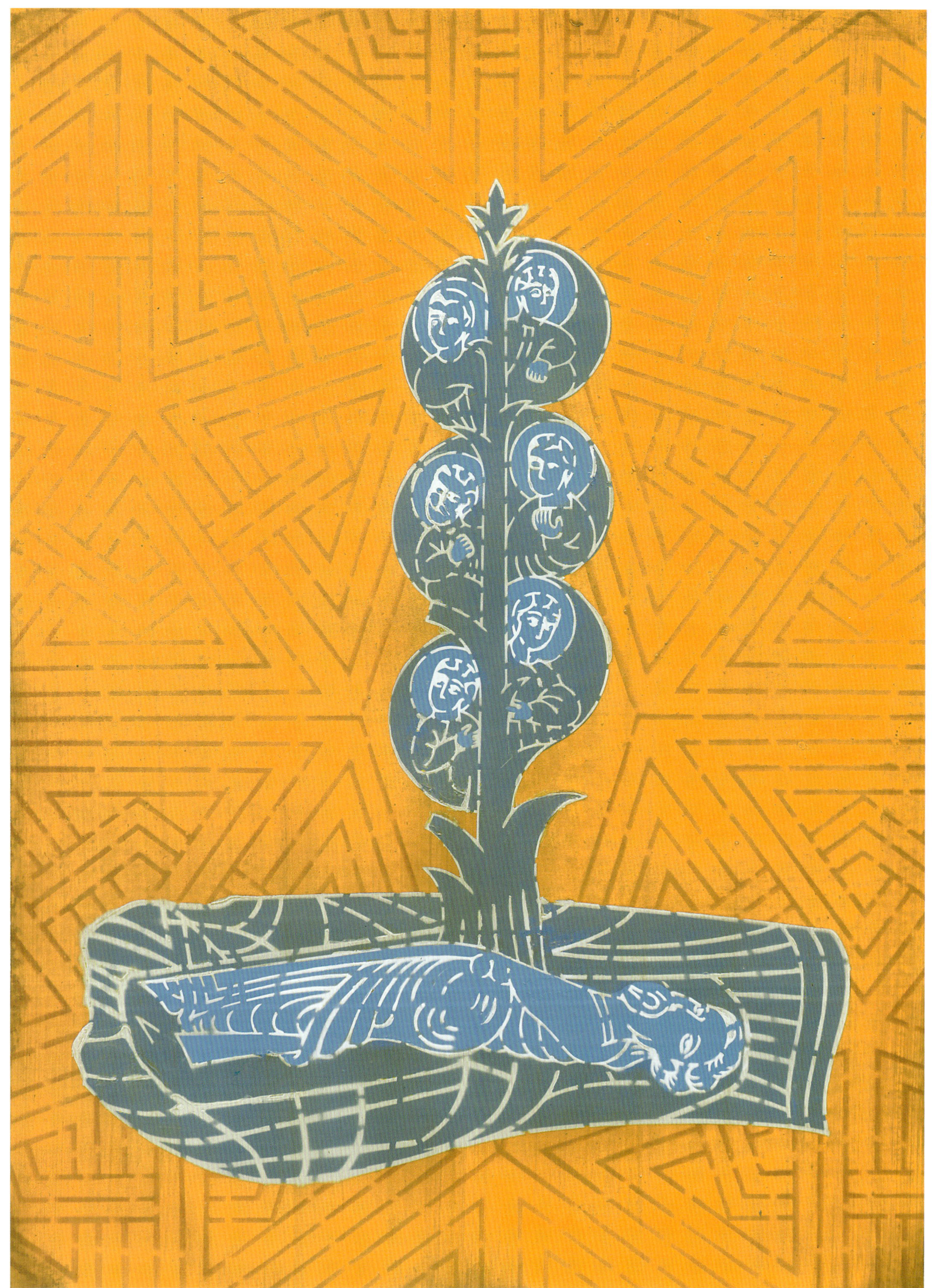

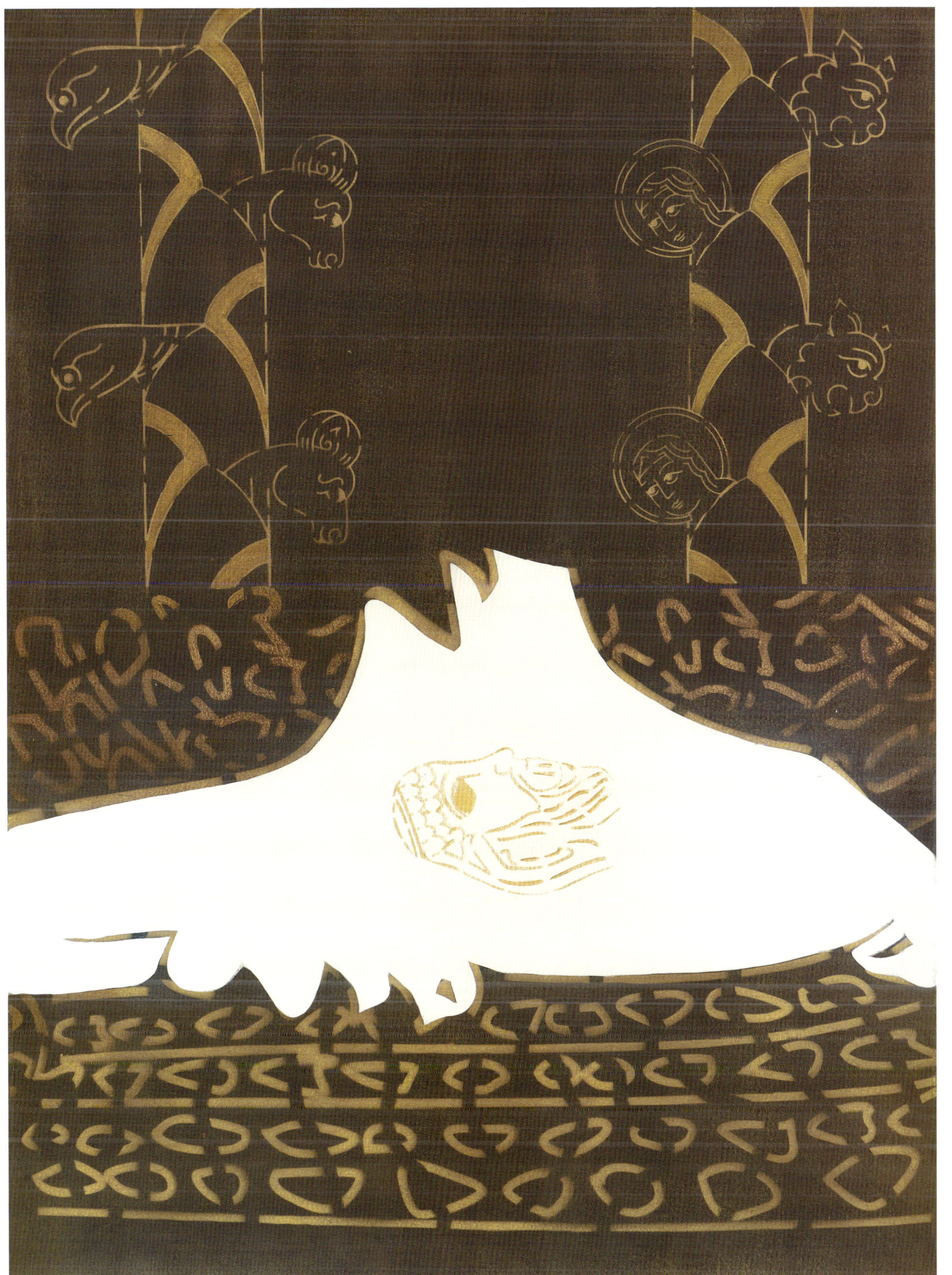

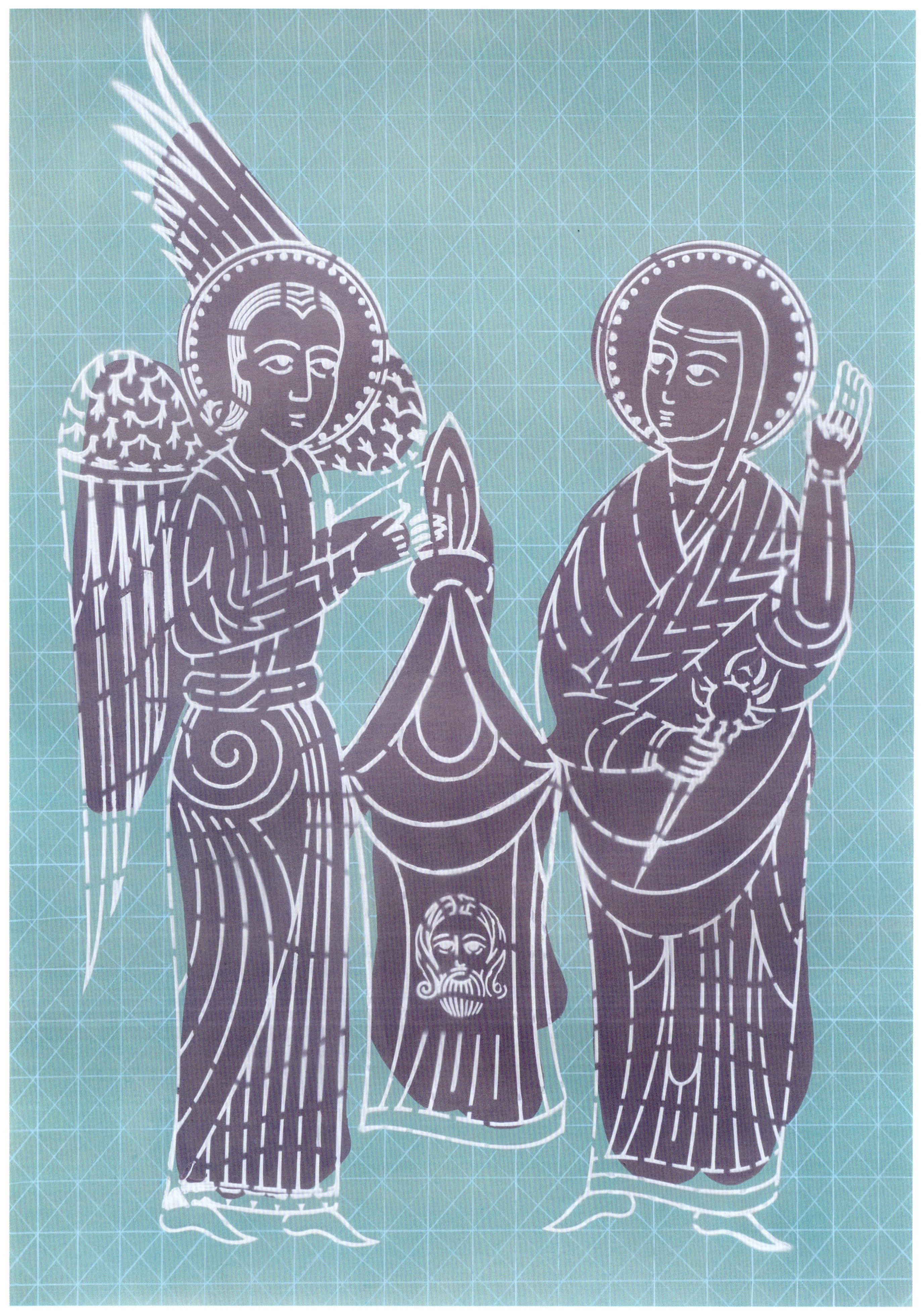

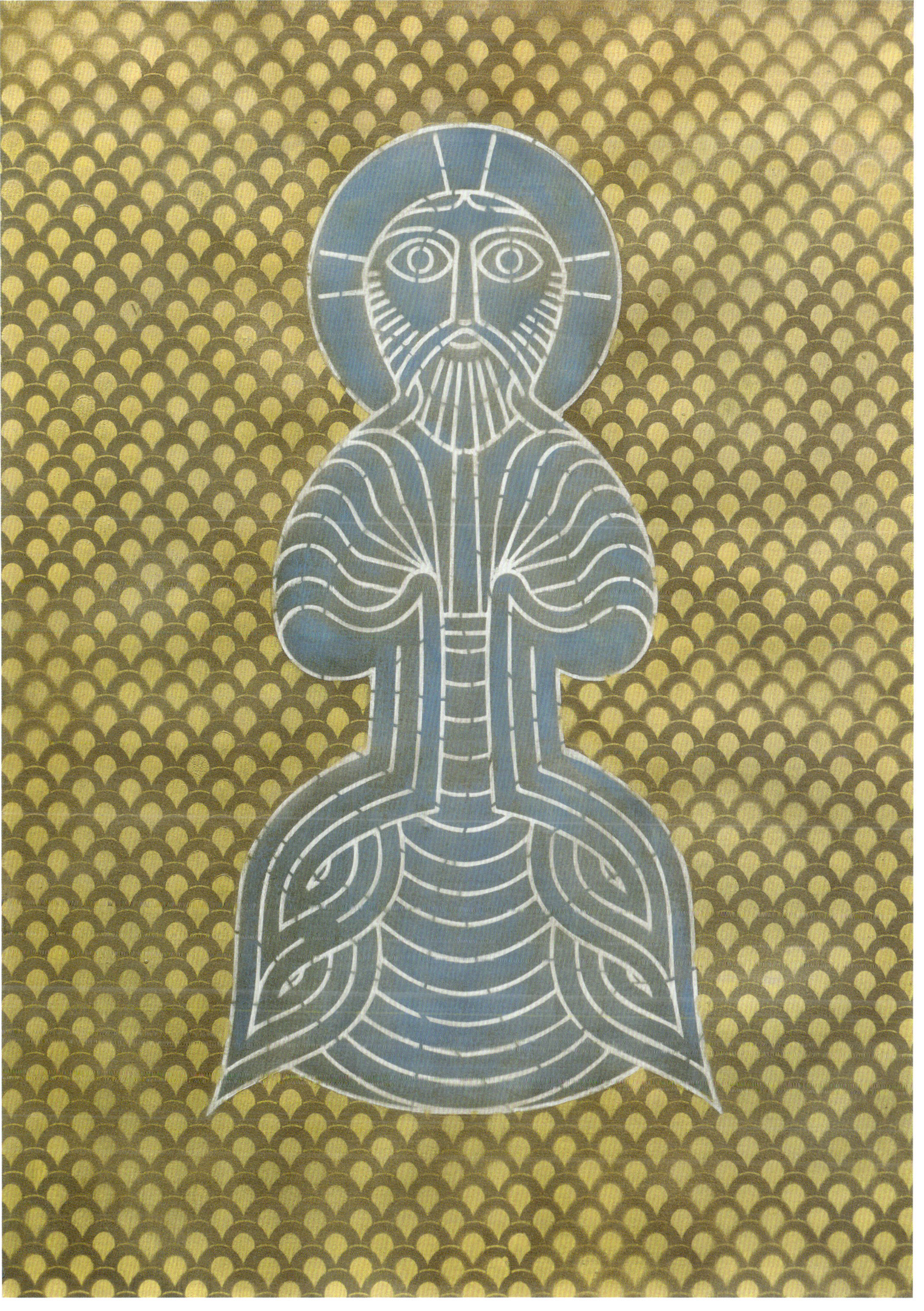

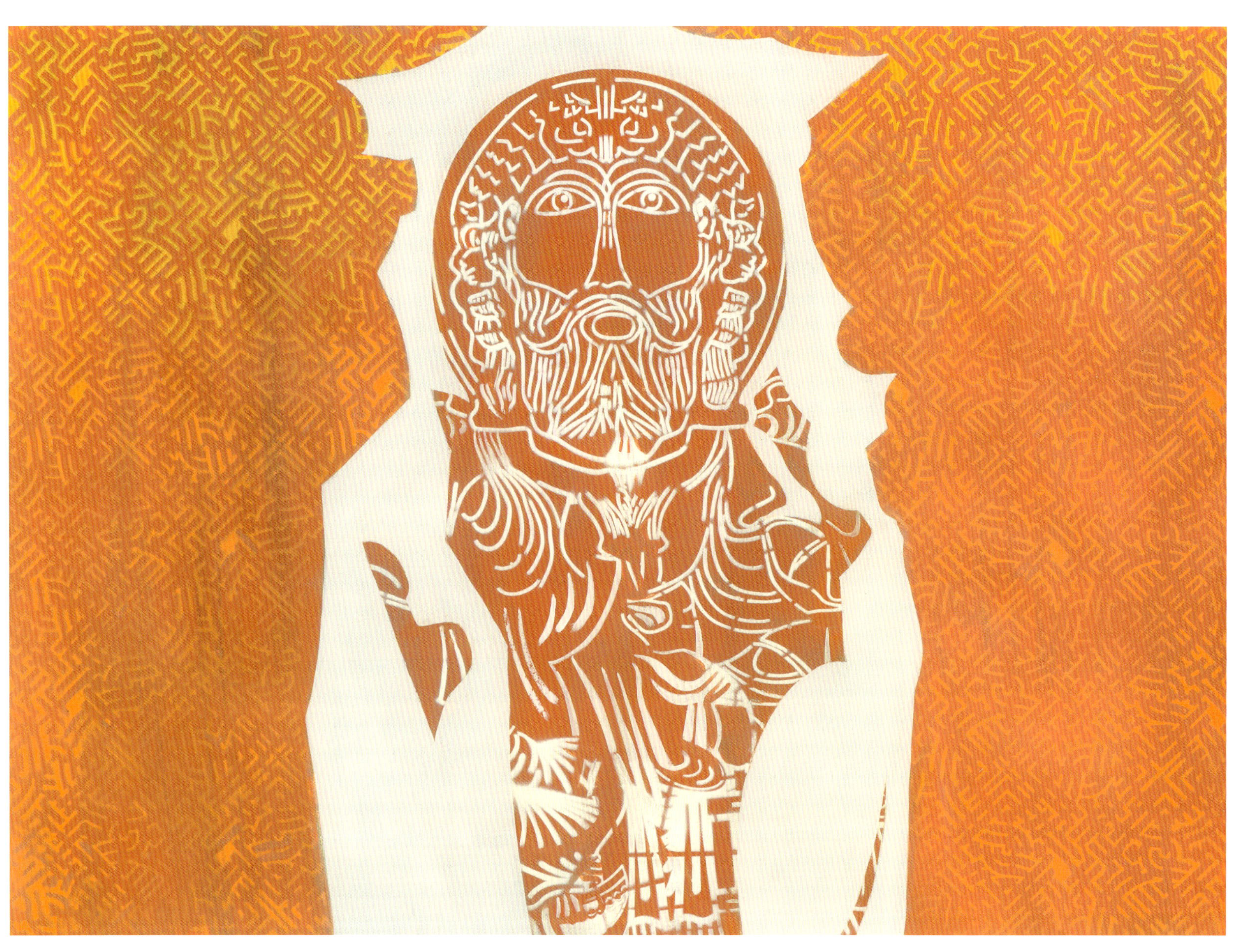

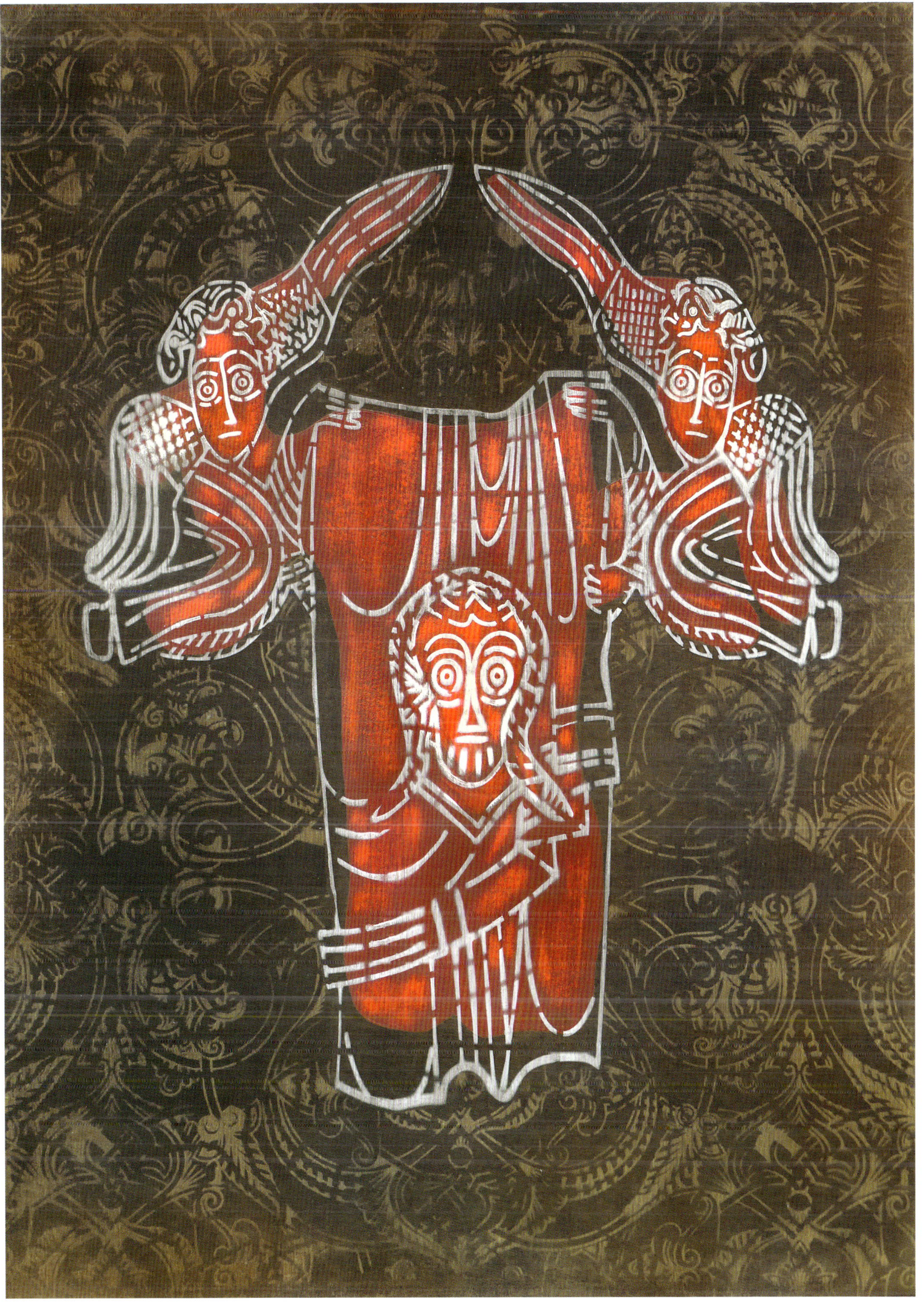

Women in Grief, 2012
Acrylic on canvas, 100 x 150 cm

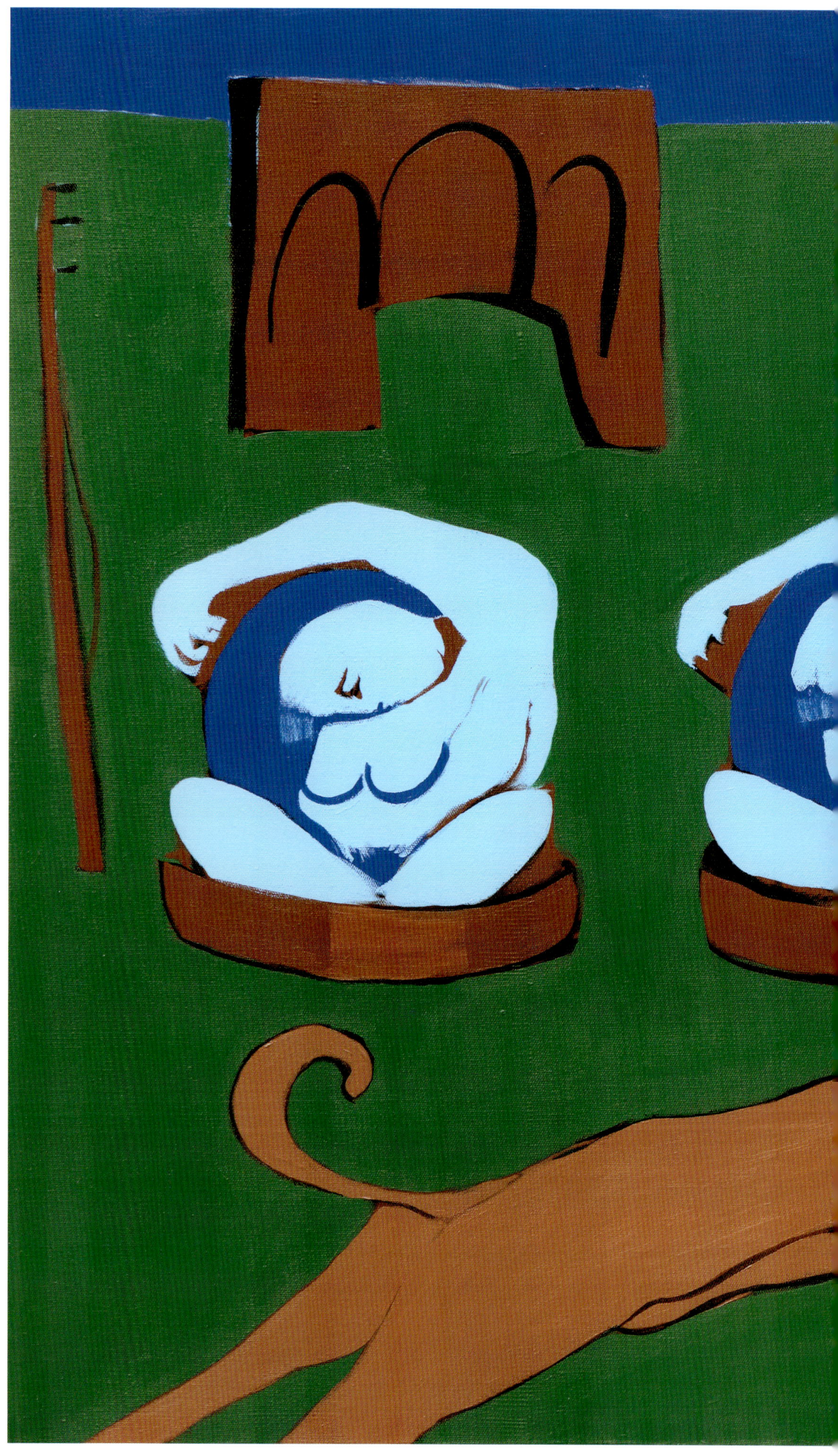

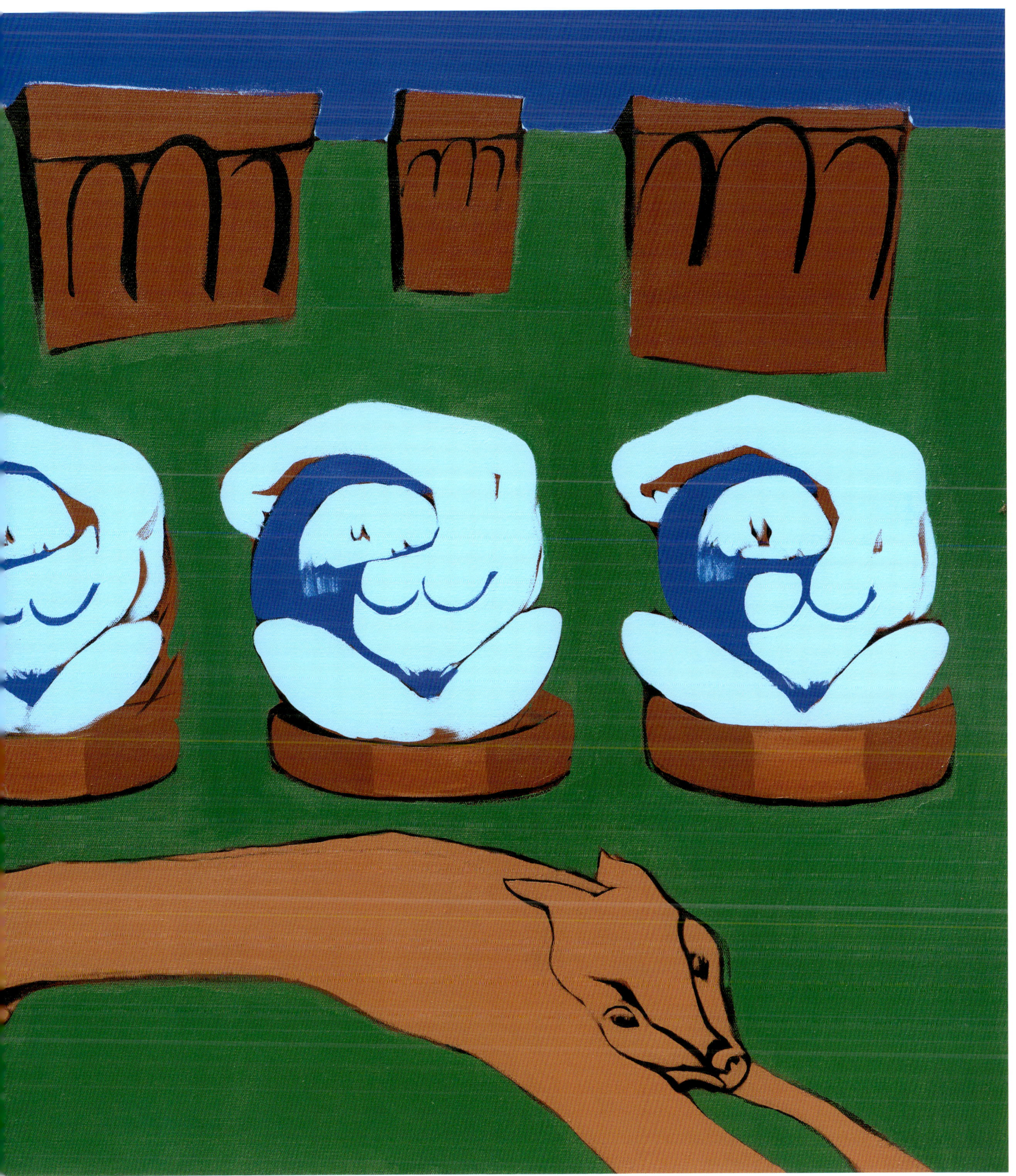

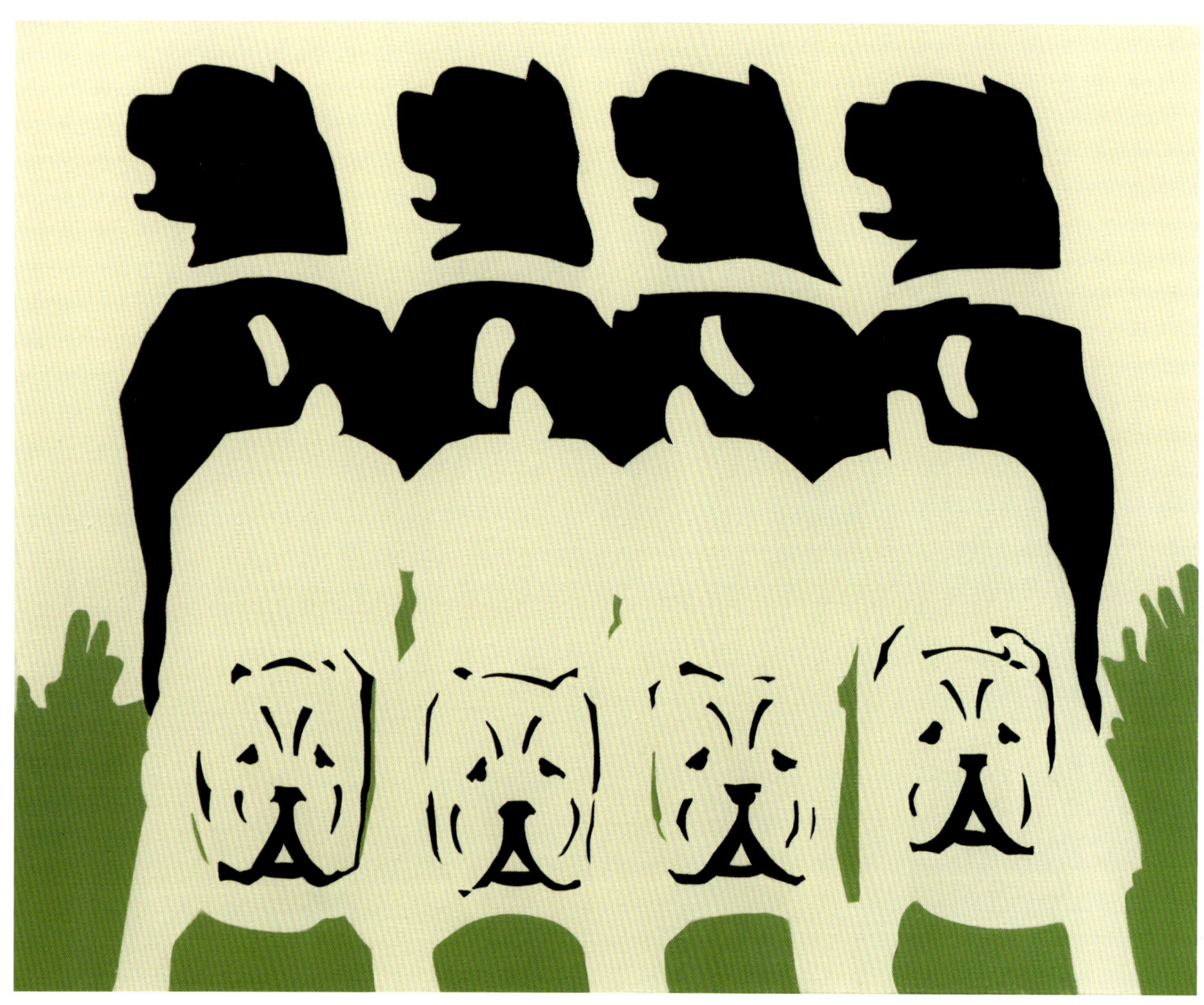

The Nature of the Dog, 2013
Acrylic on canvas, 65 x 80 cm

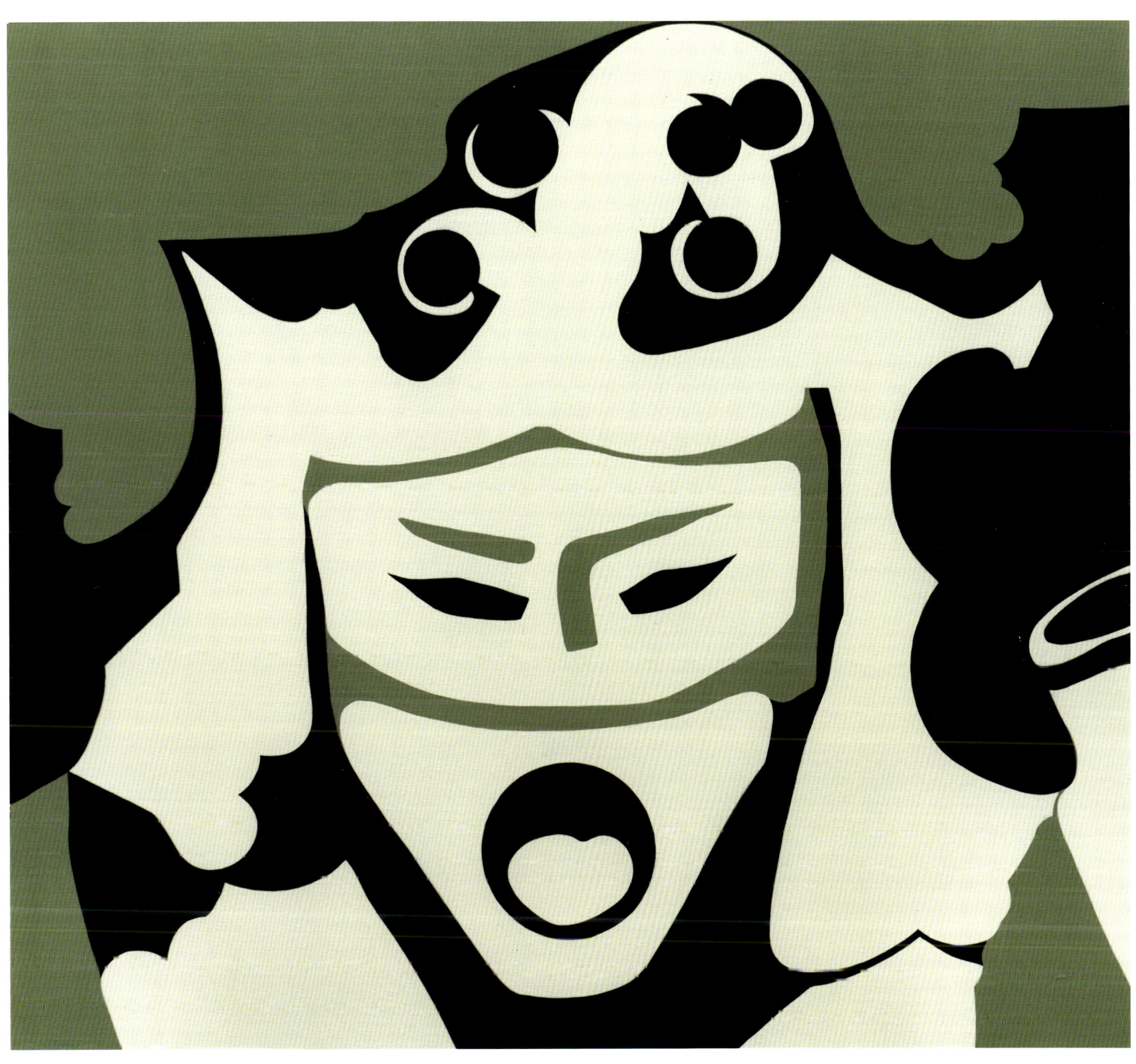

Singer, 2013
Acrylic on canvas, 105 x 115 cm

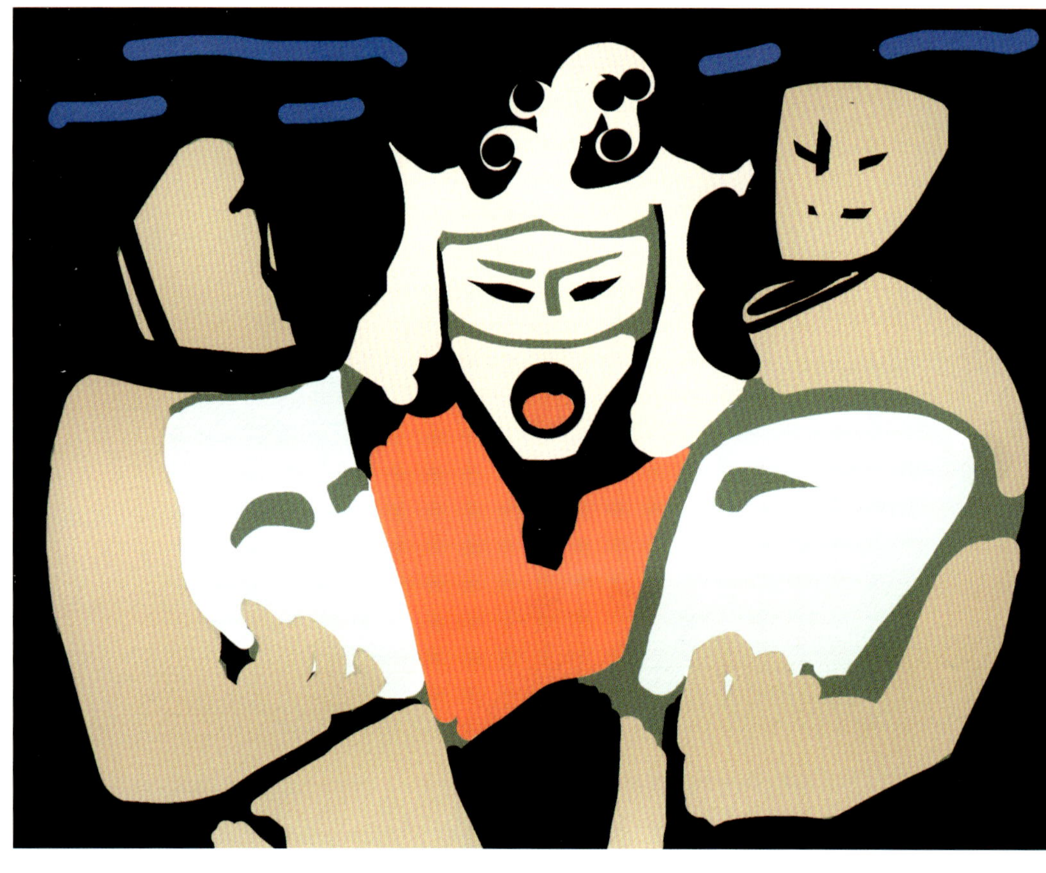

Study for *Theatre*, 2013
Mixed media on paper, 32 x 57 cm

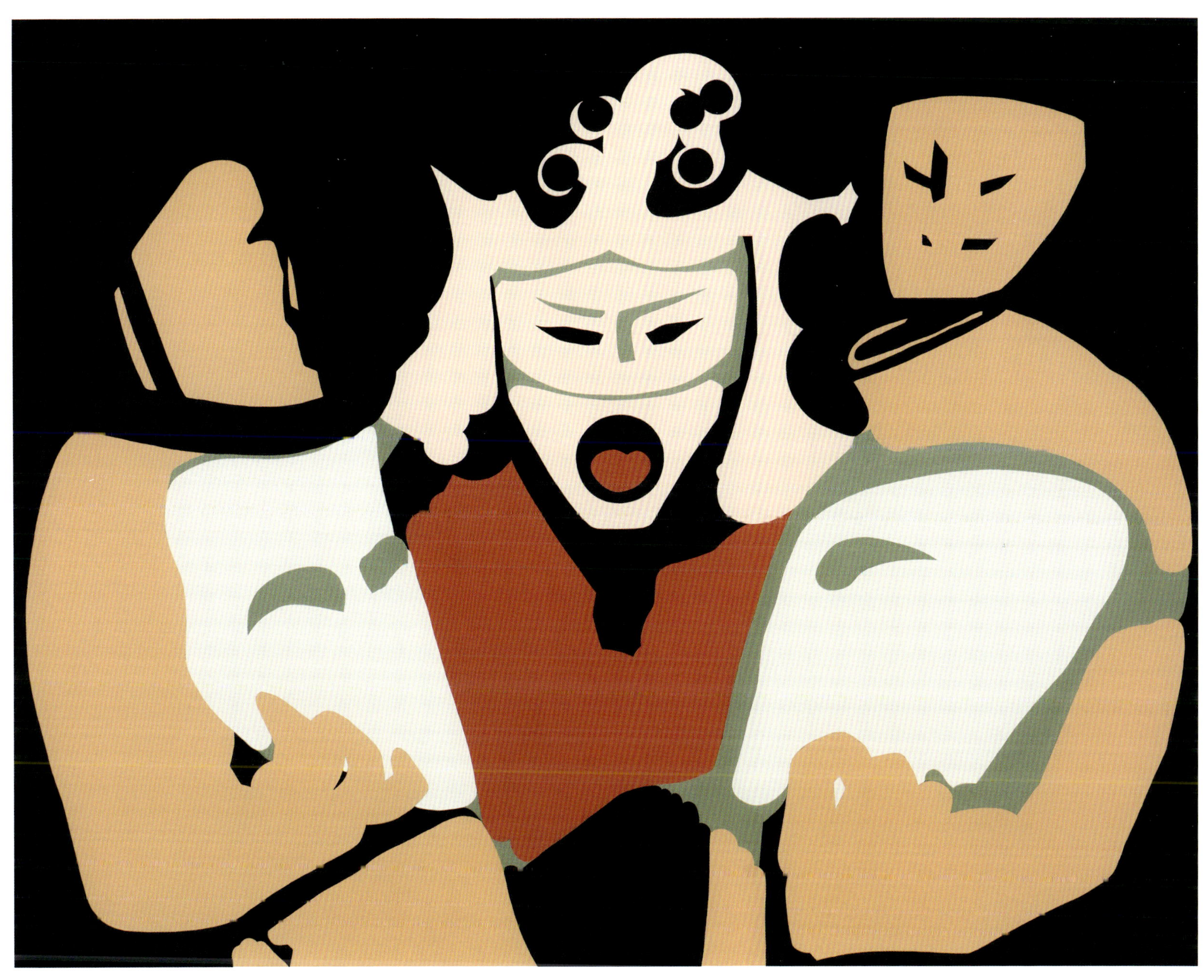

Theatre, 2013
Acrylic on canvas, 123 x 155 cm

Pages 80–81
Cedar, 2013
Acrylic on canvas, 77 x 144 cm

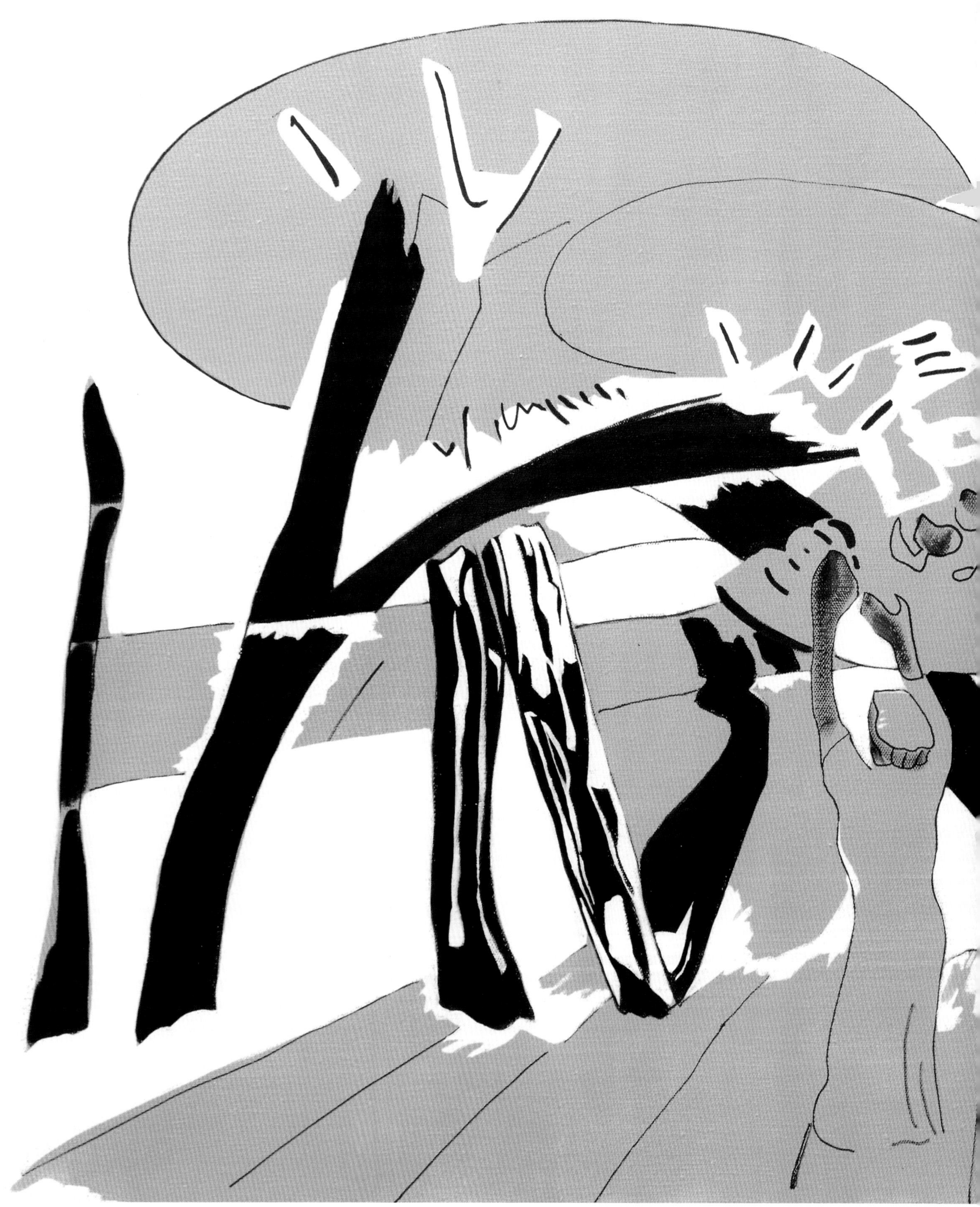

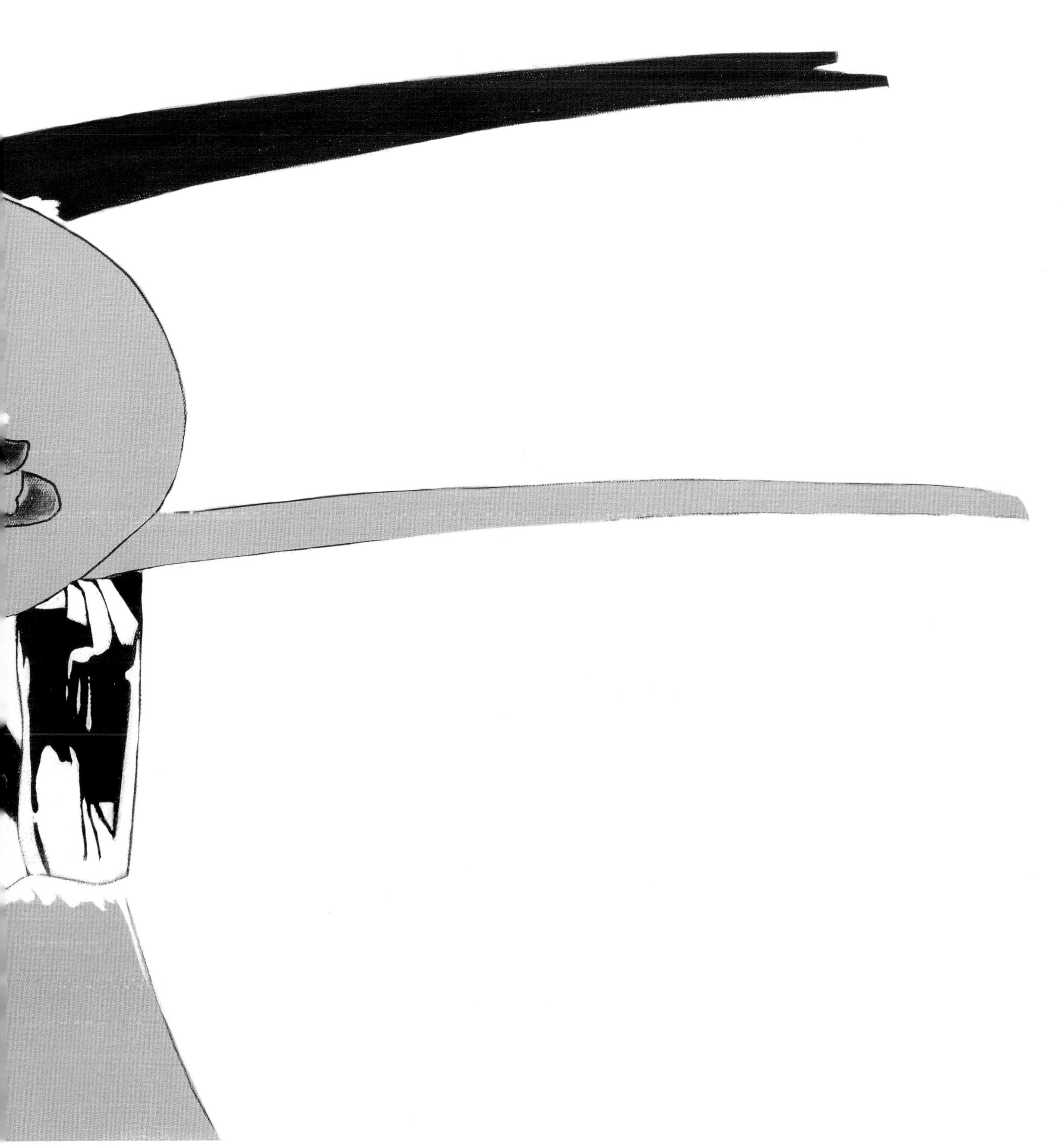

Iva, 2014
Acrylic on canvas, 80 x 65 cm

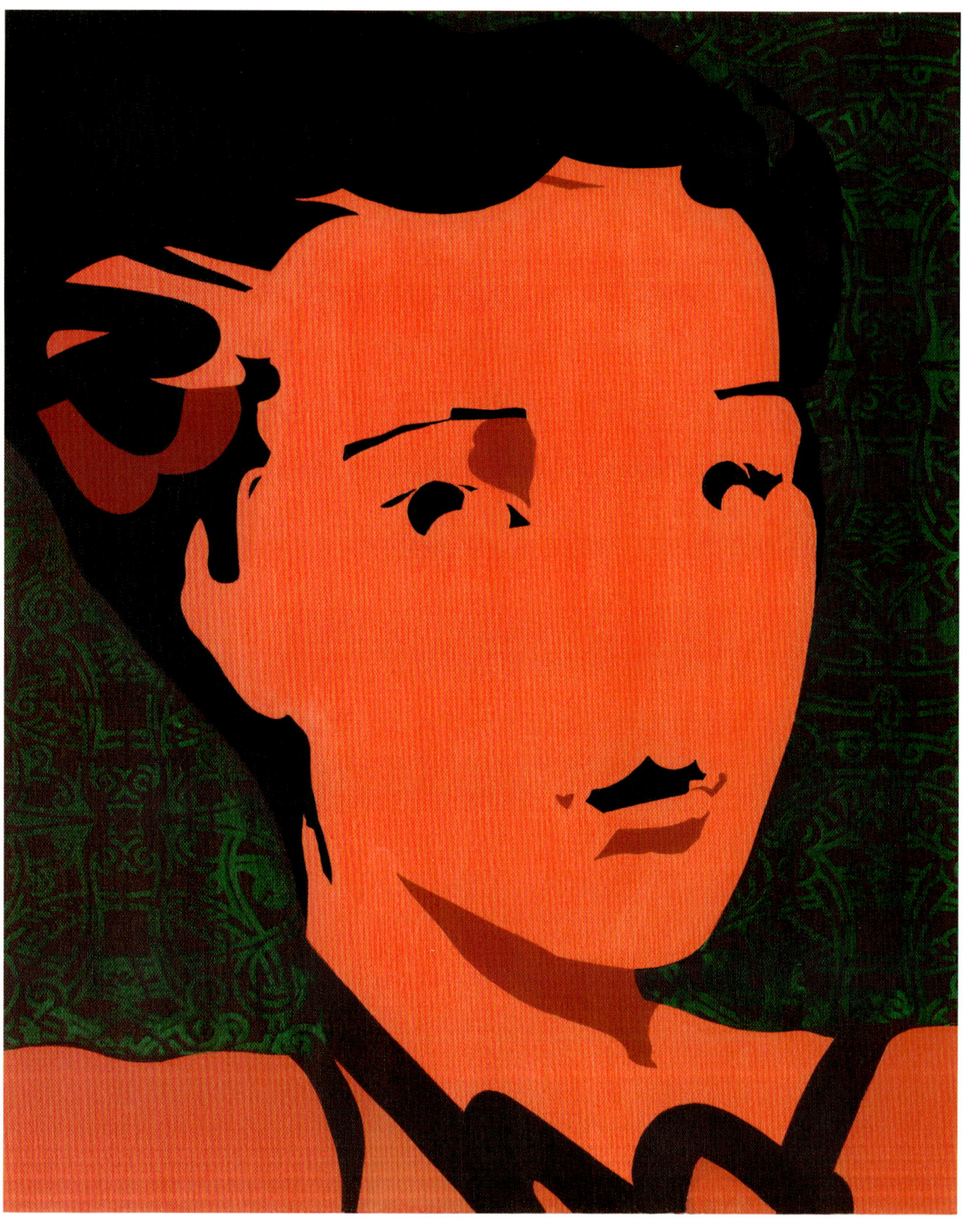

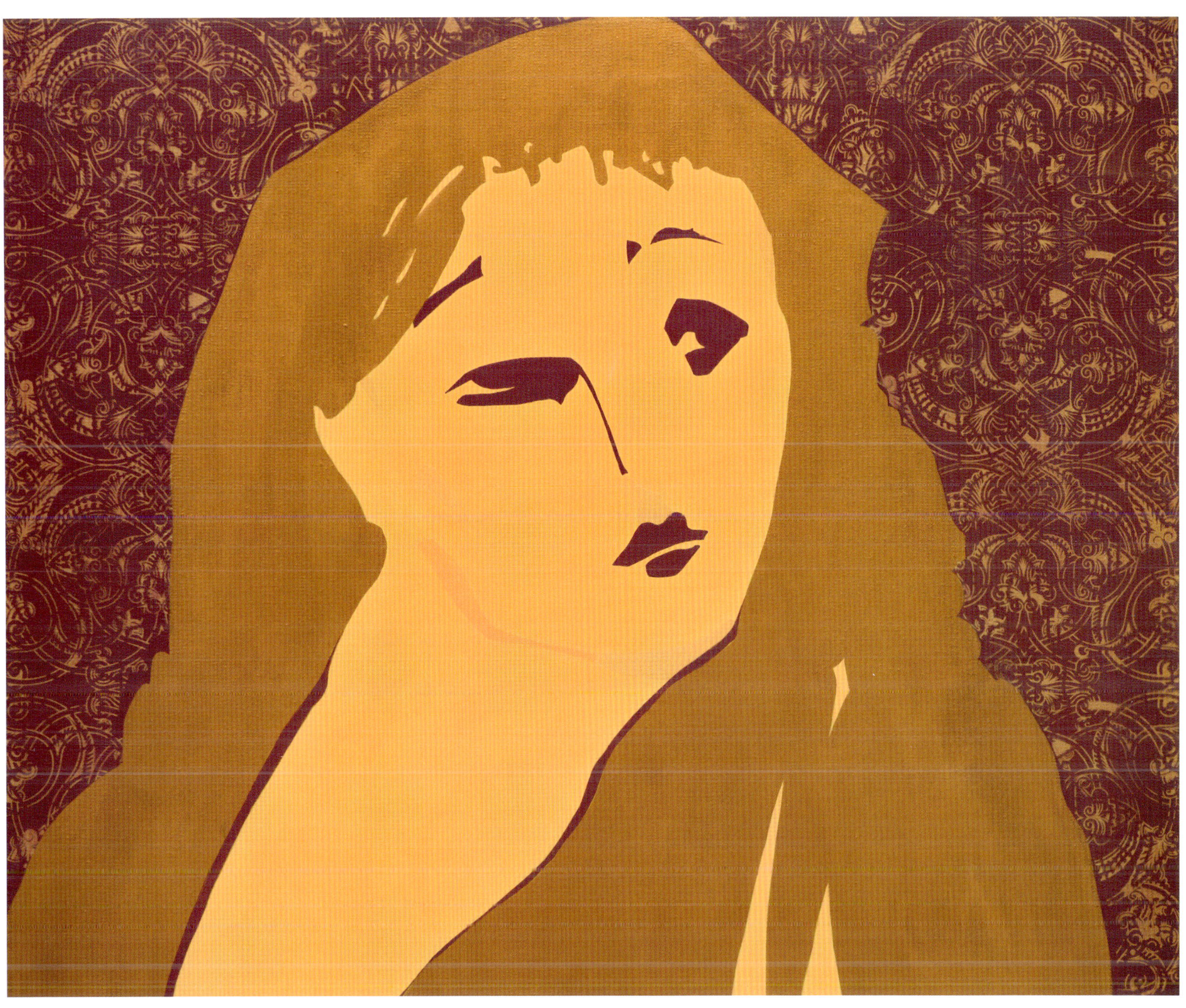

*Girl on Armenian Carpet
Background*, 2014
Acrylic on canvas, 105 x 115 cm

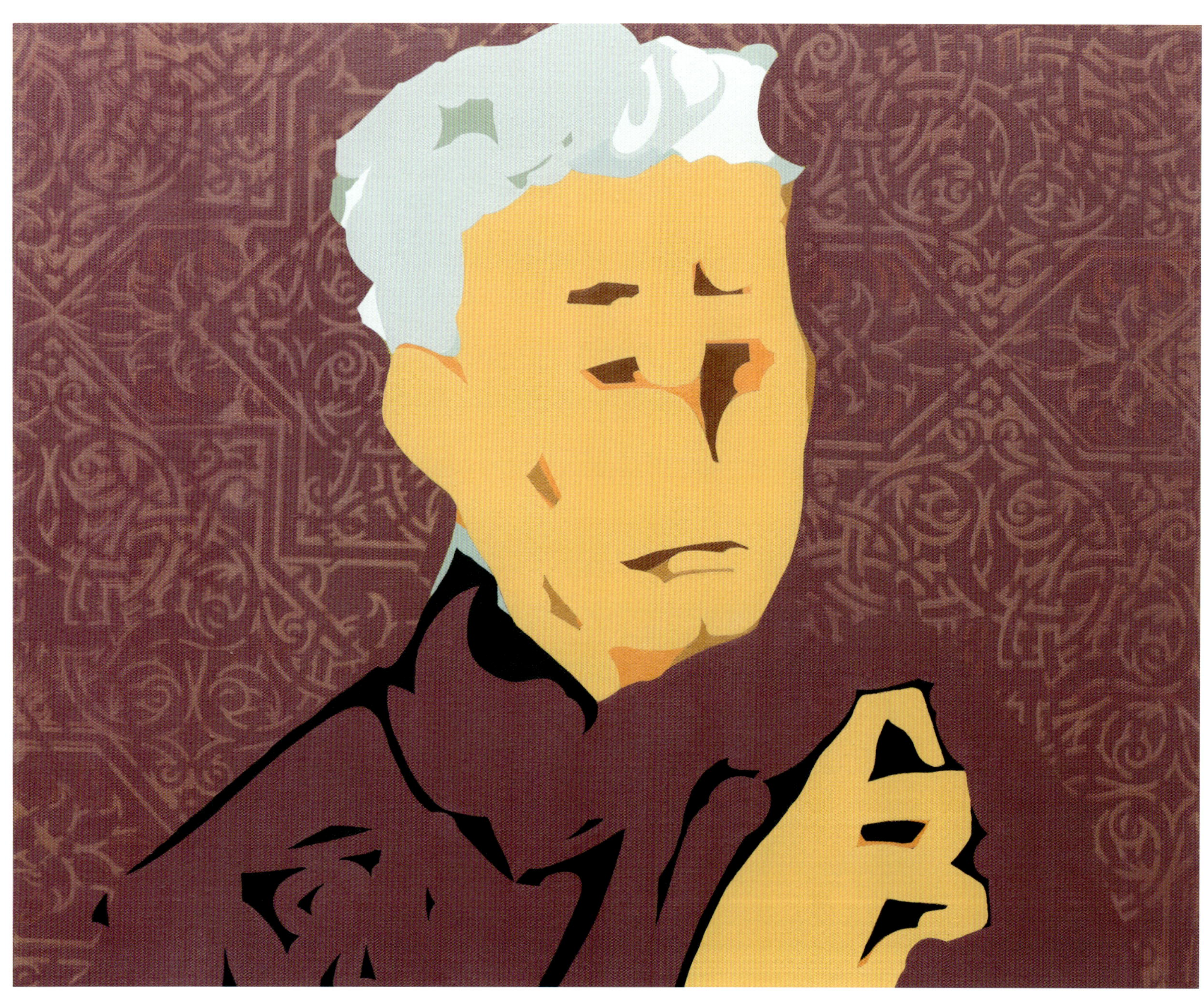

Demetrio, 2014
Acrylic on canvas, 65 x 80 cm

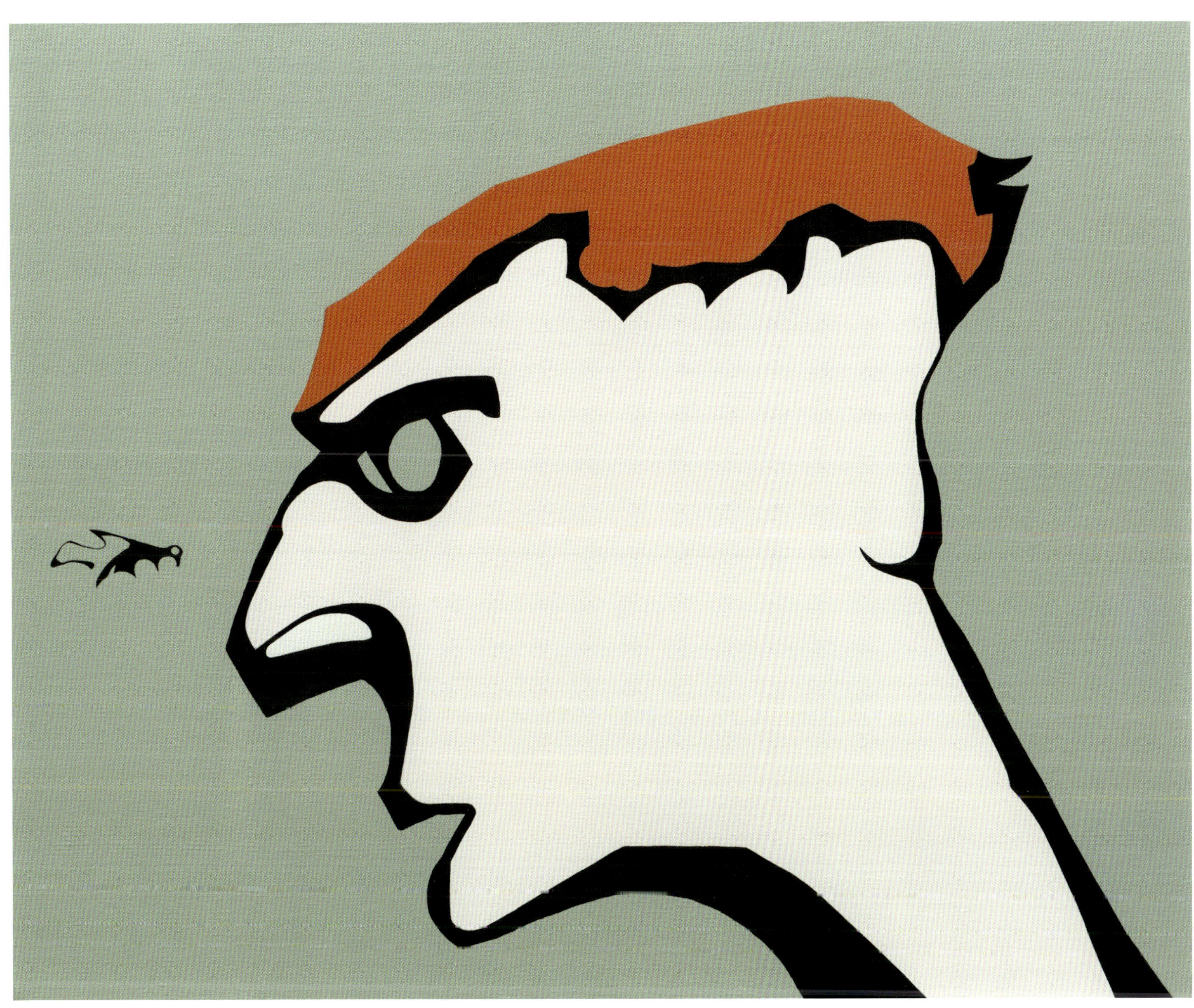

Mosquito, 2013
Acrylic on canvas, 65 x 80 cm

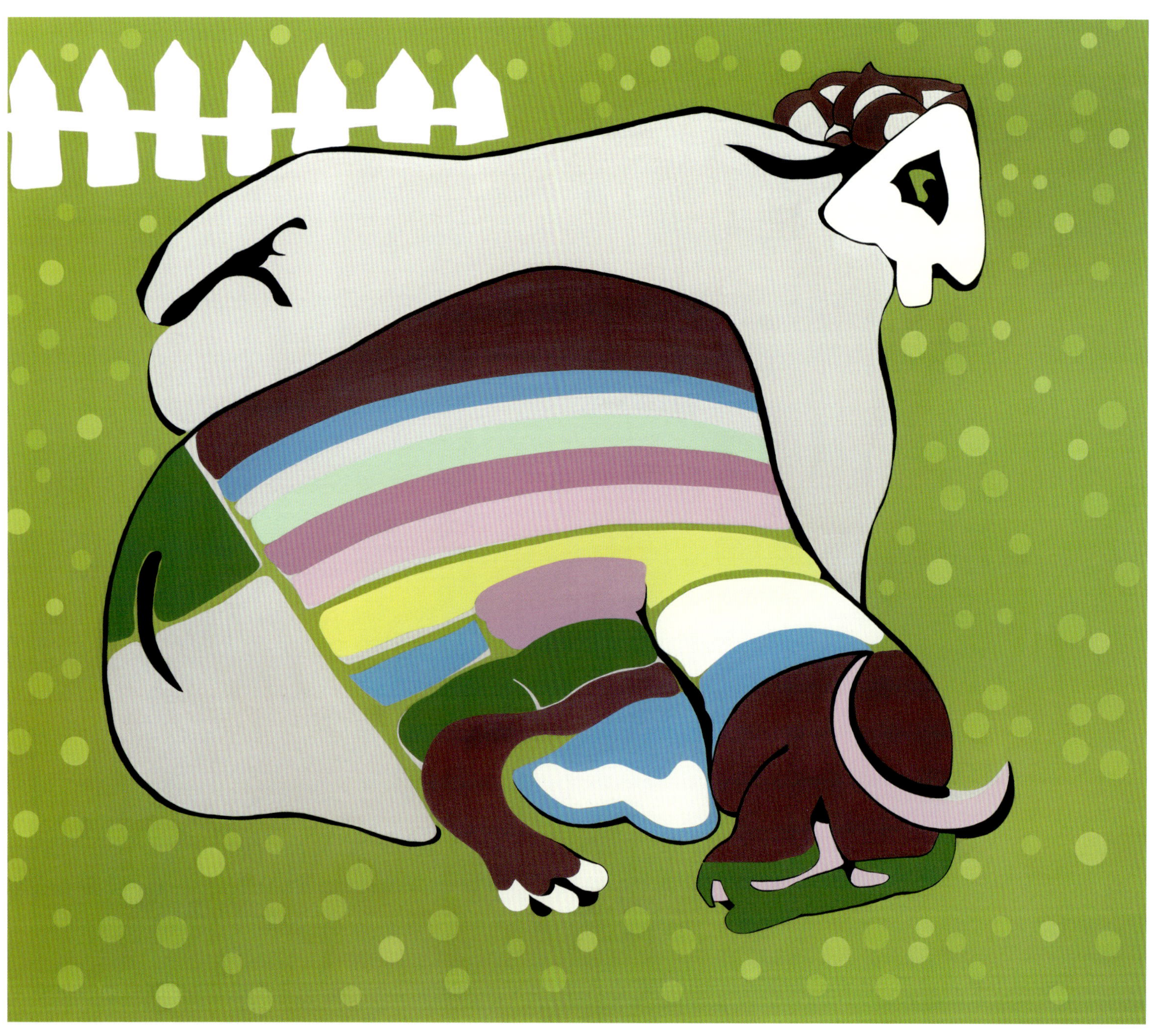

Two Bulls, 2014
Acrylic on canvas, 200 x 229 cm

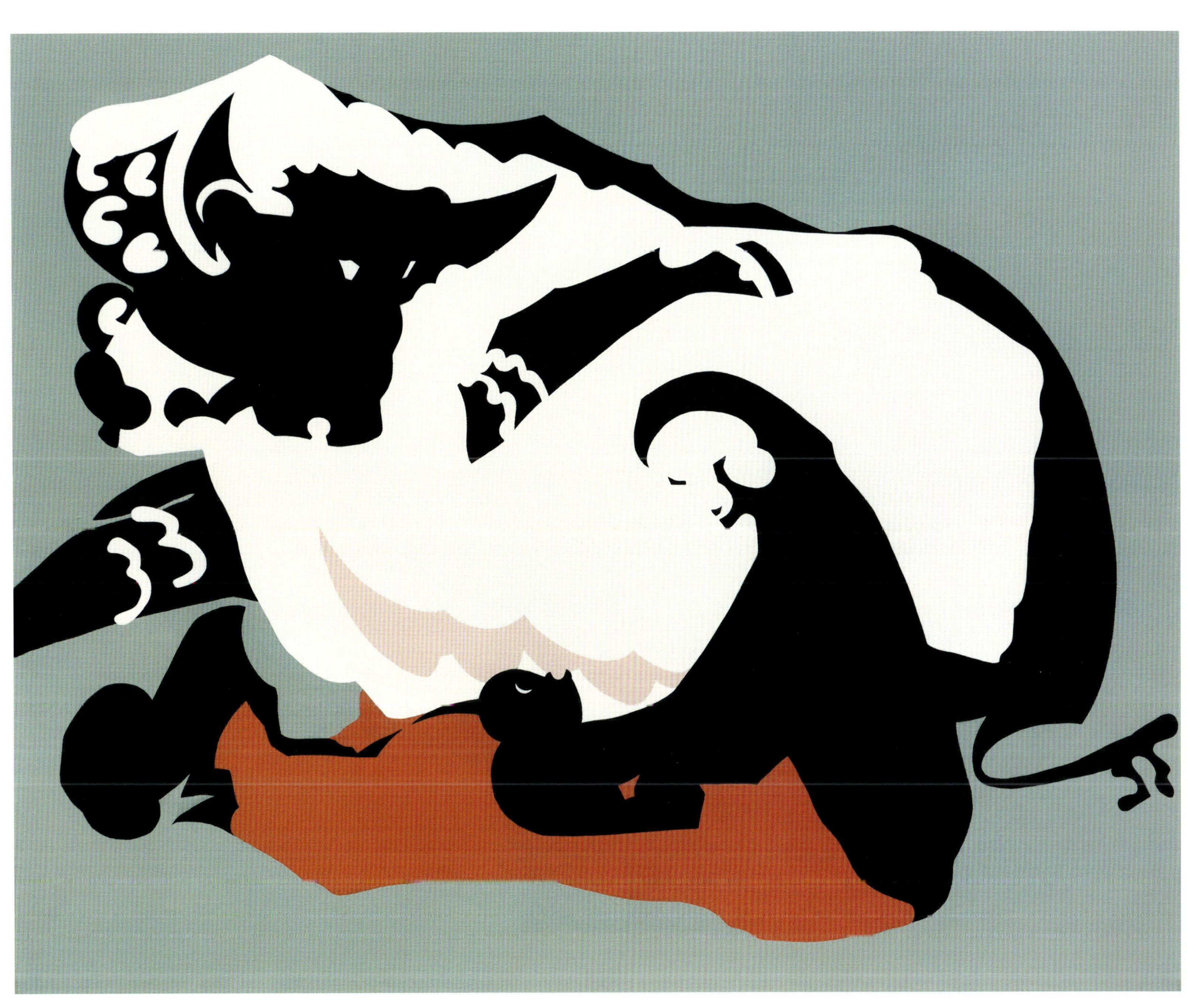

Minotaur, 2014
Acrylic on canvas, 105 x 130 cm

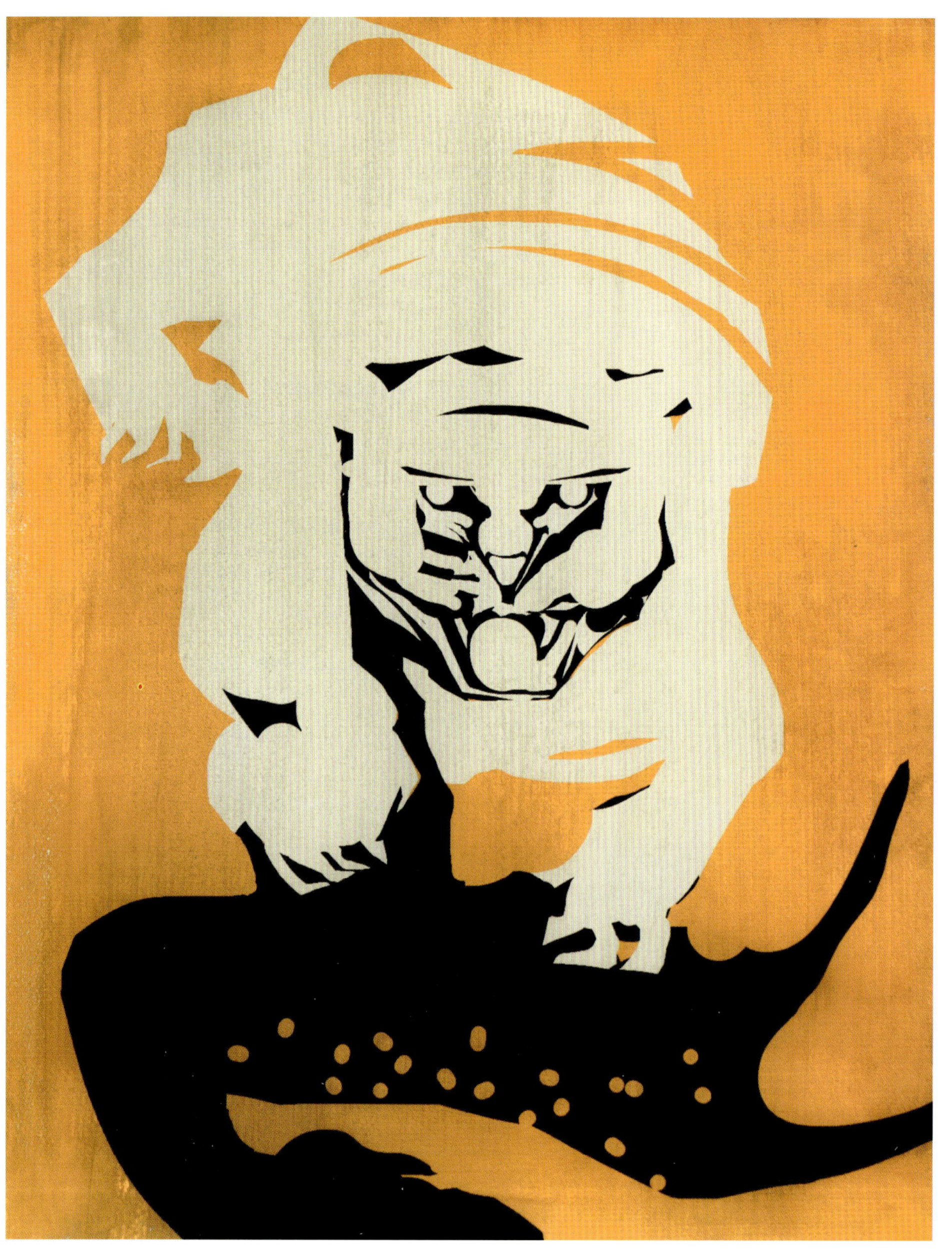

Study for *Bengal Tiger*, 2014
Mixed media on paper, 57 x 32 cm

Facing page
Bengal Tiger, 2014
Acrylic on canvas, 160 x 125 cm

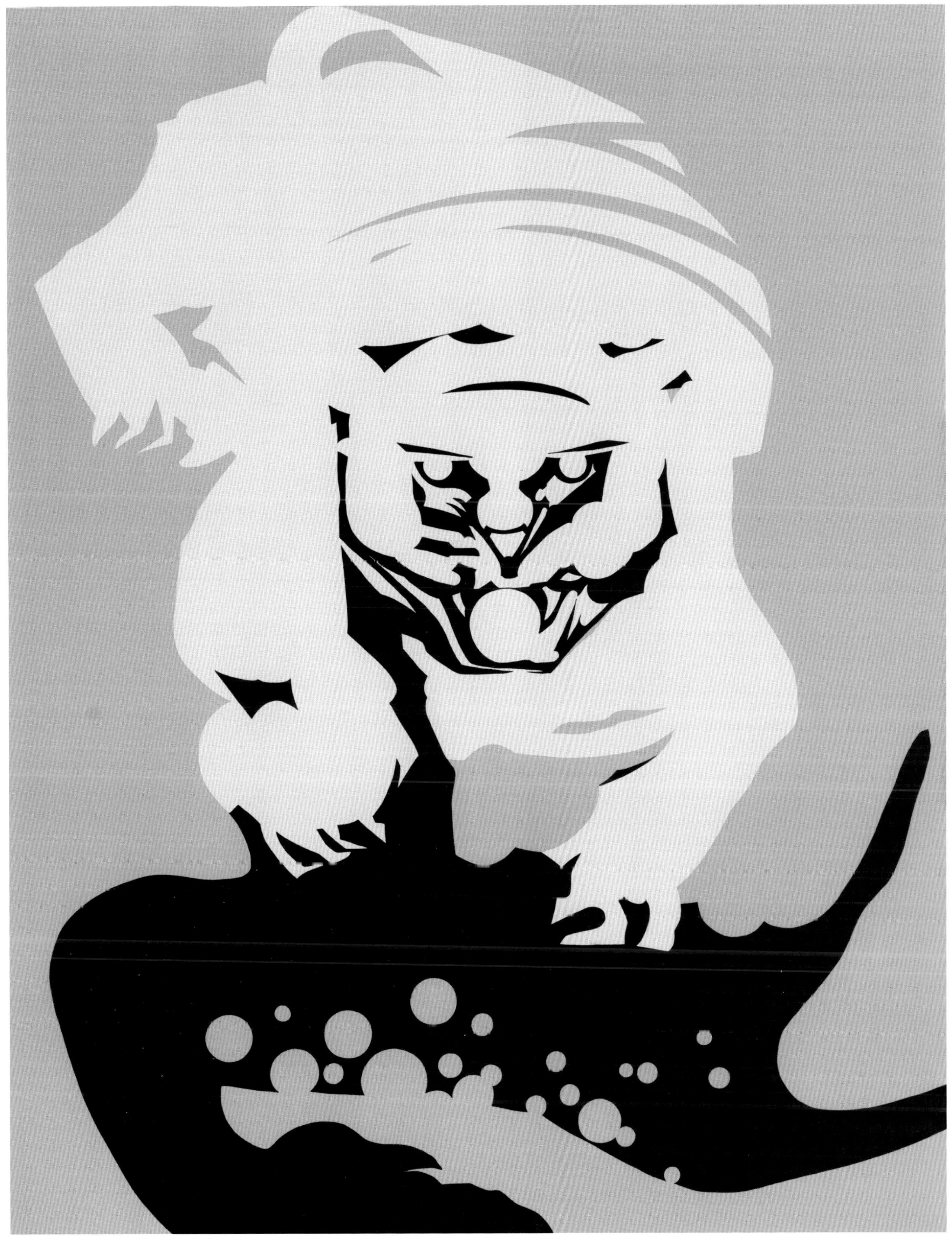

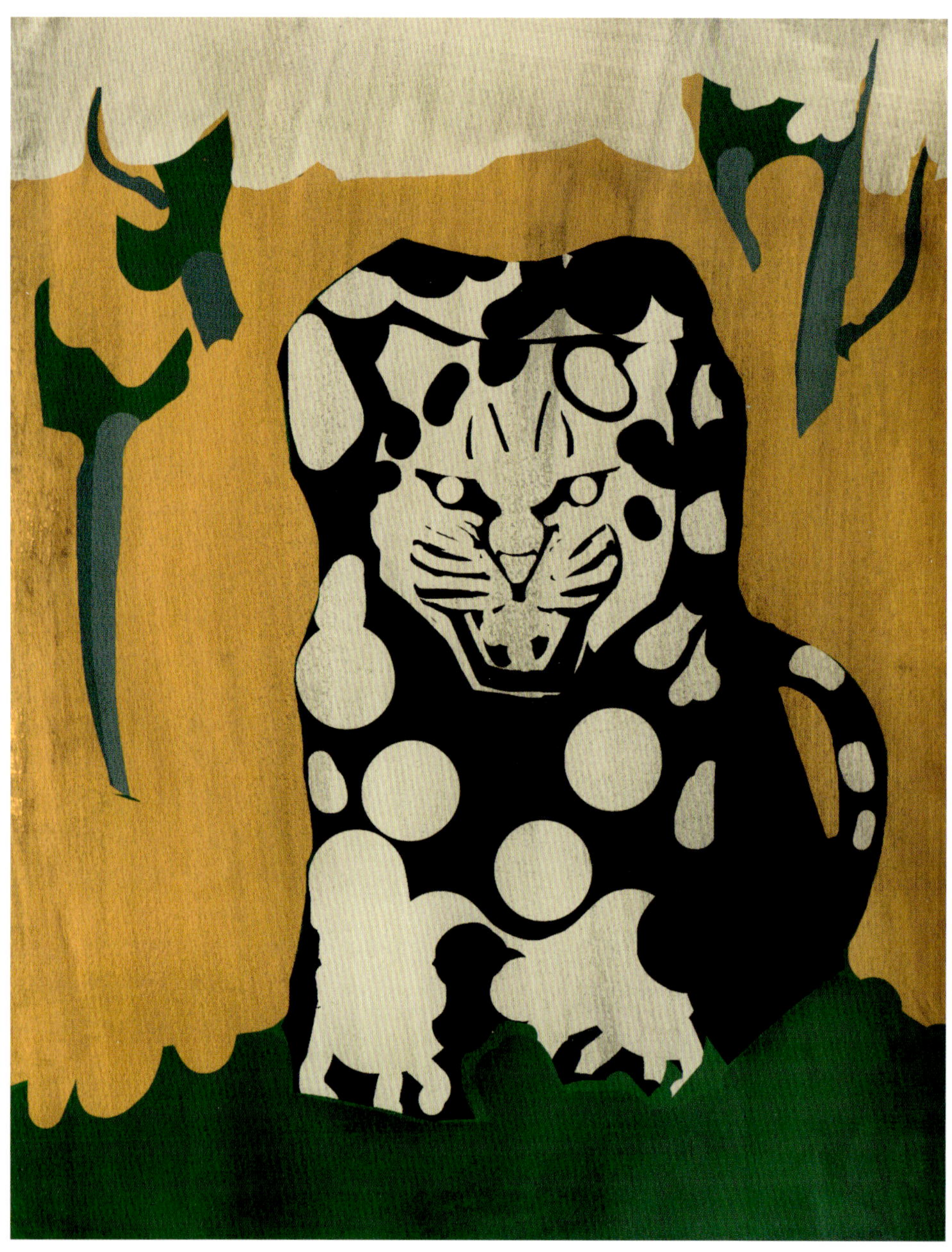

Jaguar, 2014
Mixed media on paper, 57 x 32 cm

Facing page
Jaguar, 2014
Acrylic on canvas, 130 x 105 cm

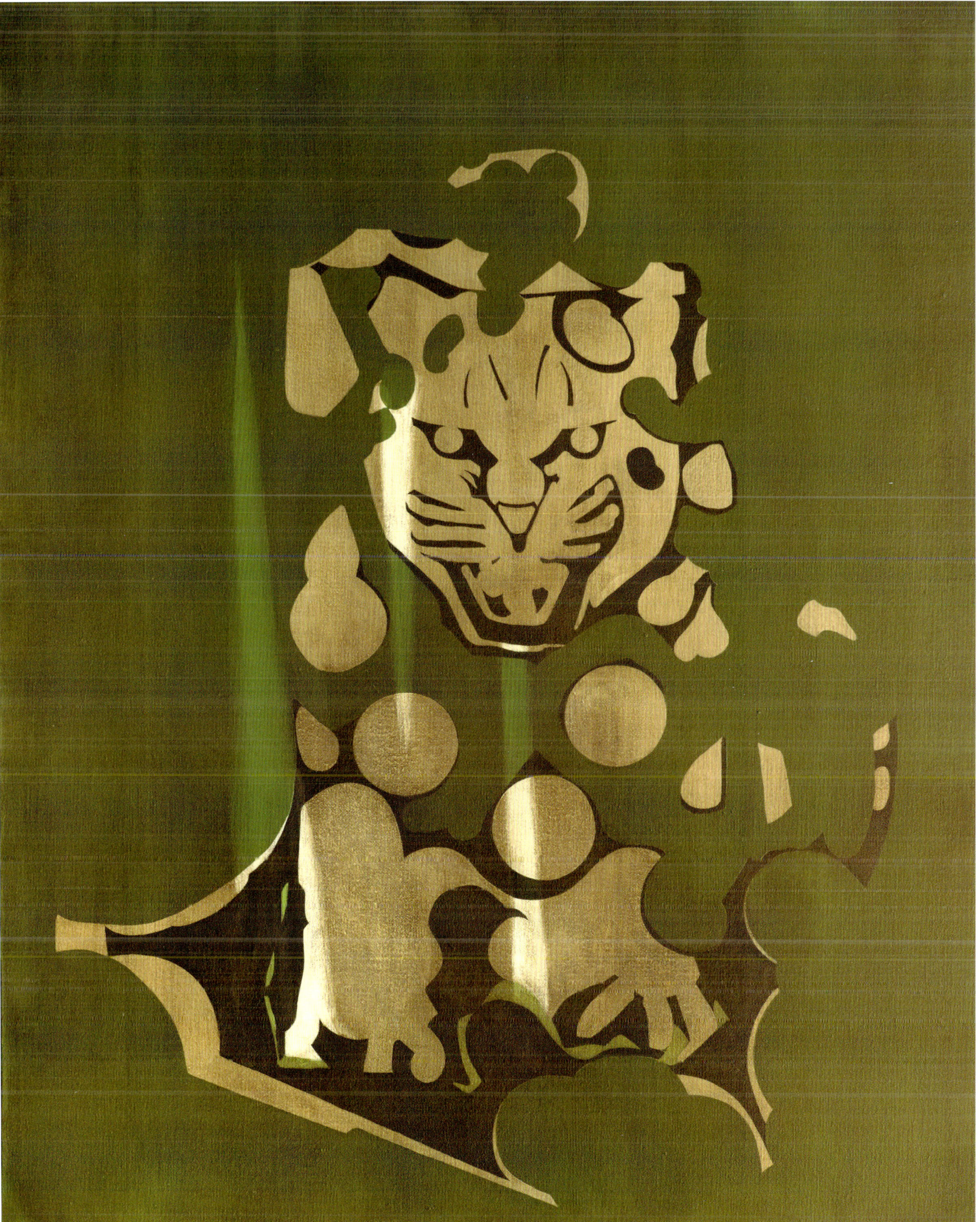

Nursing Panther, 2014
Acrylic on canvas, 70 x 110 cm

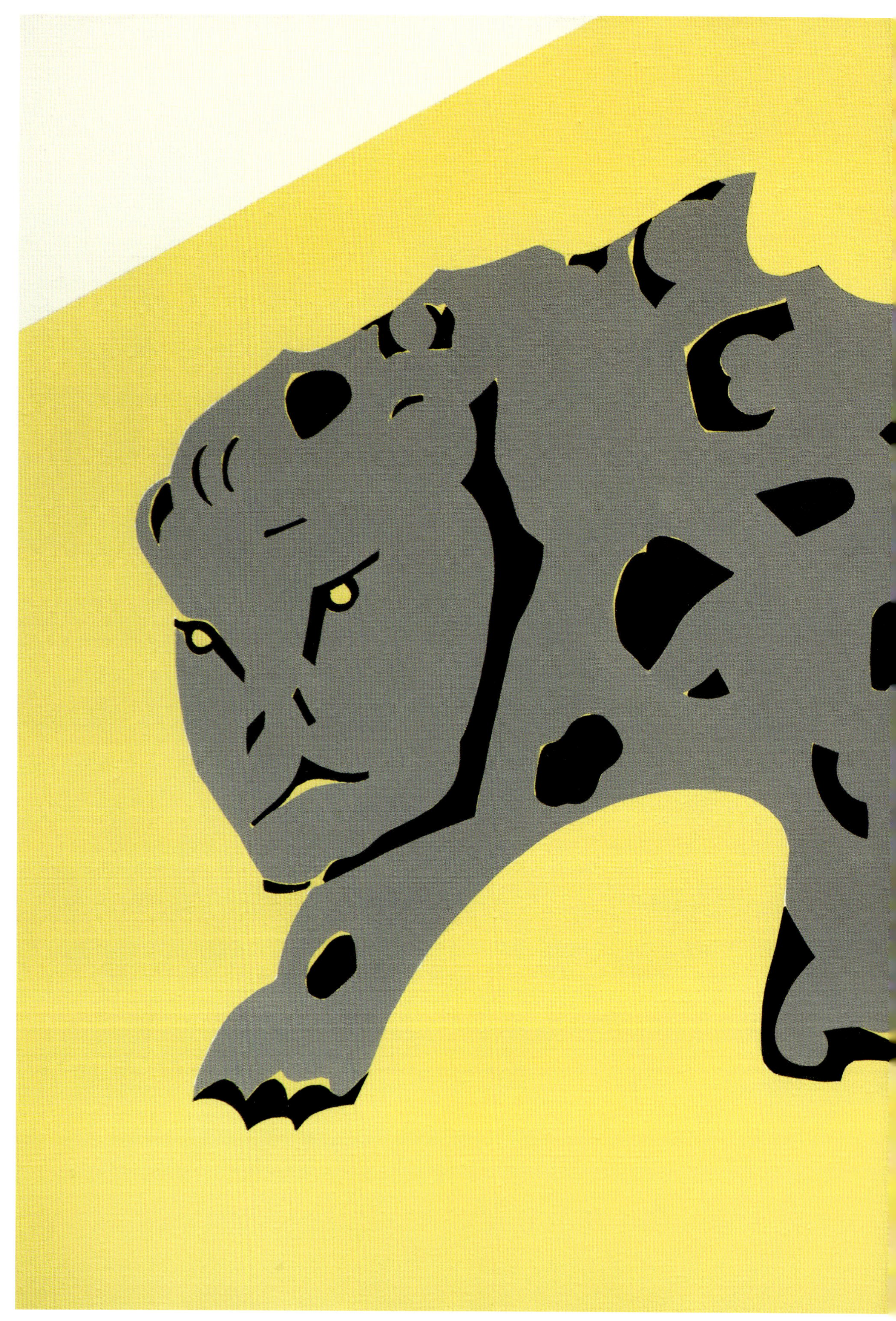

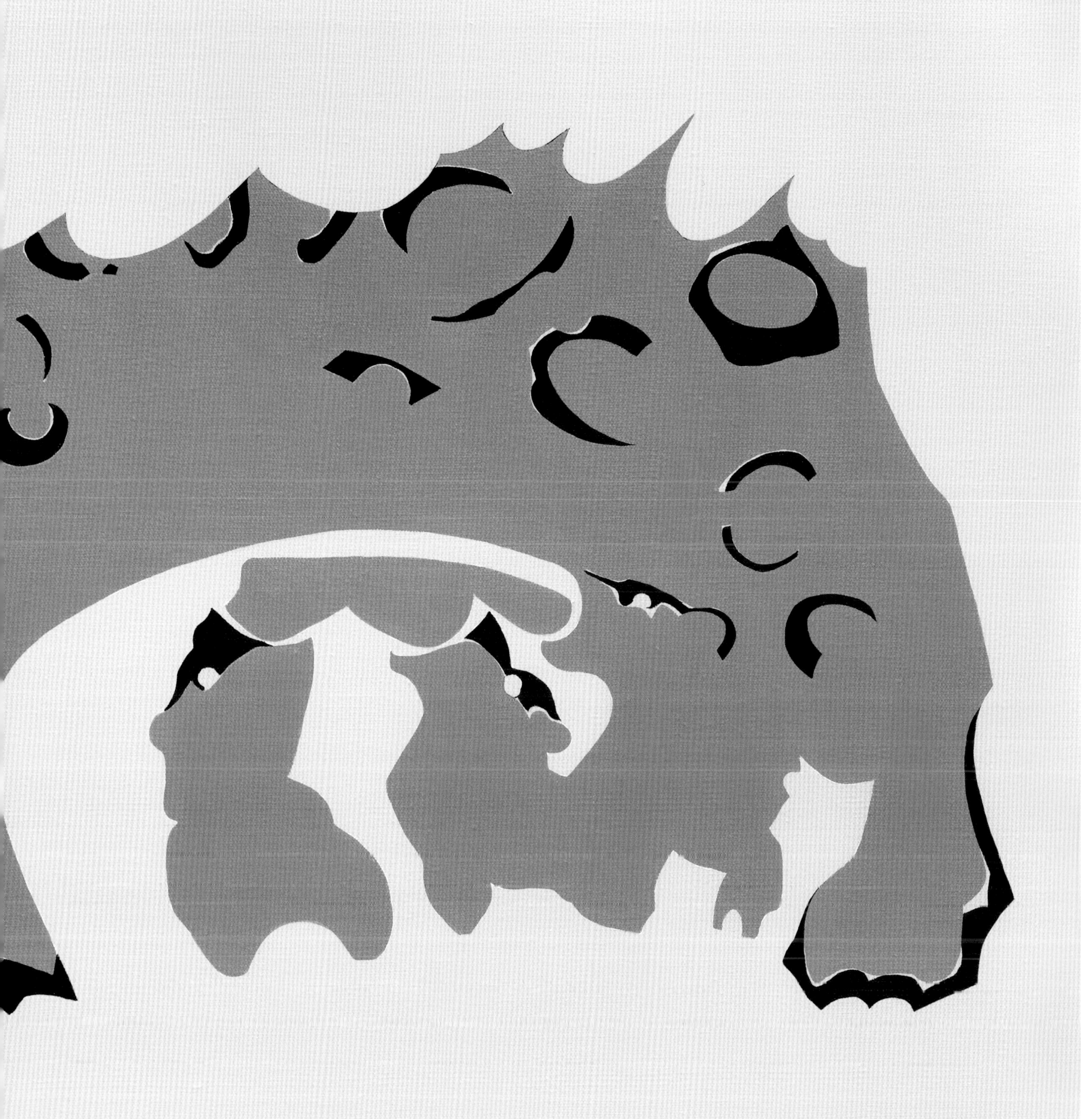

In nature, the instinct to preserve life is so strong that a panther keeps nursing her cubs even when she's soaking wet from the rain. By following this same survival instinct, the cubs suck on the milk, which in time turns into blood and bones. This, too, makes the harmony of nature.

Rafael Megall

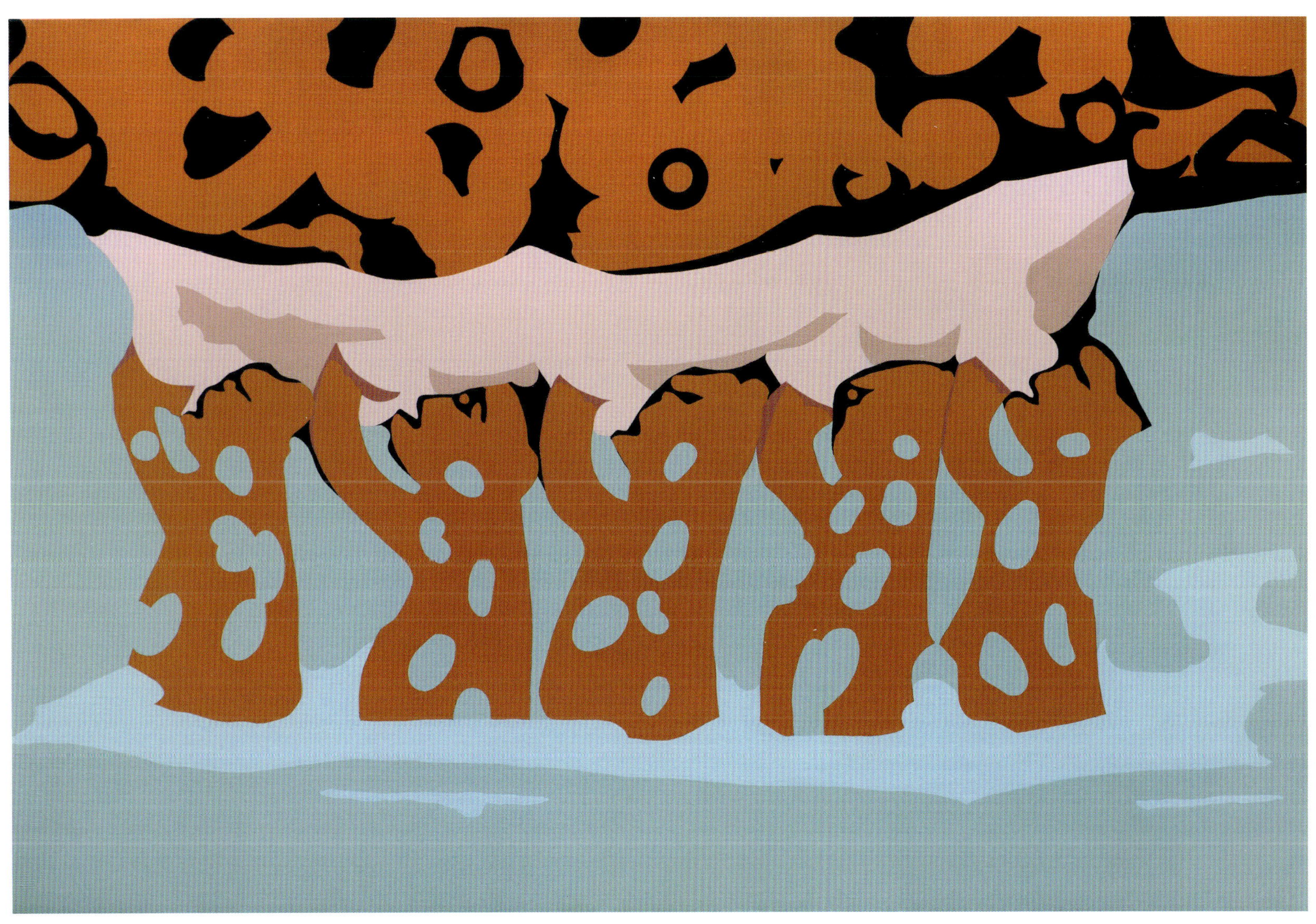

Panther with Cubs, 2014
Acrylic on canvas, 120 x 175 cm

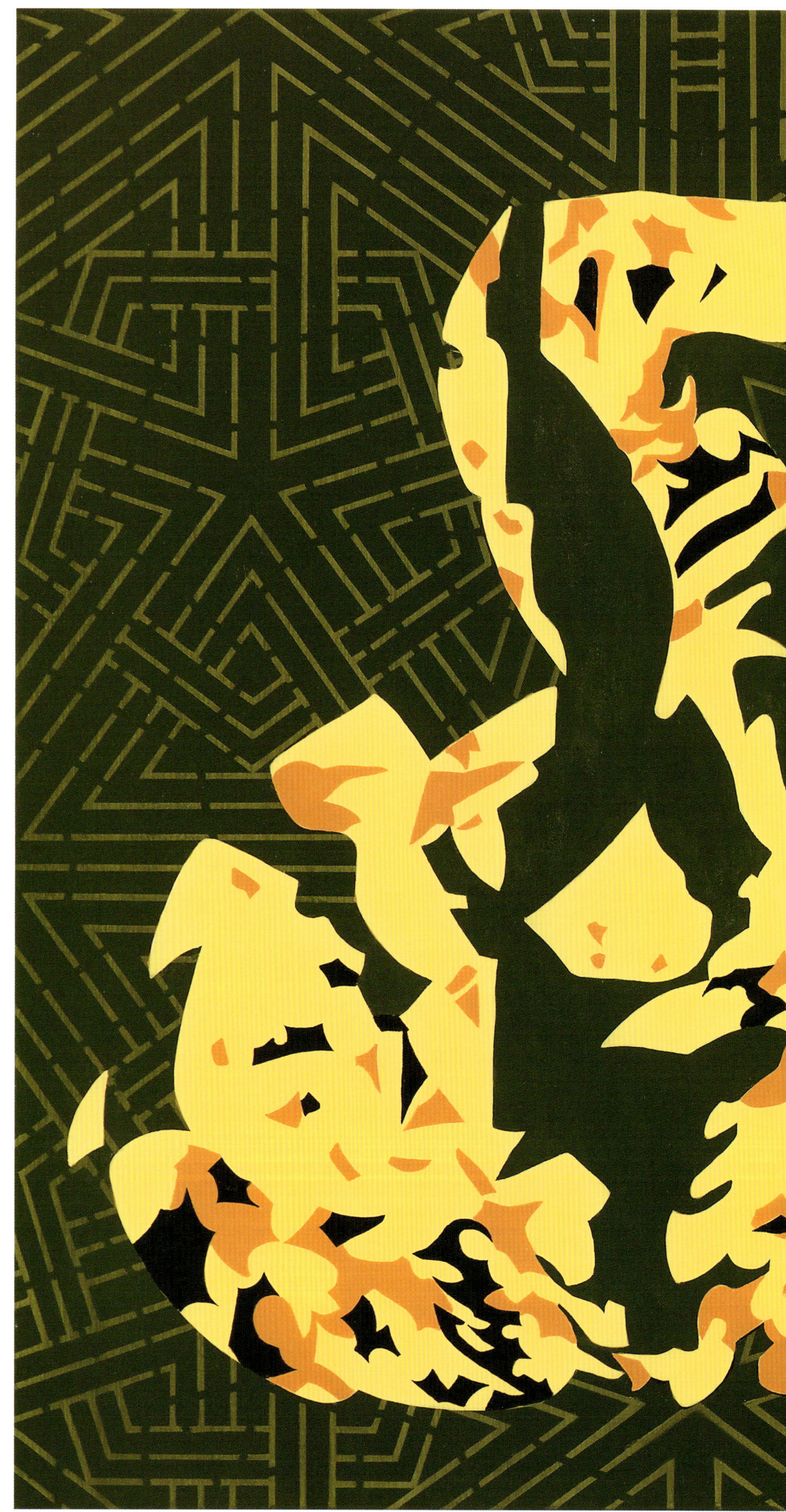

Siberian Leopard, 2014
Acrylic on canvas, 70 x 100 cm

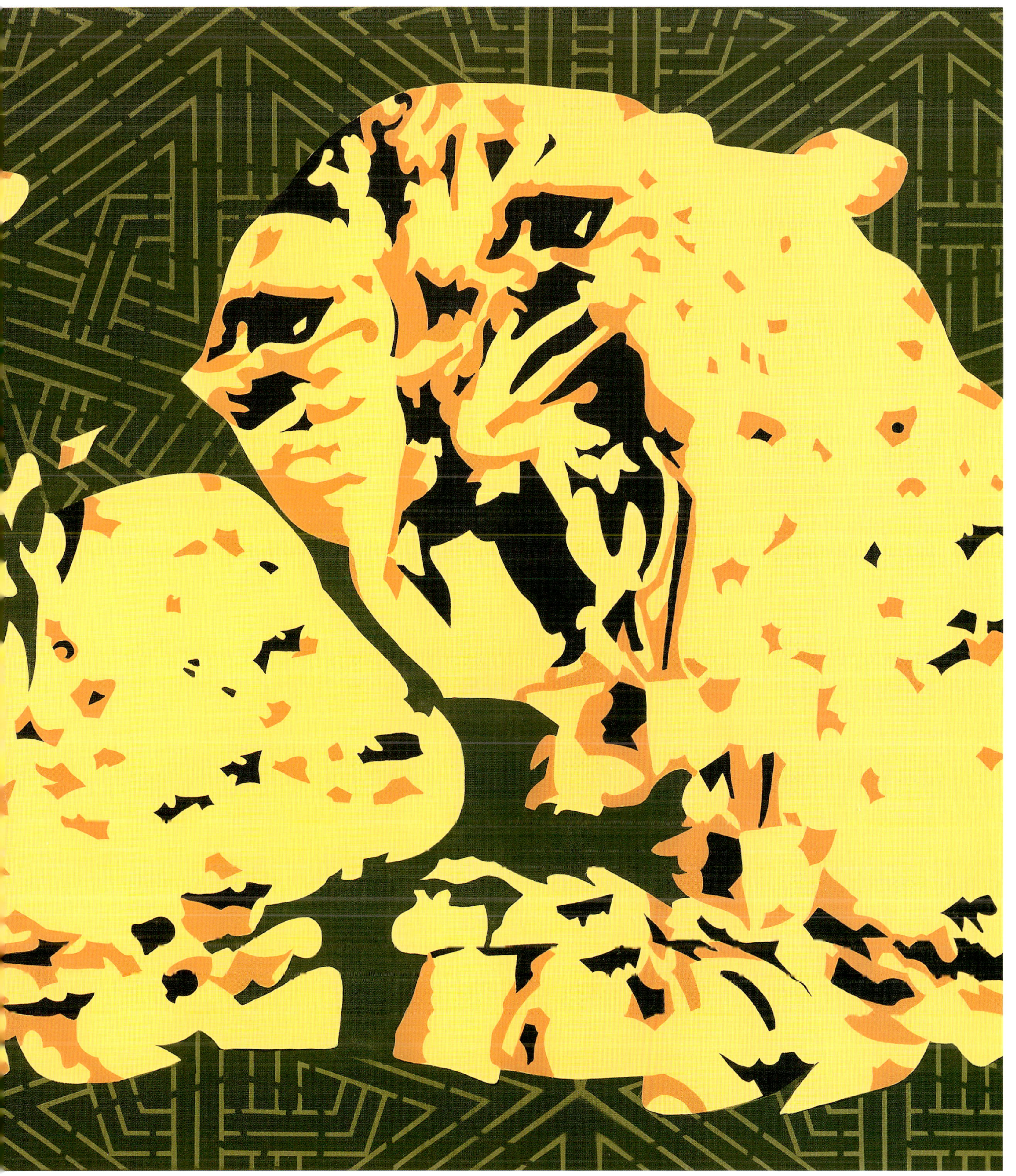

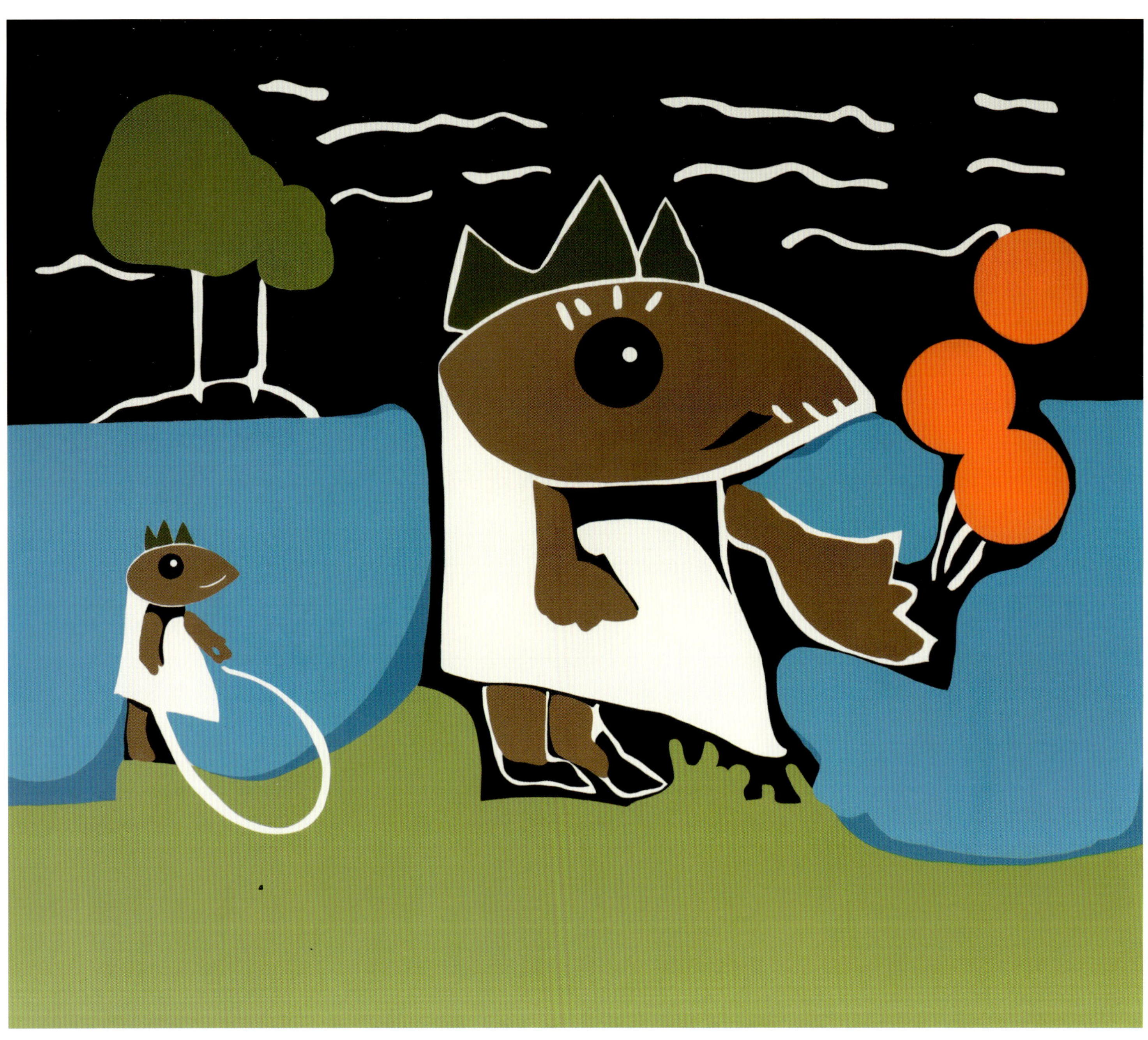

Grandfather and Granddaughter,
2014
Acrylic on canvas, 200 x 229 cm

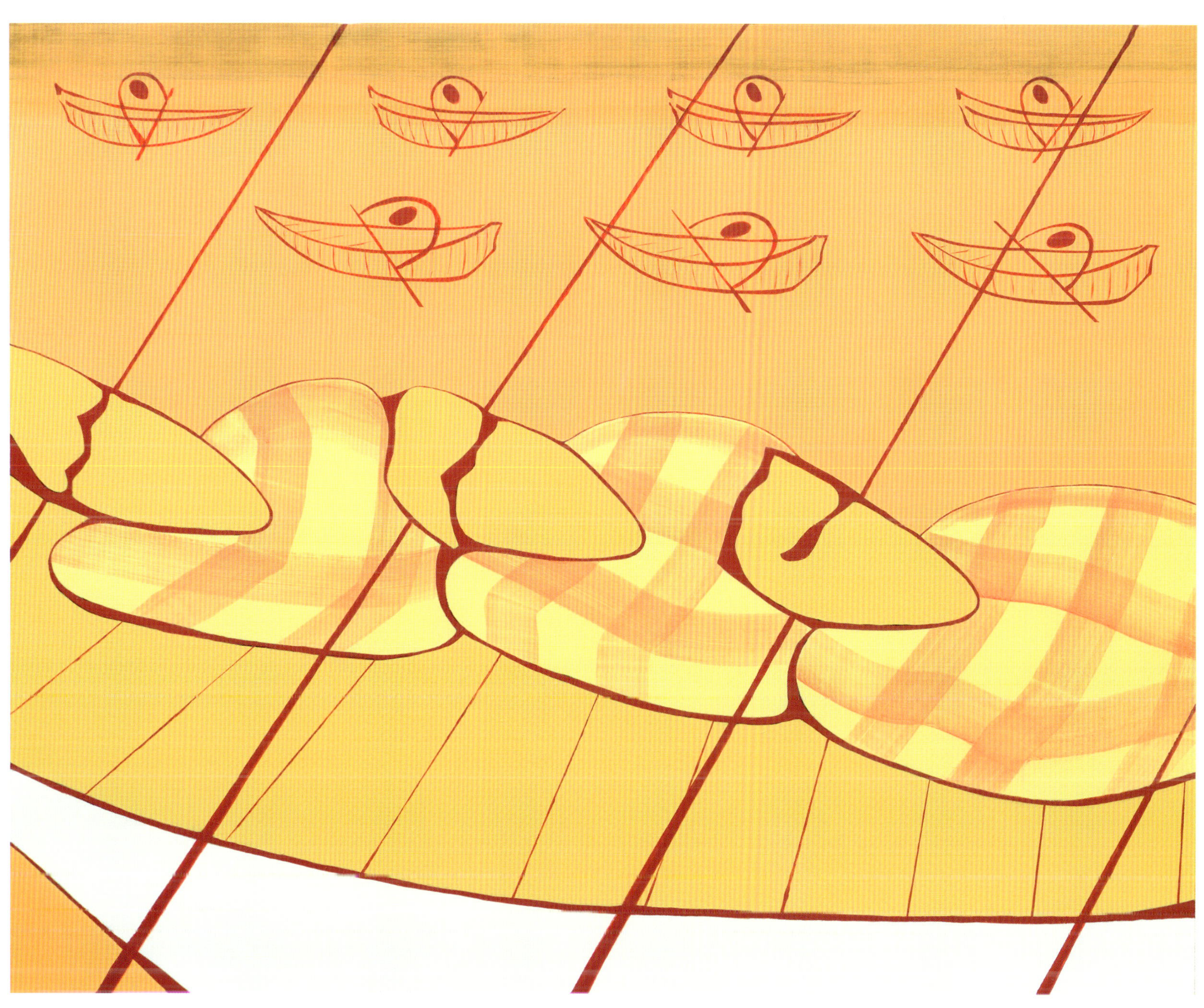

Rowers, 2014
Acrylic on canvas, 130 x 160 cm

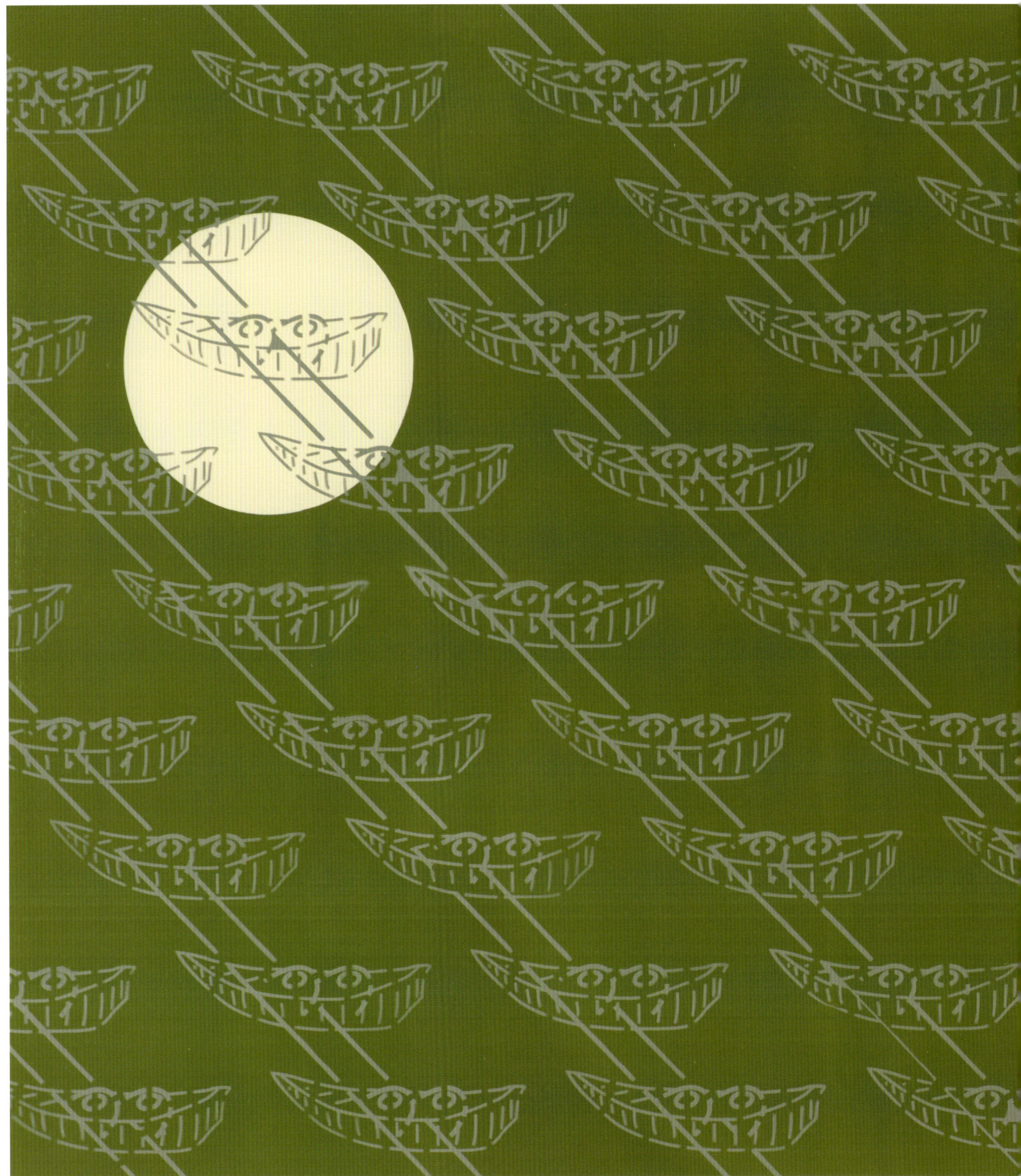

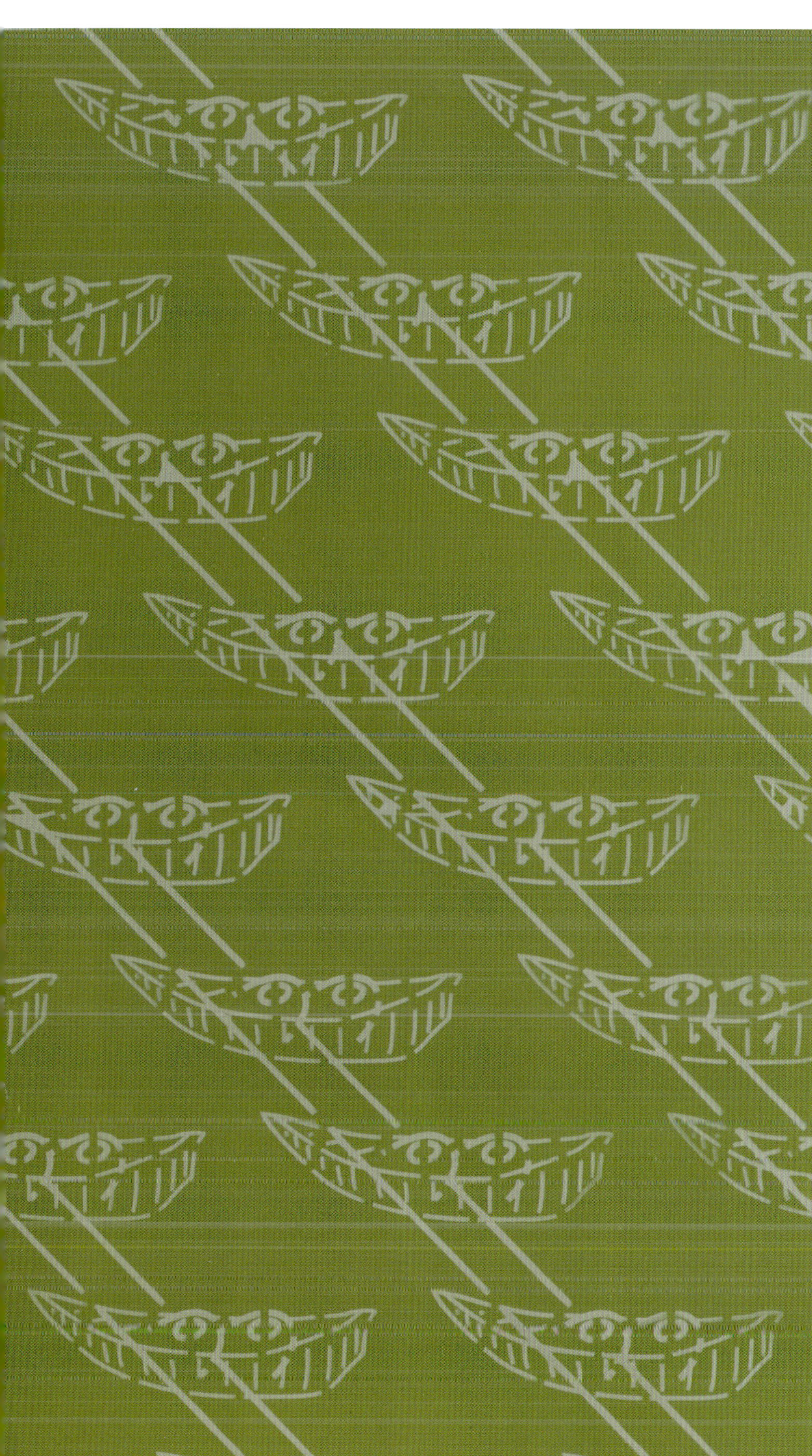

Winner, 2014
Acrylic on canvas, 70 x 100 cm

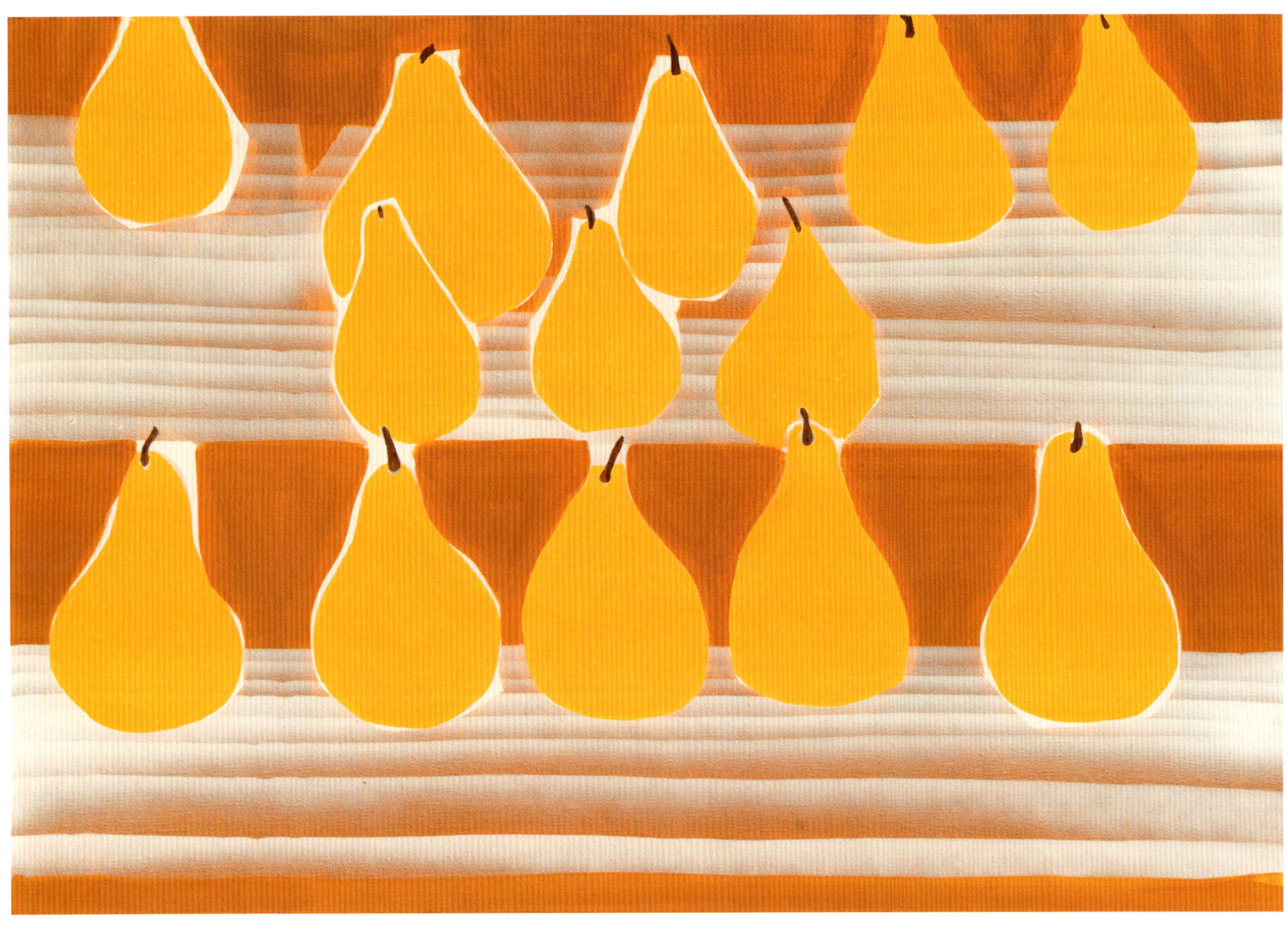

Pumpkins, 2014
Acrylic on canvas, 40 x 58 cm

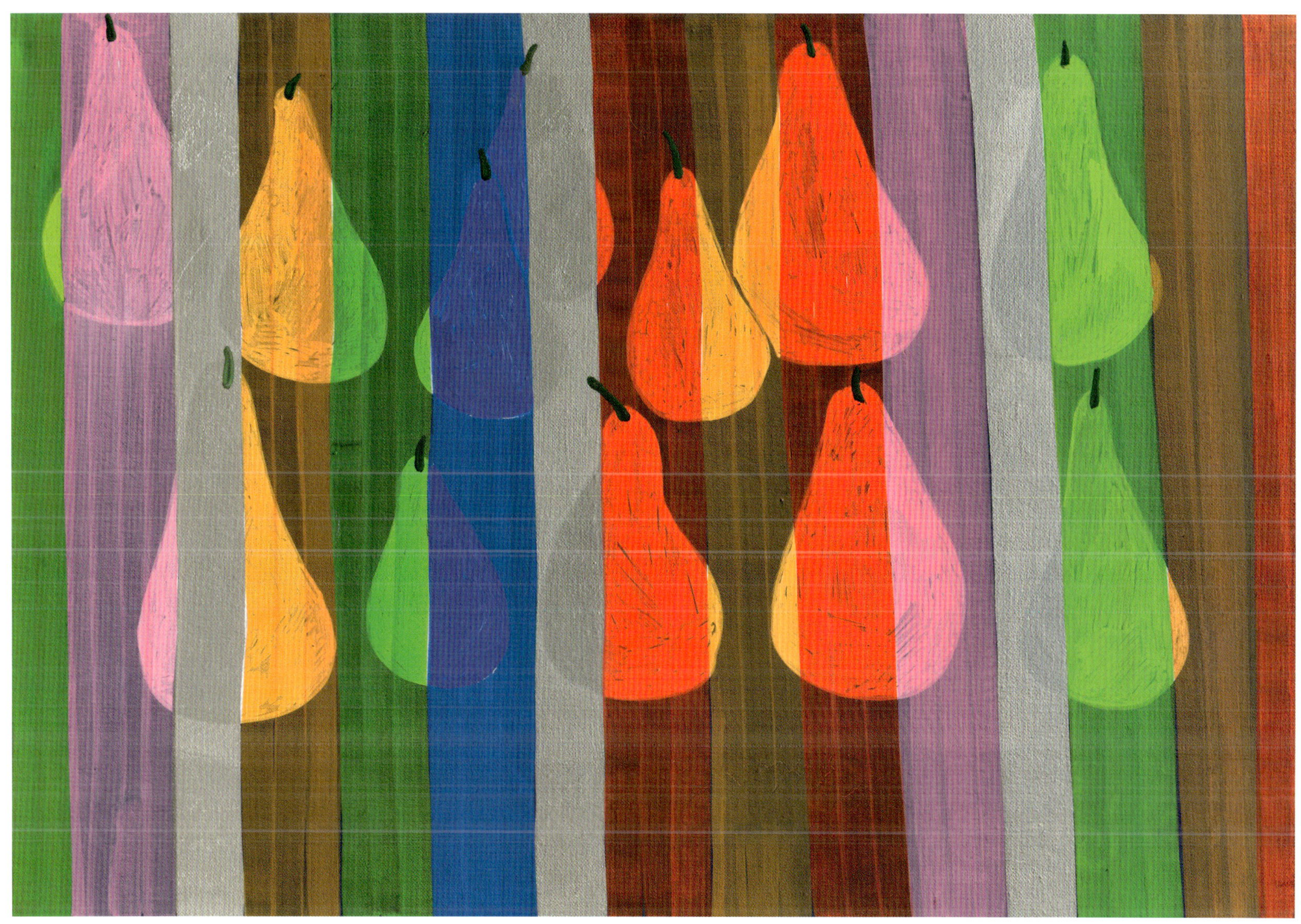

Striped Pumpkins, 2014
Acrylic on canvas, 40 x 58 cm

Plasticine Toys, 2015
Acrylic on canvas, 75 x 100 cm

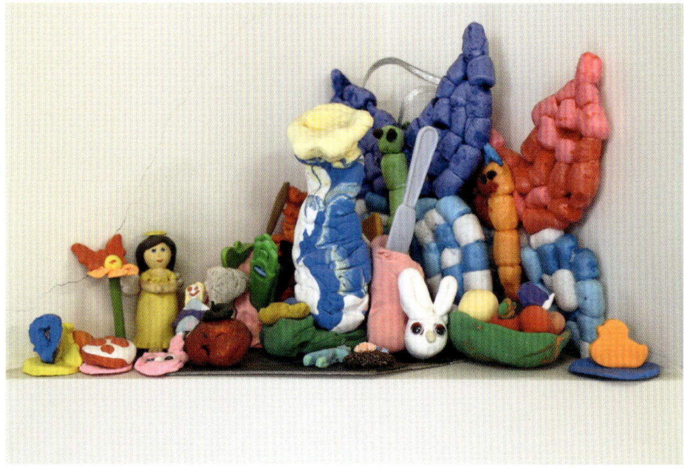

Study for *Plasticine Toys*, 2015

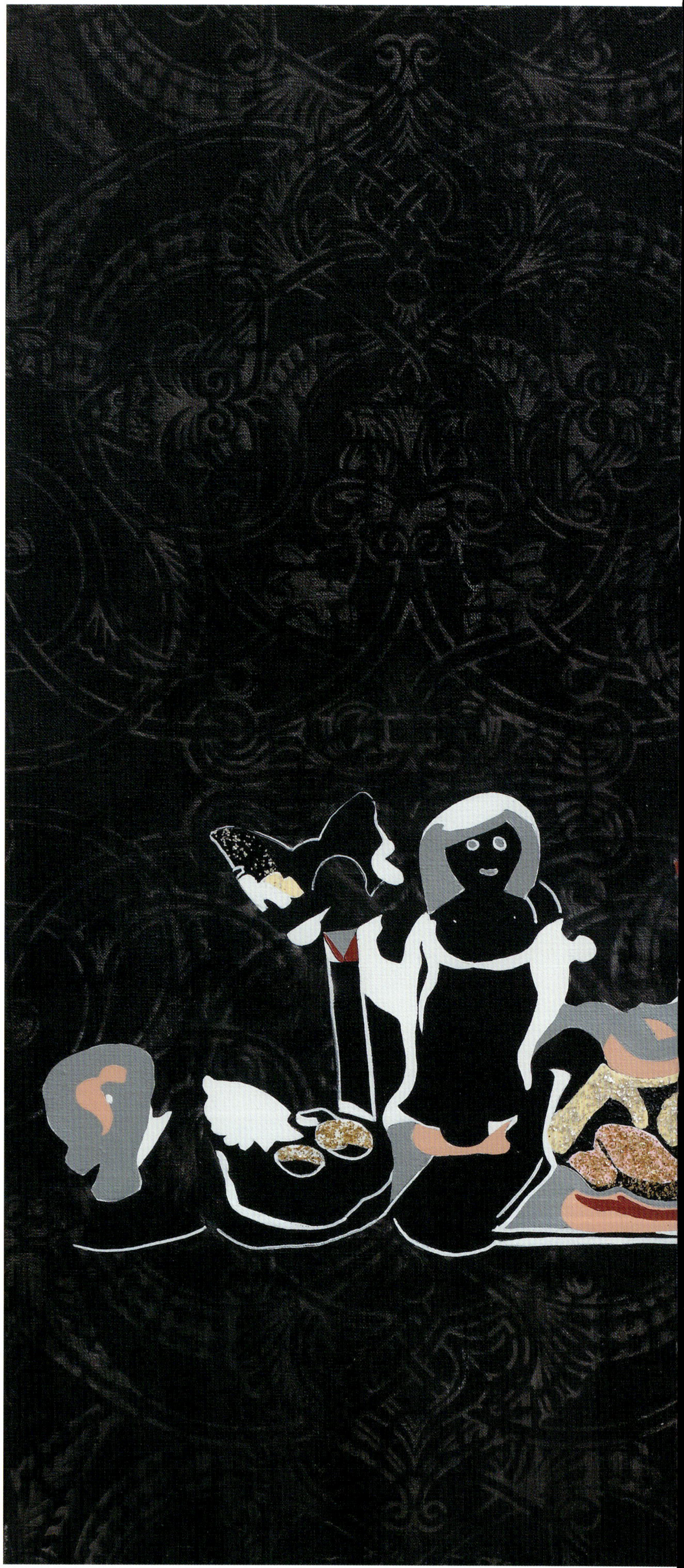

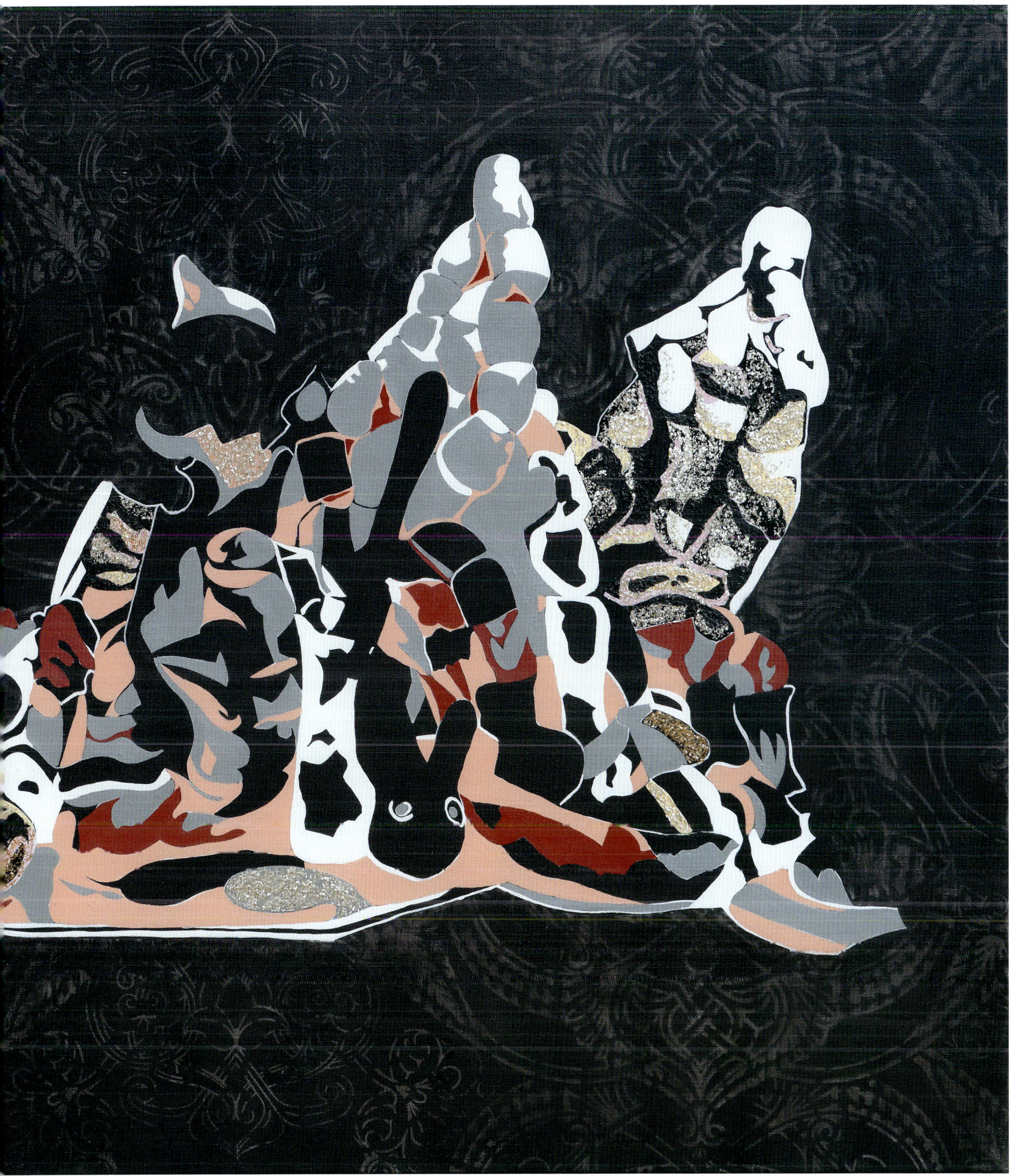

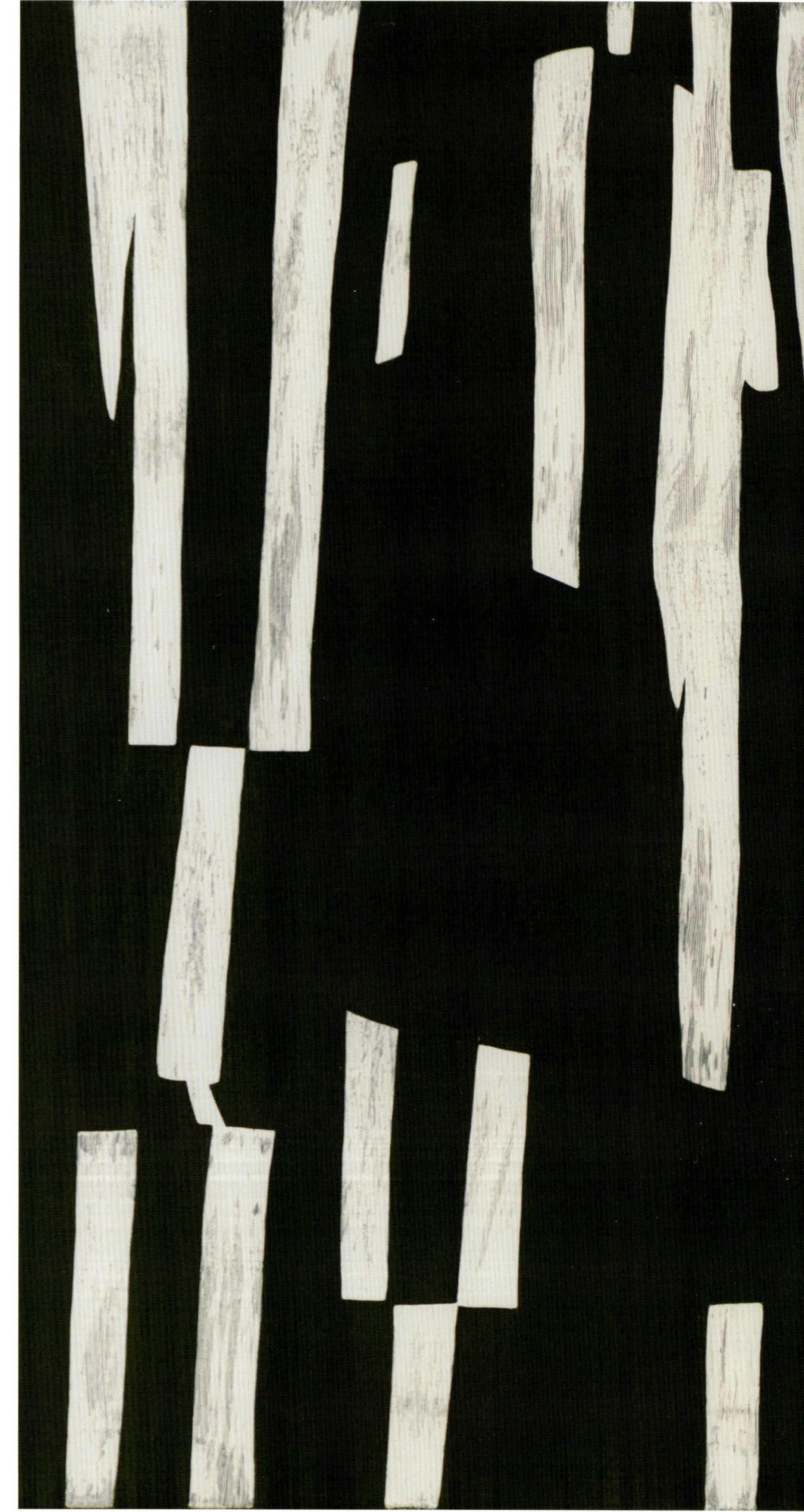

Lathe, 2015
Acrylic on canvas, 70 x 100 cm

Pages 108–109
Masks of Male and Female, 2015
Acrylic on canvas, 100 x 75 cm

Wild Cats, 2015
Acrylic on canvas, 100 x 70 cm

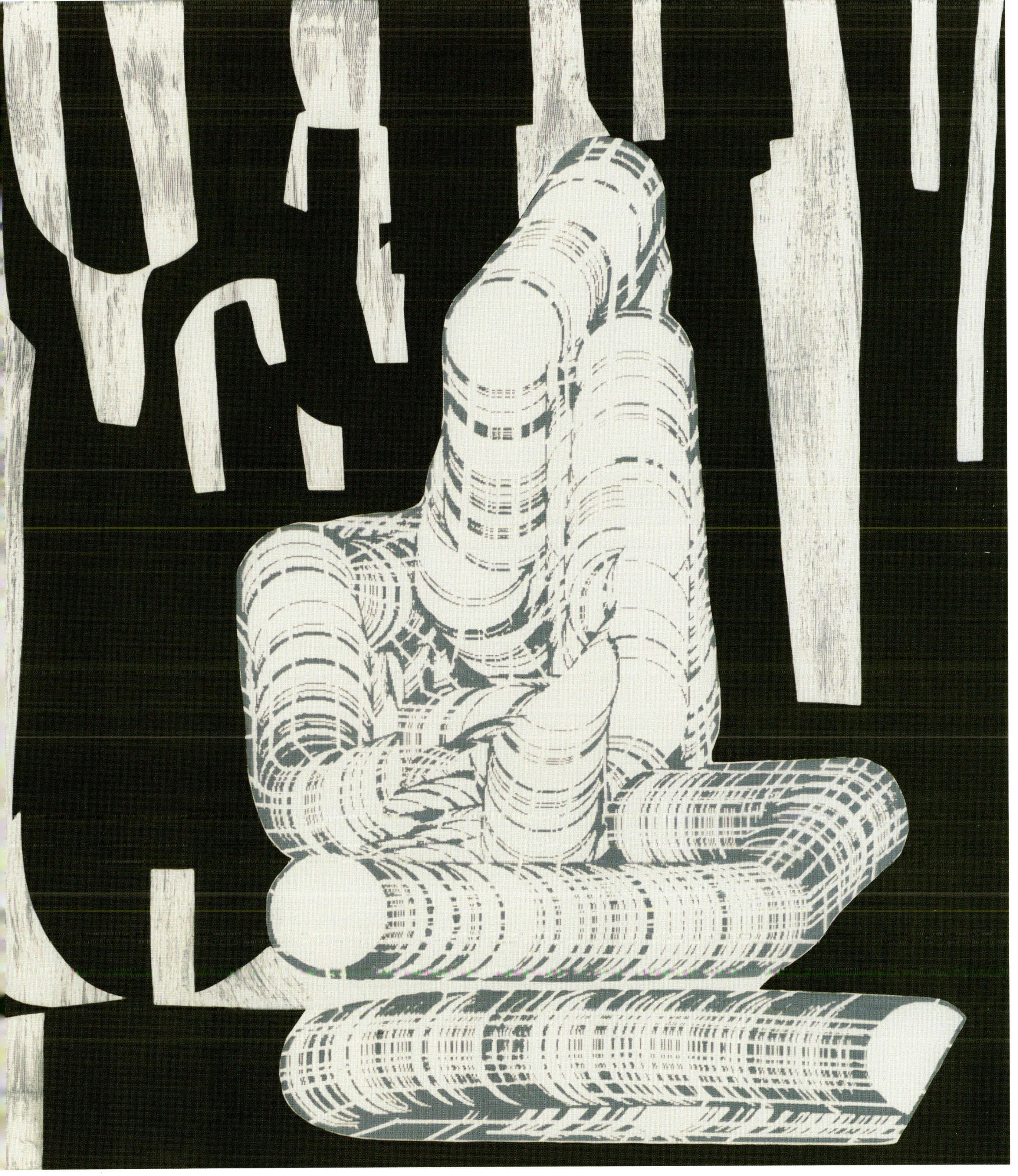

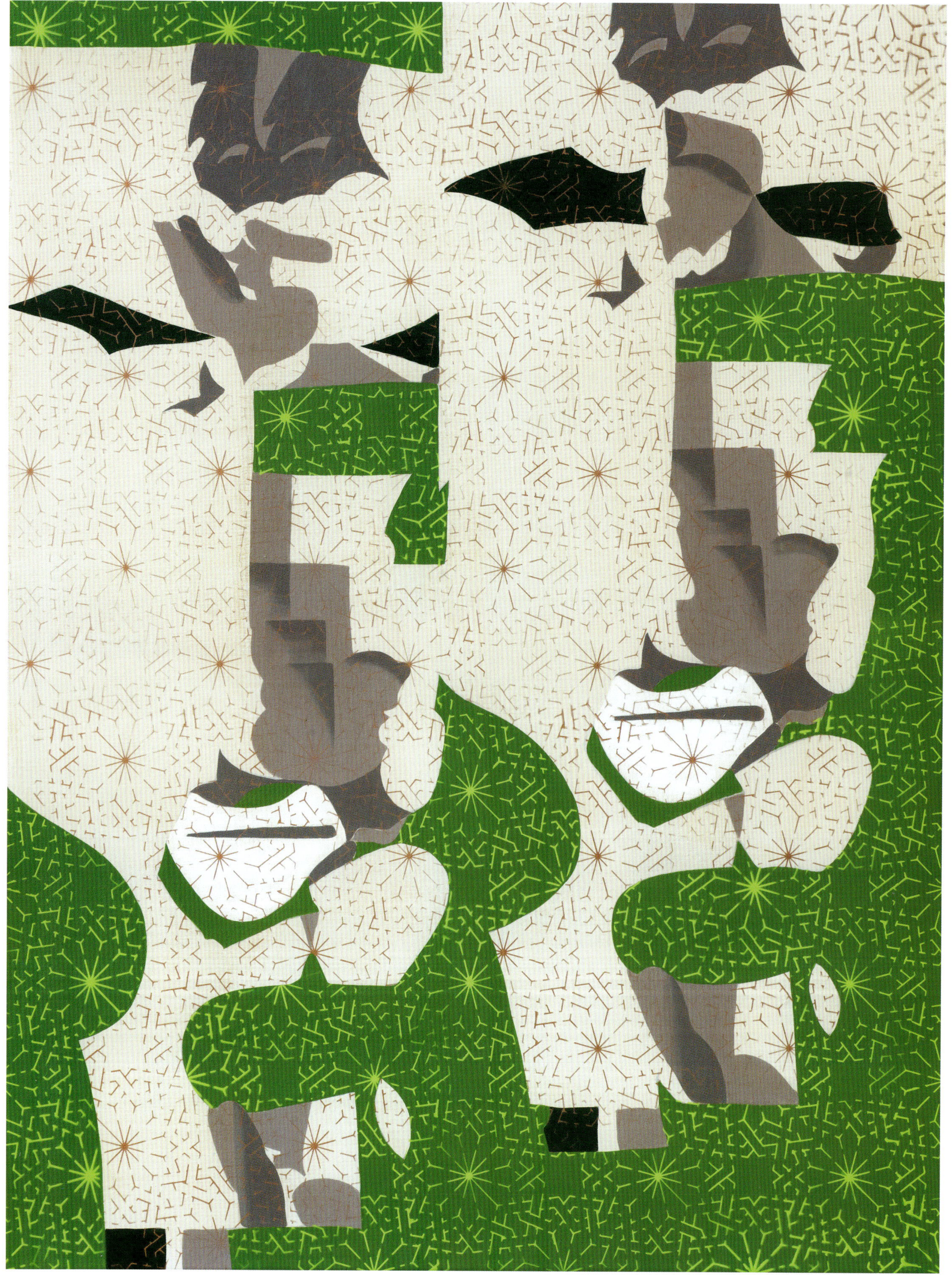

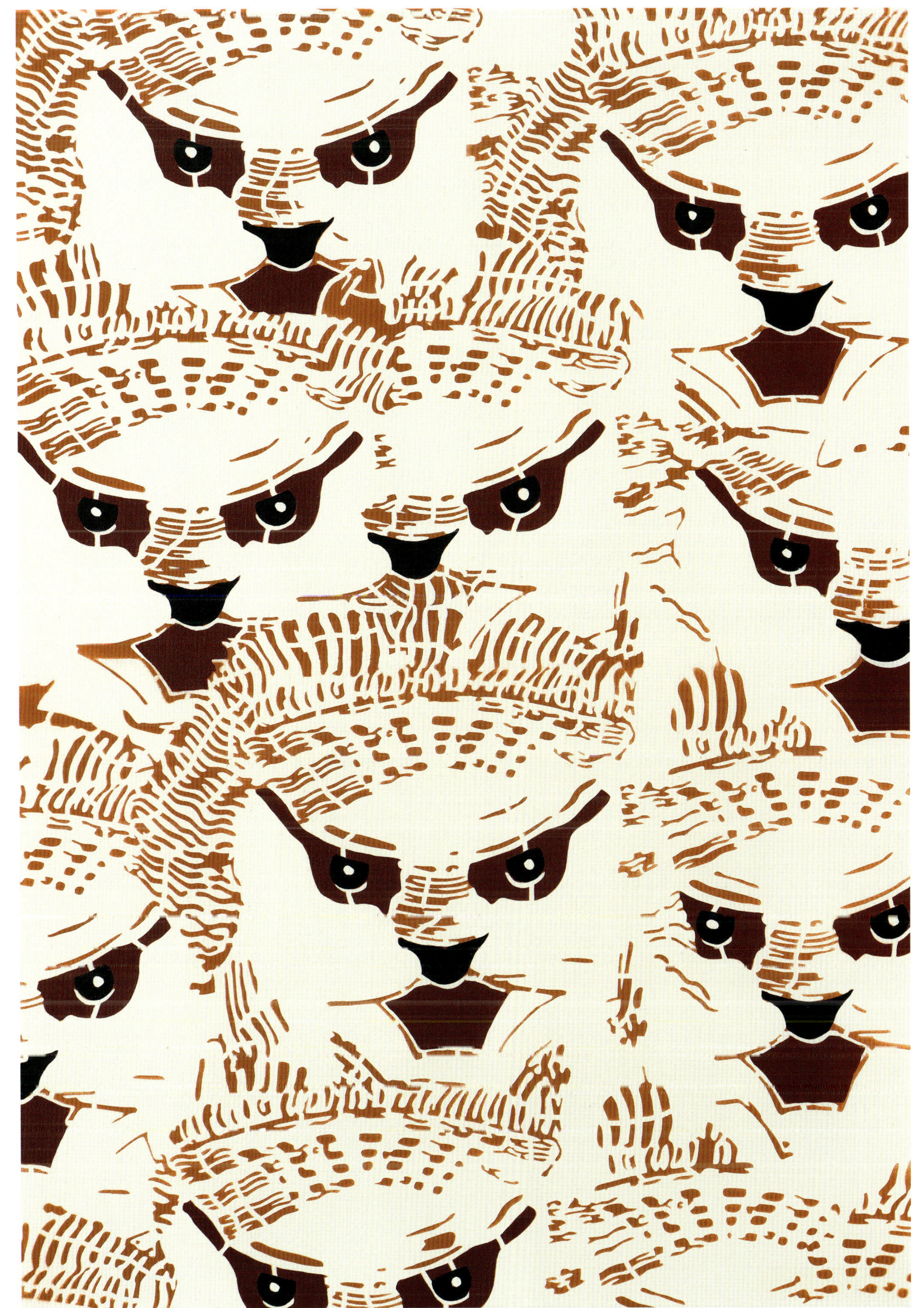

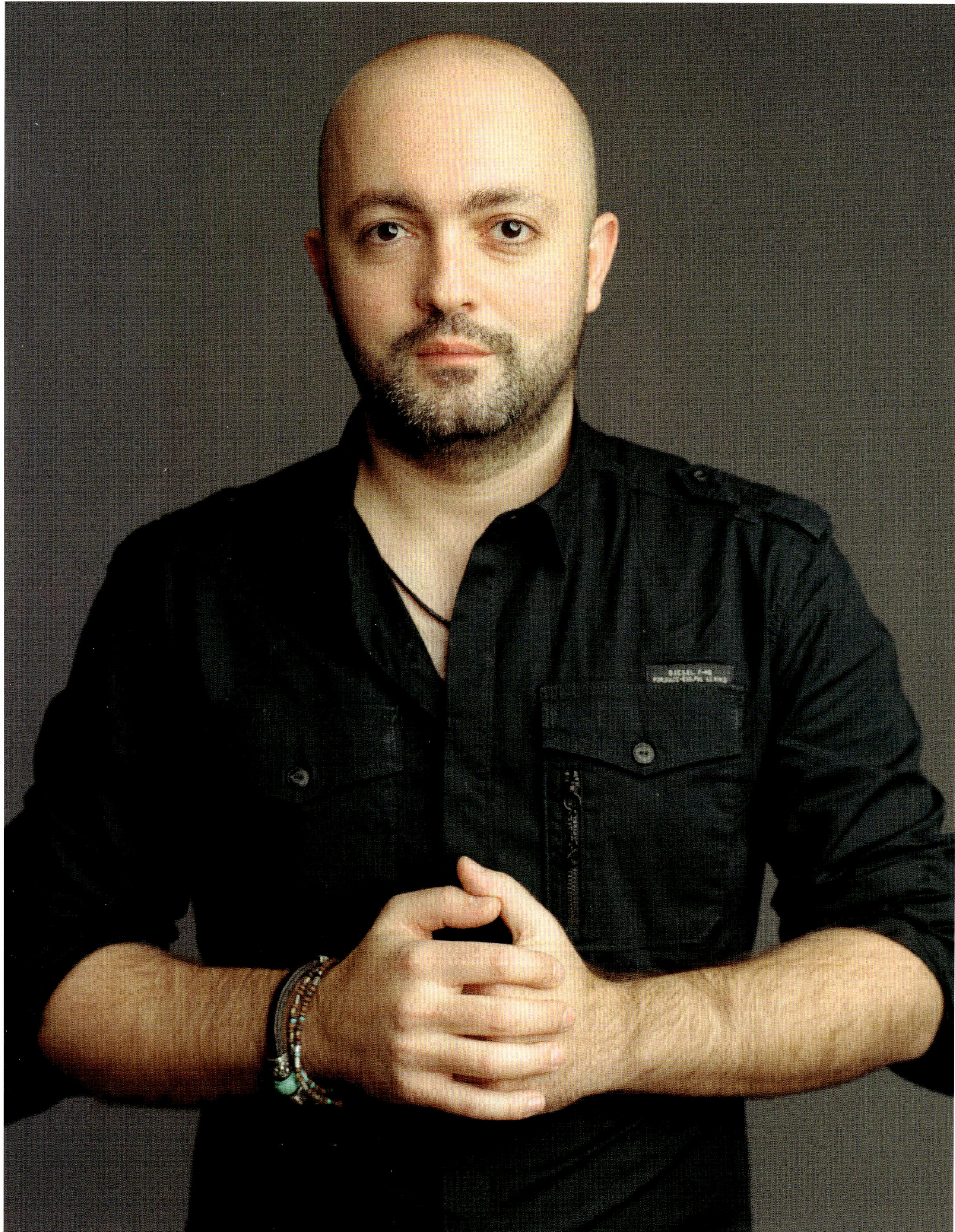

Appendix

Rafael Megall (born Rafael Melikyan) was born on January 2, 1983 in Yerevan. He started to paint when he was nine years old. From 1998 to 2004 he studied in Yerevan State Academy of Fine Arts. Since 2008 he has been a member of the Union of Artists of the Republic of Armenia. Since 2010 he lives and works in Armenia and the United States.

Solo Exhibitions

2010
• *Miniature*, Artists' Union of Armenia, Yerevan, Armenia
2011
• *The Last Works*, Gallery 8, London, UK
• *Born in Night*, Contemporary Art Museum, Yerevan, Armenia
2012
• *Turn on Emotion*, Artists' Union of Armenia, Yerevan, Armenia
2015
• *Megall*, Galleria In Arco, Turin, Italy

Group Exhibitions

2009
• Sofa New York, US
• Florence Biennale, Italy
2010
• National Gallery, Yerevan, Armenia
2011
• Armenian Contemporary Art, Museum of Contemporary Art, Kuwait
• Broadway Gallery, New York, US
• Florence Biennale, Italy
2012
• Salon d'Automne, Paris, France
2013
• Florence Biennale, Italy
2014
• Dublin Biennale, Ireland
2015
• *La Sindone e l'impronta dell'arte*, Museo di Sansepolcro, Sansepolcro, Arezzo, Italy
• Galleria In Arco, Turin, Italy
• *Frangit Nucem*, Palazzo Icimbardi, Milan, Italy

In 2012, he received the Gold Medal from the Ministry of Culture of the Republic of Armenia for his services and achievement. In 2013, the President of Armenia gave him the honorary title "Honored Artist of the Republic of Armenia." In 2013, at the Florence Biennale IX edition he received the "Lorenzo il Magnifico Award" in the painting category. In 2014, he was given the "Arshil Gorky Honorable Medal of the Republic of Armenia."

Rafael Megall, 2015
Photo Timothy Greenfield-Sanders